COVERT RESEARCH

Sara Miller McCune founded SAGE Publishing in 1965 to support the dissemination of usable knowledge and educate a global community. SAGE publishes more than 1000 journals and over 800 new books each year, spanning a wide range of subject areas. Our growing selection of library products includes archives, data, case studies and video. SAGE remains majority owned by our founder and after her lifetime will become owned by a charitable trust that secures the company's continued independence.

Los Angeles | London | New Delhi | Singapore | Washington DC | Melbourne

DAVID CALVEY

COVERT RESEARCH

THE ART, POLITICS AND ETHICS OF UNDERCOVER FIELDWORK

$SAGE

Los Angeles | London | New Delhi
Singapore | Washington DC | Melbourne

Los Angeles | London | New Delhi
Singapore | Washington DC | Melbourne

SAGE Publications Ltd
1 Oliver's Yard
55 City Road
London EC1Y 1SP

SAGE Publications Inc.
2455 Teller Road
Thousand Oaks, California 91320

SAGE Publications India Pvt Ltd
B 1/I 1 Mohan Cooperative Industrial Area
Mathura Road
New Delhi 110 044

SAGE Publications Asia-Pacific Pte Ltd
3 Church Street
#10-04 Samsung Hub
Singapore 049483

Editor: Jai Seaman
Assistant Editor: Alysha Owen
Production editor: Imogen Roome
Copyeditor: Sarah Bury
Proofreader: Jill Birch
Indexer: Martin Hargreaves
Marketing manager: Sally Ransom
Cover design: Shaun Mercier
Typeset by: C&M Digitals (P) Ltd, Chennai, India
Printed and bound by
CPI Group (UK) Ltd, Croydon, CR0 4YY

© David Calvey 2017

First published 2017

Library of Congress Control Number: 2016949496

British Library Cataloguing in Publication data

A catalogue record for this book is available from
the British Library

ISBN 978-1-84920-383-8
ISBN 978-1-84920-384-5 (pbk)

At SAGE we take sustainability seriously. Most of our products are printed in the UK using FSC papers and boards.
When we print overseas we ensure sustainable papers are used as measured by the PREPS grading system.
We undertake an annual audit to monitor our sustainability.

This book is dedicated with love to the memory of my late mother and father Rebecca and Patrick Calvey.

They are always in my heart. Rest in peace.

CONTENTS

ABOUT THE AUTHOR

Dr David Calvey is a Senior Lecturer in Sociology at the Manchester Metropolitan University (MMU). Prior to working at MMU he held teaching and research positions at the University of Manchester, Liverpool John Moores University, The Open University and was a Visiting Fellow at the University of Queensland. His publications and research interests span ethnography, covert research, humour studies, martial arts, ethnomethodology, organizational creativity, violence, private security and the night-time economy. He is a member of the British Sociological Association (BSA), a Fellow of the Higher Education Academy (HEA) and a member of the International Institute for Ethnomethodology and Conversation Analysis (IIEMCA).

ACKNOWLEDGEMENTS

This is my first sole authored book and it has been a challenging journey from its original inception in 2009 to its publication in 2017. In professional terms, thanks to Martine Jonsrud, Gemma Shields, Delayna Spencer and Alysha Owen as Assistant Editors at Sage, Professor Chris Rojek for the initial invitation to write the book, Imogen Roome in Production, Sally Ransom in Marketing and Sarah Bury for her expert guidance and remarkable detail in copyediting. Particular thanks go to Jai Seaman as Commissioning Editor who patiently and sensibly guided it through to publication over a lengthy period of time. They have all been very kind, patient and supportive with me, as have my colleagues in the Department of Sociology at Manchester Metropolitan University, who have all listened to my obsession over the years. Thanks to Dr Max Travers from the University of Tasmania for his useful comments on the draft. Particular thanks to Professor Wes Sharrock for both his continual intellectual mentoring long after I flew the doctoral nest at Manchester University and his insightful comments on the draft.

In emotional terms, thanks to all my large extended family, who, in different ways over my upbringing, shaped my being and thinking. So thanks to my siblings Dennis, Margaret, Jan, Liz, Ted, Peter, Trish and Sharon. Also thanks to my in-laws and their respective clans – Deveney, Griffin, Pattison, McFarlane, Morris and Thompson. Thanks to all my late uncles and aunts, particularly Uncle Dennis Calvey. Very special thanks to my partner and soul mate Julia Griffin, who is a constant source of hope, inspiration and creativity to me. Her sacrifices to my academic indulgences over the years have made this book possible, for which I am indebted to her. Lastly, eternal hugs and kisses to our magical daughter Mabel Griffin-Calvey, born in October 2012, for bringing so much love and joy into our world. I hope she is proud of her Daddy.

INTRODUCTION

Abstruse, bamboozle, betray, blagging, bogus, cagey, camouflaged, chameleon, cheating, chicanery, circumvent, clandestine, cloaked, closet, con, concealed, counterfeit, crafty, cunning, deceitful, deception, disassembly, disguised, dishonest, disingenuous, diversion, double dealing, double faced, dupery, duplicity, entrap, espionage, evasive, fakery, false, feigned, fictitious, fiddling, fleece, fly, fool, fraudulent, furtive, guileful, hidden, hoax, hoodwink, illusionary, imposter, incognito, infiltration, insidious, kid, lying, malingering, masked, misleading, misrepresentation, mock, mole, obscured, pretence, pseudo, ruse, scam, scheming, secret, shady, shifty, shrouded, skulduggery, skulking, slinking, sly, sneaky, snooping, spoof, spying, stealthy, sting, surreptitious, swindle, treachery, trickery, underhand, unsuspected, veiled, wily.

All the above terms, and more, are associated with undercover or covert research. There is a classic fear and fascination with covert research. It is a highly emotive and controversial area of study, which is part of the challenge and complexity of researching it. A number of questions and troubles have motivated this book over the years. Many of these I hope to answer, or at least investigate further. No doubt I shall gain some new ones on the way.

This is a book about covert research and its place in the human and social sciences. The book has a particular reasoning and rationale driving it, which is essentially one that attempts to reasonably fill the gap as regards research on covert research. For me, detailed discussions of covert research are typically glossed over and often subsumed in ethics chapters of research methodology manuals, of which there is a voluminous amount. Hence, covert research has a type of index and footnote status in various social science fields, where you have to search for a more detailed and substantive view of the covert tradition. This submerged and stifled understanding of covert research gives readers a rather crude and simplistic understanding of the complex issues involved and a limited knowledge of the rich corpus of covert work across the social sciences.

My general aim is to rehabilitate the covert research tradition in some ways and to appeal for a fairer reading of that tradition. In doing this, one recognizes and appreciates the depth and range of the covert corpus as well as the imaginative and creative role it has played in the shaping of the sociological imagination. Covert research is thus much richer and more extensive than the limited, although informative, 'usual suspects' that are often quickly identified as part of received wisdom and conventional thinking in covert research. In this way, covert research can become much more of a standard part of the methodological toolkit of the social sciences in the future rather than an exotic and maligned outcast, pariah and maverick.

Structure of the book

Turning to the structure of the book, Chapter 1 briefly explores the different contexts, definitions and uses of deception in society, namely, to broadly define and frame covert research and locate it within popular culture and the public imagination. A brief learning exercise around some key reflective questions will end this chapter.

Chapter 2 examines the roots of covert research, which have multiple strands, including investigative journalism, mass observation, psychology and sociology. It is vital to note here that covert research is neither a unified nor incremental field but one with disparate and multiple sources of origin, histories, perspectives, genealogies and philosophies. Four early case study readings, taken from different fields in the social sciences, will be explored in more detail at the end of this chapter, as a learning exercise for the reader.

Chapter 3 explores the historical debates around covert research, many of which commonly centre on informed consent and the management of ethical dilemmas in the field. This chapter also examines the more recent rise of ethical regimentation and bureaucracy surrounding field research, which can fetter and stifle the development of covert research. This chapter closes with a group learning exercise where the merits and flaws of covert research are critically discussed.

Chapter 4 explores the classical exemplars within covert research, which are the most popular and recognizable tropes across the social science community. These are what I loosely refer to as 'the usual suspects' of Erving Goffman and *Asylums: Essays on the Social Situation of Mental Patients and Other Inmates* (1961), Laud Humphreys and *Tearoom Trade: Impersonal Sex in Public Places* (1970), David Rosenhan and 'On Being Sane in Insane Places' (1973) and Stanley Milgram and *Obedience to Authority: An Experimental View* (1974). They are each examined in some depth regarding their context, key themes, motivations and influence. Some questions on the 'empathetic lessons learnt' will be explored at the end of the chapter as part of the pedagogical resource kit.

Chapter 5 deals with the eclectic and submerged fragmentation and spread of covert studies in the social sciences that are not always referred to as part of the conventional wisdom on covert research. Namely, a covert diaspora wherein several significant studies are not extensively discussed or, worse still, simply omitted in the literatures. This covert corpus, although not definitive, is viewed as a rich and diverse collection of fieldwork scenarios where the covert condition is usefully displayed. A brief learning exercise with some key reflective questions concludes this chapter.

Chapter 6 examines bouncers and the night-time economy, which is primarily drawn from my own covert case study in Manchester, England. This chapter explores the issues of danger, risk and emotion in the management of the field-work self and relates the case study to other relevant fieldwork accounts. Some moral compass-type learning exercises are also provided at the end of this chapter.

Chapter 7 explores what I consider to be a contemporary revival in covert research. For me, there are reasonable grounds to claim that the contemporary appetite and popularity for covert research is growing in the social sciences, for a number of different reasons. This chapter explores the motivations and contexts for this revival, which are not coherently interrelated, but come from multiple sources, including autoethnography, covert social networks, cyber ethnography, investigative journalism and visual ethnography. This revival does not equate, for me, to a radical paradigm shift for covert research, as it is still likely to remain a relatively niche field in the social sciences. A learning exercise consisting of some key reflective questions concludes this chapter.

Chapter 8 concludes the book and draws together key summaries and arguments from the book. These conclusions are more accurately a series of ongoing reflections about the covert condition, the continuum of concealment, moral disruption, ethical transgression and the methodological imagination and toolkit. One of the central messages here is that more general lessons can be learnt from covert research, which echo, apply, parallel and relate to the wider social scientific research community. The chapter ends with a list of key questions for students to reflect on and critically discuss in a 'before and after' manner.

1

WHAT IS COVERT RESEARCH?

1.1 Popular definitions of covert research

Turning to the initial task, it is important here to briefly survey some populist definitions of covert research from introductory textbooks because students will typically gain a basic understanding of the field from such sources, which then becomes a type of conventional wisdom on the field.

Holloway broadly defines covert research as 'research processes in which researchers do not disclose their presence and identity as researcher and participants have no knowledge of their research identity' (1997: 39). Macionis and Plummer claim: 'In sociology, the dilemma appears where the researcher conceals his or her identity and "cons" his way into a new group' (2005: 64). Giddens adds: 'Indeed, some of the most valuable data that have been collected by sociologists could never have been gathered if the researcher had first explained the project to each person encountered in the research process' (2009: 37).

Turning to the more methodological introductory texts, covert research is understandably given more detailed treatment. Bryman (2008), in *Social Research Methods*, focuses on Humphreys and Milgram as key 'infamous cases'. He then discusses a range of cases and related issues about access, legality, going native and key informants as well as the rise of visual ethnography.

Throughout various keyword books, dictionaries and encyclopaedias, covert research is defined broadly in terms of deception. Michael Bloor and Fiona Ward define covert research as: 'the undertaking of research without the consent of research subjects, by the researcher posing as an ordinary member of the collectivity, or by the experimental manipulation of research subjects without their knowledge' (2006: 43). They usefully provide a range of examples and discuss the typical advantages and disadvantages. The limitation and omission here is that they suggest that the tradition is not currently vibrant, stating: 'Although covert qualitative research projects are still sometimes undertaken, the controversy surrounding covert methods has probably made such studies less common than they were previously' (Bloor and Ward, 2006: 45).

Levine (2014) presents a voluminous multi-disciplinary *Encyclopedia of Deception*, based mainly on psychological studies about lying and deception in different contexts, from the everyday to high-profile political scandals. My work is not trying to build psychological models of deception that can be applied and tested. There is also an established literature on deception from moral philosophy (Bok, 1978, 1982; Martin, 2009) which centres on the examination of the relationship between truth, self-deception and lying, and the ethics of such behaviour in a very specific manner. Neither shall the book cover the literature on spying and espionage, much of which historically and politically analyses the more militaristic roots of espionage (Calder, 1999; Knightley, 1987; Goldman, 2006). Interestingly, some of the immediate assumptions about and mythic images of covert research are tied up with spies and spying. What Knightley (1987) refers to as the 'second oldest profession' and a still highly clandestine occupation and subculture. The more contemporary and popular images of covert research have shifted to investigative journalism, which is more accessible and one that we explore in the book. My lens and gaze on deception is thus primarily sociological although the range of deceptive scenarios that are critically explored and concepts used shall range across the wider family of social science disciplines.

1.2 Media scandals, whistleblowing, exposé documentaries and citizen journalism

What we have in broader societal terms is the contradiction between protectionism and voyeurism in society. On the one hand, we have increased our pursuit of the primacy of the private, yet on the other hand, we are intrigued by voyeuristically 'peering' and 'watching', and all the better if we remain unnoticed. The public tune in, with significant viewing figures, to various televised programmes to watch the degradation ceremonies unfold in different contexts. If the cameras are hidden or at least normalized, this seems to enhance the viewing pleasure.

Deception in public life is not new. Historically, an interesting example of deception and its unintended consequences was when the famous actor and film-maker Orson Welles broadcast *The War of the Worlds* on the radio in 1938 in Columbia, USA. The first two-thirds of the sixty-minute broadcast were presented as a series of simulated news bulletins, which suggested to many listeners that an actual alien invasion was currently in progress. This resulted in mass panics in certain quarters and an outcry by the media. Within one month, newspapers had published thousands of articles about the broadcast and its impact. Adolf Hitler, the infamous Nazi leader, even cited the panic. The hoax broadcast was repeated in Ecuador in February 1949, and resulted in local riots.

In terms of popular culture and media constructions, various comedic charac-ters trade on dupery and fakery and conduct various breaching and transgression experiments. What I call 'popular passing'. Banksy, the famous English graffiti artist is even more exotic. Without revealing his true identity, he has worked in clandestine ways over a sustained period of time in the art world.

Deceptive tactics, or what have been classically called 'muckraking', have been normalized for a lengthy period of time in the press. The Leveson pub-lic inquiry was set up by the government in the wake of the phone hacking scandal at the *News of the World*, a British newspaper, and amid wider issues of the work culture and professional ethics of the British Press. Employees of the newspaper were accused of engaging in a culture of phone hacking and police bribery (Mawby, 2014) in the pursuit of stories. The inquiry involved *News Corporation* owner Rupert Murdoch and his son being called before a parliamentary committee, and resulted in several high-profile resignations and convictions. Advertiser boycotts led to the closure of the *News of the World* in July 2011, after 168 years of publication. The Leveson Report was published in November 2012. Efforts are being made to replace the Press Complaints Commission by a new regulatory body (Cohen-Almagor, 2014).

It is clear that secrecy forms part of our popular culture and public imagina-tion. Whistleblowing at work is an established and successful way of exposing corruption, injustice, scandal and forms of wrongdoing. Indeed, whistleblow-ing has been promoted by a government national inquiry, with an anonymous telephone reporting system established, for reporting poor medical care and unacceptable professional standards in various NHS (National Health Service) hospital Trusts in the UK. This was partly a response to the *'culture of fear'* in openly reporting medical malpractice in what was commonly titled 'freedom to speak up'. Such whistleblowing is subject to the Public Interest Disclosure Act of 1998, with whistle blowers protected from potential harassment or discrimination. Whistleblowing is also linked to resistance in the workplace (Miethe, 1999; Near, 1995; Near and Miceli, 1996; Perry, 1998; Rothschild and Miethe, 1994; Tuda and Pathak, 2014). What Perry (1998), in his examination of these activities, elegantly refers to as '*indecent exposures*'. De Maria (2008) links whistleblowing and protest together and views them as important sources of ethical resistance to corruption and forms of wrongdoing. For him, the field is still largely unexplored and will likely expand.

Edward Snowden, the CIA whistleblower has caused an international storm around his claims of surveillance of the Web in 2013 by the American government. In a similarly politicized context, Julian Assange, who founded *Wikileaks* in 2006, has caused controversy by putting sensitive information, often military-based, into the public domain. It made particular global headlines in April 2010 by publishing confidential footage showing US soldiers firing at civilians from a helicopter in Iraq. In this way, *Wikileaks* represents a sort of public whistleblowing. Lindgren and Lundström (2011) view such activities as part of wider movements in 'hacktivist mobilization' and a technological 'pirate culture' which is broadly anti-authority.

Some undercover investigations have controversially hit the headlines. In September 2006, the BBC's *Panorama* programme broadcast a special investigation into corruption in English football, entitled '*Undercover: Football's Dirty Secrets*', which included meetings between agents, managers and high-ranking football club officials, filmed undercover by reporter Knut auf dem Berge, a former freelance scout, posing as a prospective football agent based in America who was looking to set up a new football agency called Dynamic Soccer. The footage purported to show agents and managers accepting backhanders and illegally contacting players under contract to other clubs, and included some high-profile clubs and managers. The strong reaction to the programme resulted in the Football Association establishing an inquiry, headed by Lord Stevens, a former Commissioner of the Metropolitan Police, to investigate the claims as well as further police investigations of bribery in 2008. More recently, in September 2016, Sam Allardyce, was forced to resign his high-profile post as national England football manager due to an undercover sting by journalists from *The Daily Telegraph* posing as overseas businessmen. Allardyce, on hidden camera, offered advice on getting around banned third party ownership in the game and was very open to taking paid offers for overseas speaking engagements.

In a different context, Margaret Haywood was a working nurse who was involved in secret filming for a BBC *Panorama* programme exposing poor care in the Royal Sussex Hospital in 2005. She was subsequently struck off the professional register for misconduct. Her case caused widespread media coverage and more academic discussion in healthcare (Belshaw, 2010; Wainright, 2009). In 2011 the BBC's *Panorama* team of covert investigative journalists discovered the systemic abuse of patients with severe learning disabilities at Winterbourne View, a residential care home near Bristol. Six out of eleven care workers who admitted a total of thirty-eight charges of neglect or abuse have been jailed. The Care Quality Commission has also launched an official government inquiry. Three former care home workers who mistreated an elderly female resident with Alzheimer's disease at the Granary Dementia Care Centre, near Bristol, were prosecuted. One received a jail sentence and two others have suspended sentences in 2013. The abuse footage was captured using hidden cameras, this time planted by the concerned and suspicious family of the resident rather than a professional journalist.

Still using '*sting*' tactics, undercover journalist Mazher Mahmood, known as the 'fake Sheik' due to his faked persona, snared former professional champion boxer Herbie Hide by getting him to supply cocaine at a hotel in Norwich, England. Despite reservations about the 'entrapment tactics' adopted by Mahmood, Hide was sentenced and imprisoned to twenty-two months in November 2013. The same journalist attempted a similar sting on a celebrity music judge Tulisa Contostavios in August 2014, but this failed. Ironically, Mahmood himself was then investigated by the police and found guilty, with his driver, of conspiring to pervert the course of justice in this case and has been sentenced to fifteen months in jail in October 2016. His various undercover investigations over the years are covered in his rather glamorized and self-styled confessions of 'the king of the sting' (Mahmood, 2008). In the political arena, two former foreign secretaries were also exposed in 2015 by undercover journalists in the '*cash for access*' scandal.

Controversial undercover investigations by female journalists faking pregnancy have been done into Crisis Pregnancy Centres (CPC) in the UK in 2014, both by *The Daily Telegraph* newspaper and independently by Education For Choice, a sexual health charity. The CPCs are not endorsed by the National Health Service and are currently unregulated by the government. There are over a hundred in the UK and are proving increasingly popular with young, particularly vulnerable and desperate, women. Such critical undercover journalistic work, although sensitive, can clearly be seen to be in the public interest.

Undercover investigations of North Korea, which many view as a rather repressive regime, were undertaken by journalist David McNeill. Posing as an ordinary tourist attending an International Film Festival, he exposed widespread poverty and illegal food markets before being caught out by the authorities in 2010. Journalist John Sweeney, who posed as a fake professor on a student exchange trip in 2013 to North Korea, also gained media attention. Sweeney's reasoning was that such covert methods are justified to explore closed and secretive societies with strong state censorship and dubious human rights records. Undercover work into the Mafia in Naples, Italy was carried out by celebrated Italian journalist Roberto Saviano, who wrote a bestselling book called *Gomorrah* (2007) that was then made into an award-winning film and television series of the same title. *Gomorrah* made global media headlines and brought attention to the use of covert methods to expose transnational corruption and crime. Undercover officers in the National Public Intelligence Unit, based in London, have recently come under formal investigation and possible prosecution for unethical practices and reckless behaviour in a number of cases. This included one officer marrying and having children with someone under investigation and another, Kennedy, who was investigating environmental activism for eight years, living as the partner of one woman in the movement under false pretences.

Citizen journalism is also known as public, participatory, democratic, guerrilla and street journalism (Allan et al., 2007; Allan and Thorsen, 2009; Domingo et al., 2008; Thurman, 2008). It is on the rise, particularly because of the widespread use of mobile technology and in situ amateur reporting of a range of different events. There are clear concerns with sensationalism, selectivity and bias but it has obvious aspects of covertness as it is an expedient form of documentation, which has either assumed consent or is purely bypassed in crowd contexts. It is usefully seen by some as a form of 'bearing witness' (Allan et al., 2007).

60 days in Jail is a remarkable documentary, similar to the Rosenhan experiment, one of the covert exemplars, except that it involves members of the public rather than trained academics, criminal justice professionals or journalists. The series was screened in March 2016 in the UK on Channel 4 and has aired in several countries around the world, with a second series already made. The series, produced by the American Arts and Entertainment Network group, followed seven people as they volunteer to go undercover for sixty days in Clark County Jail in Jeffersonville, Indiana in the USA. Their goal was to gather evidence about any wrongdoing and illegalities. There is some senior gate-keeping but the vast majority of inmates and guards are not aware of their role. They are trained beforehand and given fake but credible cover stories and criminal charges. The production team needed extensive legal advice to be able to conduct such an inquiry with the amount of concealed recording devices that were required. Despite reservations about glamorizing prison life by this intrusive media game, it puts the use of covert methodology firmly in the public eye and imagination.

A recent undercover investigation for the BBC's *Panorama*, broadcast in February 2017, reveals the harsh reality of life behind bars in the UK. The reporter spent two months in a Category C prison in Northumberland, which houses up to 1,348 male inmates. Footage shows how inmates are effectively running the prison, with many of them addicted to Spice, the popular synthetic form of cannabis. It also reveals how prison officers don't feel able to maintain control and are under enormous pressure and stress. The programme also finds little evidence of rehabilitation. It is a timely investigation as it comes at a point when the government faces repeated warnings about the crisis inside Britain's prisons as regards congestion and violence.

A range of both emotive and familiar issues have been investigated by undercover means by *Dispatches*, the Channel 4 flagship programme for televised British investigative journalism, including pensioner home care, a young offenders' institute, travel centre cheap flights and bargain priced supermarkets, to name but a few. Activist group Mercy for Animals (MRA) have also used undercover methods to investigate animal cruelty in factory farms and slaughterhouses across the world, using exposé-style websites to disseminate their findings. What is interesting to note here is that our popular conceptions of, and conventional wisdom about, undercover reporting is typically drawn from journalistic sources and not from academia.

1.3 Mock interviews and comedic pranks

In a very different comedic context, the success of comedian Sacha Baron Cohen's controversial characters Ali G, Borat and Bruno are clearly saturated in moral and ethical transgression centred on deliberate anti-political correctness. Atluri, in his useful analysis of humour and race, argues 'the charm of Cohen's characters lies in their ability to mock authority figures through playing dumb' (2009: 200).

Hamo et al. (2010) view the Ali G and Borat characters, along with other comedic characters such as Dame Edna, Mrs Merton and Dennis Pennis, as part of the 'mock interview' televised genre, which emerged in the 1980s and has been gaining in popularity since then. Hamo et al. reflect: 'This status allows the comic character to function as a court jester who is permitted to brashly break accepted norms' (2010: 250).

Similarly, we cringe at the clumsy situations and degradation ceremonies (Garfinkel, 1963) for the general public when they interact with certain comedy constructions. The range of characters constructed by Dom Jolly in *Trigger Happy TV*, Novan Cavak in *Phonejaker* and *Facejacker* and Marc Wootton in *LaLa Land* play similar games of fakery, dupery and transgression as they fool the public with their characters. Such caricatures are constructed to deliberately dupe you. Their comedic exaggeration trades on recognizability and familiarity. The line between reality and fantasy is a fine one. Deceptive breaching is clearly part of their highly appealing comedic modus operandi.

Linked to this was the prank call by two Australian radio presenters, Mel Greig and Mike Christian, in December 2012. They pretended to be the Queen and Charles, the Prince of Wales, making inquiries about the pregnancy of Kate Middleton, the Duchess of Cambridge, which tragically resulted in the suicide of nurse Jacintha Saldanha, who mistakenly disclosed information to the bogus callers at a private hospital in London. The ethical standards of radio broadcasting were then called into question and put under the global spotlight. Police investigations were made but no charges followed. This so-called 'prank call' was in an established 'shock jock' tradition and part of what Turbide et al. (2010) refer to as 'trash radio'.

1.4 Television hoaxing

The public have eagerly tuned in *en masse* to watch ordinary people being hoaxed in popular television programmes over the decades. A British version of *Candid Camera* began in 1960 and ran for seven years and then reappeared in the 1970s and 1986, with adaptations running in both Australia and Canada. With a similar sentiment, *Beadle's About* was screened to large viewing figures in the 1980s and 1990s in the UK.

Staying within the entertainment context, James Randi, the American award-winning and well-known magician, escapologist and illusionist, used deception sceptically to expose, debunk and reveal what he felt was the truth behind the trickery of various paranormal and religious organizations and leaders. He was centrally involved in Project Alpha, an elaborate hoax of a government investigation (1979–1981) of paranormal activity where two fake psychics were used. He also exposed the popular televangelist and faith healer, Peter Popoff, as fake in 1986 as well as causing a media storm in Australia for his hoax of a fake spirit medium in 1988. A documentary film about Randi's life entitled *An Honest Liar* (2014) sums up his modus operandi.

A range of both hoax and exposé undercover television programmes have increased in recent years. Successful hidden-camera prank shows include *Totally Hidden Video, Punk'd* and *Oblivious, Girls Behaving Badly, Just for Laughs, Gags, The Jamie Kennedy Experiment, Boiling Points, Howie Do It* and *The Joe Schmo Show*. More recent exposé-type undercover programmes include *Cheaters, The Real Con, Faking It, The Undercover Millionaire, The Undercover Boss, The Undercover Princess, Restaurant Stakeout, Tricked* and *Mystery Diners*, to name but a few.

Clearly much more could be said about this area, particularly for those within media studies, which is beyond the scope of the current book. Although very different from the academic focus of this book, such a popular cultural context of deception is worth noting. Such programmes seem to be on the increase, such is our appetite for deception, and, generally speaking, have been ramped up in terms of shock and degradation value.

1.5 Social media

Social media, which we are now rather normalized too, is also saturated in forms of voyeurism, eavesdropping (Locke, 2010) and deception. For Locke (2010) the nature of privacy has radically changed for the 'facebook generation' to being a more shared and collective version of it. We are typically invited, indeed expected, to 'peep' into the lives of others without their permission. The recent cases of internet trolls, on which there is growing research (Gershon, 2014; Hughey and Daniels, 2013; Jane, 2014; Shachaf and Hara, 2010), are clearly based on deception in terms of the trolls hiding behind fake or anonymous cyber-identities. What Jane (2014) elegantly refers to as 'textual hate'. Witness the rise in fake 'selfies', often taken with mobile phone cameras, by members of the public, with some depicting extreme and graphic scenes designed to shock.

Also witness the rise in incidences of fake or hoax news on social media, where misinformation and disinformation is deliberately manipulated and falsehoods are promoted for political propaganda purposes. Facebook now employ staff to monitor and censor such claims as the real consequences of such actions can be influential and harmful.

Facebook has been a topic of more recent research as regards identity formation, friendship networks and imagery (Farquhar, 2013; Sauter, 2014; Wilson et al., 2012). What Goggin (2014) describes accurately as mobile media. The recent Facebook emotional manipulation study, conducted by Kramer et al. (2014), manipulated the newsfeeds and homepages of 689,003 users for a week in 2012, without their consent, to explore mood shifts. The secrecy of the study, conducted jointly by Facebook and Cornell University, on 'massive-scale emotional contagion through social networks' caused widespread outrage and public concern, not least on the question of internet research ethics (Flick, 2016). Schroeder (2014) argues that such big data research using diverse social media will become much more commonplace in the future.

Surveillance, in various modes, is now fully embedded into the fabric of modern society but there are still sensitivities around and emotive debates about the role and extent of legitimate snooping in society. Calvert (2000) accurately refers to modern culture as a 'voyeur nation', where spectatorship and peering is an expected part of our everyday lives. The Regulation of Investigatory Powers Act 2000 gives covert police units special dispensation in their work on suspect criminal populations. The investigatory Powers Act of 2016, popularised as the highly contentious 'Snooper's charter', has significantly increased the range and intensity of covert surveillance, particularly the lawful interception of internet and social media communications. This is in the context of increasing terrorist activities on a global scale and the rise of various forms of transnational organized crime and cyber-crime. Critics feel that this is a worrying intensification of hyper mass surveillance. There is a dedicated literature on surveillance in society, which is not the focus of this book.

1.6 Practitioner undercover investigations

Corporate companies have routinely and extensively used secret shoppers and mystery customers across different sectors, including financial services, leisure services, retailing, motor dealerships, hotels and catering, passenger transportation, public utilities, and government departments, for commercial imperatives for a number of years (Miller, 1998; Morrall, 1994; Wilson, 1998). Indeed, the public can sign up easily as a mystery shopper as the large supermarket groups continually recruit mystery shoppers to gain different types of data on their employees and organizations. Store detectives are also used. They blend into their environments as normal customers, but are vigilantly watching for criminality.

The Department of Work and Pensions in the UK has expanded the amount of surveillance staff to investigate the increasing amount of fraudulent claims. Various councils use undercover agents to review the health and safety, hygiene and fair trading standards of the restaurant and hospitality industry. In the culinary world, coveted Michelin stars are awarded by covert methods, as are the routine visits of some hotel inspectors. An investigator drops in unannounced and unknown and then writes a report. There has been a rise in specialized surveillance companies across numerous countries offering private detectives to investigate workplace theft and fraud by placing trained personnel undercover in commercial settings. Some of these companies also offer male and female undercover relationship investigators exploring matrimonial infidelity and internet scams, popularly known as 'Honey Traps'. There are various national and international professional bodies in this industry, which attempt to regulate their conduct.

The medical world has also routinely used placebo experiments since their first use by physician John Haygarth in 1799. Placebo experiments, where a controlled group of patients in a clinical trial are given fake drugs with no side effects for comparative purposes, are part and parcel of the sanctioned and necessary deception in modern medical science (Beecher, 1955; Kienle and Kiene, 1997; Miller et al., 2005; Petkovic et al., 2015).

When we reflect on the secret service security organizations that most people could name, such as MI5 and MI6 in the UK and the Federal Bureau of Investigation (FBI) and the Central Intelligence Agency (CIA) in the USA, we know very little about them in detail apart from filmic myths. The Official Secrets Act, the latest revision being in 1989 from the original Act of 1911, is still currently used in the UK, Ireland, Hong Kong, India and Malaysia for legislation that provides for the protection of state secrets and information related to national security. The Free Mason Society, a secret society, still exists today and operates around the world. Freemasonry, in various forms, has a global membership estimated at six million by the United Grand Lodge of England in 2013. What Clawson (1989) elegantly describes as a process of fraternally 'constructing brotherhood' through the ages. Clearly there is a more dedicated literature on such topics, which is not the remit of this book.

1.7 Deception in police culture

Deception has played a significant role in police culture in different ways. There are clear concerns with entrapment (Panzarella and Funk, 1987; Sagarin and MacNamara, 1970), stings (Dodge et al., 2005; Marx, 1980, 1982; Panzarella and Funk, 1987), lying (Alpert and Noble, 2009; Klockars, 1980; Manning, 1974) and covert policing strategies (Fijnaut, 1995; Kruisbergen et al., 2011; McKay, 2015). As expected, the police routinely use undercover tactics for intelligence gathering and surveillance on a range of sensitive topics, such as paedophilia, drug abuse, football hooliganism, people trafficking and counterfeit goods, to name just a few. A recent case exploring the criminal underworld in Salford, Greater Manchester, which was reported in the press in November 2016, was extraordinary in terms of the undercover police officer being embedded in the local community as a café and shop-keeper for three years. He successfully infiltrated and was trusted by five crime families. Operation Damson led to 78 convictions and a number of long-term jail sentences for drugs and firearms offences, as well as a bravery award for the officer. What Loftus and Goold (2012) in their fieldwork on covert policing in the UK refer to as the '*invisibilities of policing*'. Such covert policing requires specialist training and must be sensitive to issues of entrapment.

Landmark covert insider accounts or autoethnographies of the British police force (Holdaway, 1982; Young, 1991) are discussed in Chapter 5. It is important to note here that much more active covert investigation techniques are now widely used by the police in protecting children from online grooming and sexual abuse, including cyber-stings (Gillespie, 2008; Martellozzo, 2012; Simpson, 2006; Tetzlaff-Bemiller, 2011; Urbas, 2010). What Tetzlaff-Bemiller elegantly describes as 'undercover online: an extension of traditional policing' (2011: 813).

In his pioneering work on exploring undercover police work in the USA, Gary T. Marx (1980, 1982, 1988) cogently argues that 'secret police behaviour and surveillance go to the heart of the kind of society we are or might become. By studying the changes in covert tactics, a window on something much broader can be gained' (1982: xxv). Mac Giollabhui et al. (2016) add, in their recent overt ethnographic study of UK covert policing: 'the growing importance of covert police investigation has profound implications for the relationship between citizen and the state in a democratic society but it is relatively unexplored by police researchers' (2016: 630). Clearly, academic access to this occupation is very sensitive and highly restricted.

Based on interview and observational data of undercover American and Canadian police officers, Sara Schneider (2008) explores artefacts of identity, muddied identities and identity breakdowns. For Schneider, undercover operators are ones who 'construct their trick identities through the scripting and safeguarding of their cover stories' (2008: 8) in what she calls 'craft and artifice'. Schneider, coming from a performance art academic background, talks about the interaction between self and scene. Under the heading of 'elementary collusion', Schneider argues that 'Western culture has long dallied with the identity players' (2008: 4).

Related to this are various first-hand insider accounts of undercover work, which are often glamorized and gritty, by former police and security industry professionals and experts, some of which have been popularized in films. Included in this autobiographical genre are Paul Doyle's (2004) investigation of the Boston criminal underworld as an undercover agent, William Queen's (2005) two-year investigation of a violent American motorcycle gang as a special agent, Valarie Wilson's (2007) twenty years as a covert CIA agent and Bon Hamer's (2008) twenty-six years as an FBI agent.

In a British context, Duncan Maclaughlin (2002) recounts his memories of his undercover work for Scotland Yard, David Corbett (2003) reflects on his experience with the Glasgow undercover police unit, Christian Plowman (2013) recalls his sixteen years' service as an undercover specialist with the London Metropolitan Police, as does Pete Ashton (2013) after his ten-year service with them.

In a filmic context, some of which have been big screen Hollywood hits, the award-winning film *Donnie Brasco: My Undercover Life in the Mafia* (1988) was based on the autobiography of Jospeh D. Pistone, an FBI agent for twenty-seven years who investigated the New York Mafia. Another film was the story of Frank Serpico, the undercover policeman who was a celebrated whistleblower on corruption in the New York Police Department in the 1960s and 1970s. The film *Serpico* was adapted from the best-selling biography *Serpico: The Cop Who Defied the System* (1973) by Peter Maas. Similarly, *Prince of the City* (1981) was a crime film based on the biography of New York Police undercover detective Robert Leuci. In the UK context, James Bannon (2013) explored his covert investigations of hooliganism at Millwall Football Club, on which the British film *ID*, released in 1995, was based. More recently, the film *Imperium* was released in 2016 which is based on the real life undercover investigations of white supremacist and neo-Nazi organizations in the USA by former FBI agent Michael German. His investigations spanned fourteen years and were published in his book *Thinking Like a Terrorist: Insights of a Former Undercover Agent* (2007).

The undercover operations of Robert Mazur, who worked for the United States Customs Service and the Drug Enforcement Agency, has also been recently turned into a film, *The Infiltrator*, released in 2016. Mazur infiltrated Pablo

Escobar's Colombian based international drug cartel over a five year period in the mid-1980s. Eighty-five arrests of drug lords and corrupt bankers were made as well as the collapse of the Bank of Credit and Commerce International, which was a legitimate institution involved in money laundering. Mazur changed his identity for some years after a large bounty was placed on him. The film is based on Mazur's book *The Infiltrator: Undercover in the World of Drug Barons and Dirty Banks Behind Pablo Escobar's Medellin Cartel* (2009).

The filmic context, although clearly driven by different goals, logic and imperatives, has been another way to embed covert work into the popular imagination and public consciousness.

1.8 Conclusions

The insider, police, media and journalistic contexts of deception are, in different ways, more practically motivated and have different imperatives and approaches on legal issues of entrapment and public justification than academic ones. Clearly, such contexts and scenarios present a different order of problems from academic ones, but deception plays an important and intriguing role in all these contexts.

It is reasonable to claim, then, from a brief review of these different settings, that deception is profoundly interwoven into the fabric of everyday life and has a familiar place in popular culture and the public imagination. If we stop and think about the covert aspects of eavesdropping (Locke, 2010), which has been routinely used by social scientists over the years, it is something we take for granted in ordinary language. Many of the assumptions about and images of covert research are somewhat evocative ones drawn from such populist contexts rather than from academic sources. Our focus here is more with the academic context, although understanding the reactions and responses to it relates to wider movements in society.

1.9 Learning exercise

1. Define covert research.

2. What image of covert research immediately springs to mind and what sources do they come from?

3. What is the importance of understanding the different contexts within which covert research has been used?

4. What is your initial 'gut reaction' response to doing covert research?

2

THE ROOTS OF
COVERT RESEARCH

There are various forms of early covert research in the social sciences, from a diverse and disparate range of intellectual sources. I have grouped them into four broad categories of investigative journalism, mass observation, psychology and sociology. As expected, there are considerable and dedicated literatures on these fields, and a review of each is clearly not the purpose of this current book. I will be examining specific aspects of these fields that are relevant to our concerns about the early roots of covert research in a broadly chronological fashion. I will explore four key case studies – Nellie Bly (1887), Paul Cressey (1932), Leon Festinger et al. (1956) and Melville Dalton (1959) – from these different fields in the learning exercise at the end of the chapter. These case studies could easily be classified as classic exemplars themselves, although they are not as popular as the 'usual suspects', which often constitute conventional wisdom in the field. But, for me, these case studies are additional 'covert gems' that deserve to be recovered and discussed. These early covert roots are not unified, integrated, cross-fertilized or incremental sources in any way but are, in most cases, unrelated and divergent developments. Hence, there is no settled, single source of origin, which makes it a challenging but worthwhile task to study these 'covert gems'.

2.1 Investigative journalism

In the nineteenth century, a series of pioneering feminist investigative journalists went undercover to expose the brutal and oppressive working conditions for girls and young women in factories in the United States. Eva Gay, under aliases Eva McDonald and Eva Valesh, explored the bag and mattress factories, shirt factories and laundries of Minneapolis by posing as a factory worker herself. Gay published a series of newspaper articles, 'The Toiling Women', 'Song of the Shirt' and 'Working in the Wet', in the *St Paul Globe* in April 1888, which saddened the nation. Similarly, Nell Nelson exposed various garment, dry goods and paper box factories in Chicago by working there undercover. A twenty-three-part series of articles called 'City Slave Girls' was published by her in the *Chicago Daily Times* between July and August in 1888. Lucy Hosmer did the same in shoe factories in St Louis. Her article 'Factory Girls in a Big City' was then published in the *St Louis Post-Dispatch* in November 1896. Marie van Vorst explored a Massachusetts shoe factory undercover, while her sister-in-law Bessie van Vorst went undercover in a knitting mill in New York. Five pieces were published under 'The woman that toils' in *Everybody's Magazine* between September 1902 and January 1903. They were later published as a book.

Upton Sinclair, an early American exposé journalist, wrote *The Jungle* in 1906, after it had been published in serial form the year before in the socialist newspaper *Appeal to Reason*. It was from a broadly socialist political perspective and aimed to expose corruption in government and business. He dedicated the book to 'the working men of America'. A large section of the book focused on the bad practices, brutal working conditions and effective wage slavery in the meatpacking industry of Chicago, where many new immigrants worked. Basically, this was a 'survival of the fittest' situation in the workplace, often without union regulation. The book was based on undercover work undertaken in 1904 when Sinclair spent seven weeks undercover after being commissioned to do so by the socialist newspaper *Appeal to Reason*. After several rejections from publishers, he funded the first printing himself and then found a publisher. The book was turned into a film in 1914. The public outcry about the book, which came to be seen as a social protest novel, led to the 1906 Meat Inspection Act and The Pure Food and Drug Act. There is a blur between fact and fiction in the book, with some critics viewing it as a work of socialist propaganda.

In his book *What's On The Worker's Mind: By One Who Put On Overalls To Find Out* (1920), journalist Whiting Williams spent seven months working undercover as a labourer in various locations, including a steel mill, a rolling mill, a coal mine, a shipbuilding yard, an iron mine and an oil refinery. He changed his name throughout and dressed according to the occupation in his attempt to understand the strained relations between Labour, Management and the Public.

In the 1940s and 1950s, Stetson Kennedy, a journalist, writer, human rights activist and folklorist from Florida, USA, infiltrated the *Ku Klux Klan* (KKK) headquarters chapter in Atlanta, the extreme right-wing racist organization, and exposed and ridiculed their secret rituals. He also interacted with other racist groups, such as the Nazi Columbian Brown Shirt and Christian Crusaders organizations. He wrote about racism in his various books, including *I Rode with the Ku Klux Klan* (1942), later reissued as *The Klan Unmasked* (1954).

Kennedy famously described the members of the KKK as 'home grown racial terrorists'. Kennedy infiltrated the KKK rather creatively by using the name of a deceased uncle who had been a member. In this way, he gained quick entry and established a level of trust with them. He managed to rise up the KKK hierarchy to Kleagle, a senior rank. Kennedy was providing information to the Federal Bureau of Investigation and testified in court cases against the KKK. Despite the reservations by critics about fabrication and exaggeration, this was a brave project by Kennedy, who feared exposure and recriminations throughout his life from the KKK. He acknowledged later in his career that some of his covert materials were from a close colleague who had also infiltrated the KKK but did not want to be named.

John Howard Griffin is an American journalist who was involved in extreme passing, as a white male posing as a black male, in the racially segregated southern American states. Under medical supervision he artificially darkened his skin for the undercover project. He kept a diary of his six weeks spent travelling on coaches and hitchhiking around at a time when race relations tensions were running high. He published his story in *Black Like Me* (1961), which was later turned into a film, released in 1964. The book, which became very influential, documented his experiences of racism and prejudice, including being excluded from certain places and receiving threats of violence. Griffin passionately stresses 'I offer my account in all its crudity and rawness. It traces the changes which occur to heart and body when a so called first class citizen is cast on the junk heap of second class citizenship' (1961: 13).

2.2 Mass Observation

Another early source of covert work was the UK-based Mass Observation project, which was established in 1937 by Charles Madge and Tom Harrison. Simply put, it was established to study how ordinary members of the British public went about their everyday life and daily activities (Hubble, 2006). What Sheridan et al. (2000) refer to as a type of *'writing ourselves movement'*. Early work included the recording of daily life in London's East End and in northern English towns like Blackpool and Bolton (Gurney, 1988) as well as a *'day-survey'* of significant cultural events like the coronation of George VI (Calder, 1995).

These early studies established the reputation of Mass Observation as a highly competent social research organization. For a short period in the early phase of the Second World War, between 1940 and 1941, the organization was also commissioned by the government to monitor and record the morale of the British people covertly. Thus, the morale of citizens would be captured in factories, pubs and air raid shelters by a type of mass surveillance and snooping. Clearly, some of the early observations of public behaviour would be covert, although a multiple range of methods were used.

The Mass Observation organization extensively used a panel of volunteer observers to keep diaries and complete periodic questionnaires. It became famous for this mode of self-documentation and popular autobiographical diary method. In 1947, Mass Observation UK was registered as a limited company and began to undertake essentially commercial work. It was not until 1981 that the mass use of volunteers recording their own experiences for detailed sociological and anthropological research was again taken up. In that year the Mass Observation Archive (MOA) was established as a non-profit social science body.

Since the Archive began operation, thousands of volunteers have contributed autobiographies on a diverse range of topics, including some that were relatively undocumented at the time, such as everyday accounts of poverty. What Sheridan (1993) broadly characterizes as '*popular autobiography*'. The data also displays interesting lay accounts of the gender roles and the sexual division of labour (Stanley, 2008). Understandably, the data are very diverse and there have been debates about its value and reliability (Bloome et al., 1993; Hubble, 2006). The interesting duality for Summerfield (1985) was that Mass Observation represented both social research and a social movement, with much of its data on social life still remaining unpublished.

The Mass Observation group was one of the early organizations to conduct systematic studies into mass leisure activities, including holidays, drinking in public houses, dance crazes and visiting the cinema. Typically, therefore, there was the adaptation of a range of unobtrusive, participant observation measures, such as mingling and eavesdropping, to record phenomena. The central issue here is the covert observation of public, often collective, crowd behaviour. Seaton (1997), within the tourism field, calls for a 'Mass Observation Revisited' in that the standard tools of questionnaire surveys are best augmented with 'unobtrusive, direct observational measures' (1997: 25).

More recently, Purdam (2014) argues that there are parallels between certain aspects of Mass Observation using volunteers to gather data and the modern ideas of citizen social science and citizen data where volunteers collect digital and online data about their daily lives. Purdam argues: 'This new role for citizens can link to the policymaking process and contribute to a redefining of the interfaces between citizens, knowledge processes and the state' (2014: 387).

2.3 Psychology

Various branches of psychology have a long history of deception. In his exploration of prejudice and discrimination, Richard LaPiere (1934) travelled throughout the United States with a Chinese couple, stopping at about 250 restaurants and hotels. Only one establishment refused them service. Six months later, LaPiere wrote to each establishment and requested reservations for a Chinese couple and more than 90 per cent rejected the reservation based on a policy of a non-acceptance of Orientals. This field experiment was repeated with black people at a later date, with very similar results (Kutner et al., 1952).

Henle and Hubble (1938) transgressed standard experimental conditions and used extreme methods of concealment to record conversations and measure egocentricity, which caused much outrage and controversy. As they state: 'they concealed themselves under beds in students' rooms where tea parties were being held, eavesdropped in dormitory smoking-rooms and dormitory wash-rooms, and listened to telephone conversations' (1938: 230).

Asch (1955) studied group conformity by employing actors to pretend to be research participants, a common practice in social psychology experiments. The duped participants could then be observed under the group pressure of six or seven confederates who were trained to respond identically. Berkun et al. (1962) were similarly interested in the stress and performance of military trainees. By using trained confederates they faked that the plane was going to crash while the trainees were airborne over the sea. The pilot and ground ambulance staff were involved in this rather extreme hoax, as they prepared the runway for emergency action.

In an experimental study of public honesty, Merritt and Fowler (1948) observed the pecuniary honesty of the public in how they responded to fake lost letters that the researchers placed on different days in different cities. The letters were opened, ignored or delivered. Farrington and Kidd (1977) similarly undertook a series of covert dishonesty experiments with members of the public. Namely, opportunities to offend were presented in the form of coins dropped on the pavement, with hidden observers taking notes. Farrington and Knight (1979, 1980) continued that tradition more recently with money found in faked lost letters.

Honesty and moral compass issues with children were investigated by Brock and Guidice (1963) in their study of stealing by children. The researchers asked the children to go into another room to take part in an experiment. On arriving, the fake female experimenter would be distressed, with her purse and a set amount of money scattered on the floor. She then left the room for a short period, having asked the children to collect the money and place it in her purse. The money was then counted to measure any dishonesty.

Darley and Latané (1968, 1970), two famous social psychologists, were motivated by the shocking murder of a young woman in New York City in 1964. The murder had extensive news coverage, which pointed alarmingly to the alienation and dehumanization of city dwellers. They designed experiments to test intervention in emergencies and the diffusion of responsibilities in what would become classically known as *'the bystander effect'*. Like so many others of its kind, this classic experiment, which is much quoted in social psychology textbooks, relied on deception in various ways. To test their propositions it would be necessary to fake or 'stage' a situation in which a realistic 'emergency' could plausibly occur, including fake epileptic seizures or fits, a room full of smoke, reactions to shoplifting and a female student in distress asking for help. Some of the experiments involved collusion and contrivance with other students. In a similar vein, Piliavin et al. (1969), in their famous Philadelphia 'subway Samaritan experiment', caused particular controversy. This involved a confederate collapsing, with and without bleeding from the mouth, to observe and measure bystander apathy.

A more modern extension of these psychological field experiments has been those done on helping. At the University of Kansas in the USA, Batson et al. (1978) designed a field experiment to assess the effect of being in a hurry to our willingness to help a stranger, namely, the *'Good Samaritan'* situation. Accordingly, a fake male undergraduate played a distressed victim on the stairs of a university building as forty male undergraduates involved in computer laboratories were intentionally directed his way. Some undergraduates were strongly encouraged to get to class promptly while others were told the opposite. These manipulations were seen to directly affect the incidences of help.

Weinberger (1981) explored the influence of age on responses to asking for help in New York City. Twelve confederates, mixed in terms of age and gender, were employed to play the role of the help seeker in the field experiment. Weinberger did not find any evidence of ageism. Levine et al. (2001), in an attempt to understand cross-cultural differences in helping strangers, conducted field experiments in twenty-three large cities around the world. They were interested in forms of 'spontaneous non-emergency helping' and to see if there was any cultural variability in the helping of strangers. Three different faked scenarios were explored, including alerting a pedestrian who had dropped a pen, offering help to a pedestrian with a hurt leg who was trying to reach a pile of dropped magazines and assisting a blind person to cross the street. A clear gender limitation is that the study used only male students as those seeking help in the field experiments.

What is particularly noteworthy here is the relative normalization of deception in experimental methodology, where researchers have deceived subjects about the intentions of their research. Murray (1980), exploring his own training as a social psychologist, argues that researchers would aim 'routinely to frighten, provoke, insult and depress and generally lie to the subjects of their experiments' (Murray, 1980: 367). Bailey and Ford (1994) also argue that theatricality plays a vital role in such deceptive laboratory experiments as the experimenters adhere closely to roles and scripts, akin to actors performing on the stage.

2.4 Sociology

Several early covert studies emerged from various corners of sociology. The Chicago school of sociology housed some key ones, but importantly not all of them. The Chicago school is the conventional 'ethnographic Eden' for qualitative social researchers and has become synonymous with urban ethnography, participant observation and direct fieldwork. There is a voluminous literature on the Chicago school, which I do not intend to engage with here. I want to specifically draw on some selected covert examples from the early Chicago school of sociology as well as from other strands of sociology.

Robert E. Park, who was a trained journalist, encouraged his students and peers in what has been described as 'street corner methods'. He was a seminal and pioneering figure at the University of Chicago, whose classic dictum was 'go get the seat of your pants dirty in real research' (in McKinney, 1966: 71), which is still thankfully much quoted today. The early exemplar studies of this school were *The Ghetto* (1928) by Louis Wirth, followed by *Street Corner Society* (1943) by William Foot-Whyte. This was part of Park's more general '*tours of exploration*' philosophy, which effectively involved walking the streets to gain impressions and familiarity with the urban culture. *The City* (1925) by Robert Park, Ernest Burgess and Roderick McKenzie elegantly captures some of the methodological reflections of early Chicago researchers. Not all of this urban research was covert, but some covert elements are clearly discernible.

The Hobo: The Sociology of the Homeless Man (1923/1961) by Nels Anderson, one of the classic early Chicago ethnographies, was biographically driven; although most of the collected materials were life history, some would have been covert participant observation. Anderson reflects on his biographical motivation to study the hobo, which directly relates to his and his father's nomadic past, as: 'I was in the process of moving out of the hobo world. To use a hobo expression, preparing the book was a way of "getting by"; earning a living while the exit was under way. The role was familiar before the research began' (Anderson, 1923/1961: xiii).

Charles Rumford Walker, a Yale graduate who had served in the US Army, graphically described his experiences, and particularly the toll of the twelve-hour day in a steel factory, in *Steel: The Diary of a Furnace Worker* (1922), before he became an academic. Similarly, Frances Donovan could also be described as an amateur rather than professional sociologist. She waited tables in a range of restaurants for nine months, worked as a department store clerk for four months and spent thirty years as a school teacher. Her auto-biographical accounts, using participant observation of these three different occupations, had covert features and provided very early studies of women's work that influenced her long-time acquaintance Everett C. Hughes, the sem-inal sociologist from the University of Chicago. They were published as *The Woman Who Waits* (Donovan, 1919), *The Saleslady* (Donovan, 1929) and *The Schoolma'am* (Donovan, 1938).

Turning to the early landmark studies in industrial sociology, Elton Mayo's input came in the classic Hawthorne Studies of the late 1920s and early 1930s, which examined productivity, involved significant deception. When difficul-ties arose with making accurate observations, Mayo (1933), who was based at Harvard Business School, alongside the researchers F. J. Roethlisberger and W. J. Dickinson, established a small dispensary in the plant with a qualified nurse, who opportunistically collected data through the confidences of several factory workers who visited her for medical assistance.

There is an entire field and industry dedicated to the analysis of Howard Becker's work, the famous second-generation scholar from the University of Chicago. Drawing on examples from his early work, his study of dance musicians began around 1947, when he himself was working as a jazz musician as well as being a college student at the University of Chicago. The paper 'The Professional Dance Musician and his Audience' (Becker, 1951), formed the basis of his MA in Sociology. Becker briefly reflects on his eighteen months of fieldwork, involving interviews and observations: 'My research was disclosed to few people. In gen-eral, I was accepted as just another young piano player by most of the men from whom this material was gathered' (1951: 137).

Clearly, Becker exploits autobiographical and retrospective participant obser-vations and memories he made while working as a musician at parties, dance halls and jazz clubs. As Becker reflects later in his famous book *Outsiders: Studies in the Sociology of Deviance*:

> Most of the people I observed did not know that I was making a study of musicians. I seldom did any formal interviewing, but concentrated rather on listening to and recording the ordinary kinds of conversation that occurred among musicians. (1963: 84)

Sullivan et al. (1958) conducted a participant observation study of Air Force recruit training programmes. The three researchers were from the Universities of Buffalo, North Carolina and Wichita. This research had a pragmatic aim in reducing disciplinary problems, increasing enlistment and improving training performance. The study of the training programme lasted four months. Sullivan et al. reflected on their covert stance, where Sullivan himself enlisted as a basic trainee: 'he would be a full-fledged member of the group under study, his identity, mission, and role as a researcher un-known to every one' (1958: 661).

Sullivan took fieldnotes secretly when the other recruits were sleeping and met with the other researchers on leave weekends. Sullivan not only faked his identity but constructed a new personality. The study of the training programme lasted four months. In terms of preparation for the demanding field role, for nine months Sullivan was 'coached in the ways of the adolescent sub-culture' (Sullivan et al., 1958: 663).

Such embedded and embodied work was emotionally demanding. As Sullivan et al. stress: 'In deliberately cultivating a second self the research-observer was engaged in something superficially like intelligence work or espionage' (1958: 664). This was a rather extreme form of passing in that the researcher falsified family history and education, lost thirty-five pounds in weight and had some minor plastic surgery in order to be presented as a nineteen year-old, when his real age was twenty-six. For Sullivan et al. it was an innovative way 'to gather a body of previously unavailable information' (1958: 664) and moreover was a 'new approach that might probe beneath the surface in a revealing way' (1958: 667).

Donald F. Roy's (1959) 'Banana Time' was a study of job satisfaction and informal interaction with machine operators in a garment factory in New York. This was a study of how workers managed monotony and boredom and was the basis for his doctorate at the University of Chicago. Roy sums up the situation: 'The next day was the same: the monotony of the work, the tired legs and sore feet and thoughts of quitting' (1959: 160). This study was influential to many researchers within industrial and occupational sociology in exploring shop-floor informal work cultures, the analysis of time in the workplace and conflict at work. Roy reflects on the deceptive dimensions of his research role over an eleven-month period as a drill operator in a machine shop in an earlier journal paper:

I noted down the data from memory at the end of each workday, only occasionally making surreptitious notes on the job. … I did not reveal my research interest to either management or workers. I remained 'one of the boys on the line', sharing the practices and confidences of my fellows and joining them in the ceaseless war with management. (1952: 427)

In a British context, industrial sociologist Enid Mumford, explored small work group behaviour by working undercover as a catering assistant in the three canteens at Liverpool Docks. Her work on human factors and socio-technical systems became very influential in industrial and occupational sociology. Mumford described her early covert role as 'concealed participant observation' (1959: 137) that 'would not significantly disturb group behaviour and attitudes' (1959: 137).

Julius Roth, who is associated with the second generation of Chicago researchers, while hospitalized as an actual patient with tuberculosis, studied his own treatment situation, including the innovatory analysis of the passing of time from the patient's perspective, for eleven months in two hospitals in the 1950s. He was encouraged to keep a regular diary by his mentors, Everett C. Hughes and David Riesman, which eventually resulted in *Timetables: Structuring the Passage of Time in Hospital Treatment and Other Careers* (1963), which was a groundbreaking book in medical sociology. The study was later given grant support and extended, wherein Roth took on a formal overt role as a sociological observer. Roth reflects on his biographical motivation and covert character of the initial study in a later journal paper:

> I realized that I could make it part of my career by using it as an opportunity for on-the-spot observation of social interaction in an institutional setting. ... There was no formal interviewing or other directed form of data collection, though I sometimes steered conversations to areas of special interest to me. The patients and the hospital staff did not know that I was collecting information on them. (1974: 347–348)

A different type of sociology, although still sociological, has also used covert tactics in its early development, at Harvard University initially and then at University of California, Los Angeles (UCLA). The originator of ethnomethodology, Harold Garfinkel, pioneered the use of what have been popularly called 'breaching experiments', although Garfinkel referred to them variously as 'tutorials', 'teaching instructions' and 'classroom demonstrations'. These 'experiments' are a set of provocations deliberately designed to break the mundane, routine, implicit, tacit and taken-for-granted social rules in a setting. For Garfinkel, trust is a vital condition for stable social actions and in these breaching experiments trust could be demonstrated to have been violated. These so-called 'breaching experiments' are low-level disruptions of ordinary scenes where people then use reasonable explanations to repair the situation.

Typical breaching examples would involve students in taking shopping from a stranger's basket in a grocery store, standing very close to a person while otherwise maintaining an innocuous conversation, saying 'hello' at the termination of a conversation, treating customers as waiting staff in a restaurant, haggling over goods in a shop with fixed prices and acting as lodgers in the parental home.

Such breaching experiments are conceptually driven studies of how social order is maintained and restored, but they clearly had covert elements of disguise, dupery and fakery. Initially, for Garfinkel, these disruptive role-playing experiments displayed rather dramatic results or what he called 'massive effects' (1963: 220) in how we accomplish social order. For Garfinkel, the breaching experiments made the familiar strange, and in turn makes social order visible. For Garfinkel, these field activities were a series of demonstrations not experiments. Lynch (1993), trading on the same intellectual tradition, argues that these troublemaking exercises were more akin to practical jokes than formal social-psychological experiments. What Gregory usefully calls 'incongruity procedures' (1982: 49).

Wolff (1973), inspired by both Goffman and Garfinkel, was interested in the extent to which public behaviour is collectively coordinated. In his investigation of the public behaviour of pedestrians, Wolff conducted an experiment where two researchers, one female and one male, deliberately go on a collision course with a targeted pedestrian in a busy New York street and observe the effect by filming it from above. The researchers wore dark glasses to eliminate eye contact. Ironically, the research was conducted originally by Wolff in 1969 as assessment material for a university course run by the famous social psychologist Stanley Milgram.

Pleasants (1998) makes a comparison between Garfinkel's breaching experiments and the controversial obedience to authority experiments conducted by psychologist Milgram, although some feel that the comparison is flawed because they are from very divergent traditions. Pleasants argues that 'Garfinkel's and Milgram's experiments were very much alike in that both constructed a 'phenomenal micro world and both had to deceive their subjects on the true aim of the experiment and identity of the experimenter' (1998: 20).

Watson usefully refers to the breaching experiments as 'interventions, that is, into the normal stream of daily life as members experience it' (2009: 479). In contrast to those who viewed these somewhat notorious experiments crudely as frivolous, malicious, mischievous or ethically dubious, Watson stresses that there was 'a profoundly serious methodological reason for them' (2009: 479). Thus, for Watson, trust arrangements are a vital part of Garfinkel's very distinctive notion of a sociology of everyday life.

2.5 Conclusions

The early roots of covert work are disparate, non-incremental and clearly not rigorously cross-fertilized. What is very obvious from this review is the diverse body of early covert work. It is also partly a reflection of different ethical

29

times and, in some ways, is in stark contrast to the current climate of ethical hypochondria. Four case studies from different fields were considered in more detail in this chapter. These case studies are, for me, covert gems which need to be rehabilitated for wider consumption and, hopefully, appreciation. In this way, our understanding of the usual suspects of covert research could be diversified and usefully expanded.

2.6 Case study readings

I have listed the case studies chronologically. In disciplinary terms, case study 1 is from investigative journalism, case studies 2 and 4 are from sociology, and case study 3 is from psychology. The sections below are brief summaries of the readings and some comments to guide your thinking about them. Clearly, reading the original material is suggested to develop your own ideas further.

Case study 1: Nellie Bly (1887) *Ten Days in a Mad-House*

For many, the godmother of exposé and crusader investigative journalism must be Nellie Bly (1864–1922), which was an alias for Elizabeth Jane Cochrane. She undertook progressive and brave pieces of covert work, which are still referenced today by some feminist writers and investigative journalists but are generally not widely cited in academic covert work, which is regrettable. It has also been made into a big screen Hollywood film, with the same book title, recently in 2015, which should increase the popular exposure of her work. She was a pioneering feminist journalist and passionate humanitarian, who started her journalism with the *Pittsburgh Dispatch*, where she got her pen name. Under commission by *The World* newspaper in New York City, where she was the first female reporter, twenty-three year-old Bly had herself involuntarily committed to the Women's Lunatic Asylum on Blackwell Island for ten days. This was one of her first undercover assignments.

After a night of practising deranged expressions in front of a mirror, she checked into a boarding house. She refused to go to bed, telling the boarders that she was afraid of them and that they looked crazy. The next morning they summoned the police and she was taken to a courtroom, where she pretended to have amnesia. The judge concluded she had been drugged. She was then examined by four expert doctors, who all declared her to be insane and suffering from hysteria, and committed her.

Committed to a very large asylum, which housed 1,600 inmates, Bly experienced its conditions first-hand. When speaking with her fellow patients, Bly was convinced that some were as sane as she was. Bly recounted stories of brutality, neglect, sleep deprivation, ice cold baths, beatings and forced feedings. Bly struggled to get released from the asylum and needed the support of *The World* newspaper to verify her story as a genuine journalist.

Her case attracted media attention. The articles by Bly aroused public outcry, brought on much needed asylum reform after a grand jury investigation, and were so popular that Bly turned seventeen provocative chapters into an acclaimed and popular book, called *Ten Days in a Mad-House* (1887). The Grand Jury invited Bly to assist and their report recommended some of the changes she had proposed. The report resulted in an $850,000 increase in the budget of the Department of Public Charities and Corrections. The Grand Jury also recommended that future admissions checks and procedures were much stricter and more monitored so that only the seriously ill went to the asylum.

Bly also wrote a regular column for the *New York Evening Journal* after returning from being a reporter on the front lines in Europe covering the First World War. Bly is commonly regarded as an iconic feminist by many commentators, who salute her bravery and innovative approach as a journalist. As Kroger's (1996) journal title cogently exclaims, '*Nellie Bly: She Did It All*'.

Case study 2: Paul G. Cressey (1932) *The Taxi-Dance Hall: A Sociological Study in Commercialized Recreation and City Life*

Cressey, while serving as a case-worker and special investigator for the Juvenile Protective Association, in the summer of 1925 was asked to report on the new and then unfamiliar phenomena of 'closed dance halls', which were open to male patrons only, and their recreational value for young people in Chicago. Moral crusades had closed several of them down and they had been under public scrutiny for some time. In the author's preface, Cressey explains both the motivations and strategies to study the topic, where case material was gathered over a five-year period from the experiences and observations of a team of investigators. Cressey outlines the rationale for the deliberate covert strategy: 'It was apparent that this study, if it were to be completed, had to be conducted without any co-operation from the proprietors and despite the deliberate opposition of some of them' (1932: xix).

Cressey elaborates on the methodological rationale for a collaborative team approach:

> Observers were sent into the taxi-dance halls. They were instructed to mingle with the others and to become as much a part of this social world as ethically possible … The investigators functioned as anonymous strangers and casual acquaintances. (1932: xix–xx)

These 'underground' taxi-dance halls, which were often concealed under 'dancing school' or 'dancing academy' titles, increasingly featured in several large American cities. Cressey stresses the commercialization of the female dancers rather poetically: 'Like the taxi-driver with his cab, she is for public hire and is paid in proportion to the time spent and the services rendered ... It is a mercenary and silent world – this world of the taxi-dance hall. Feminine society is for sale, and at a neat price' (1932: 3/11).

For Cressey, the taxi-dance halls were a distinct social world with certain codes and techniques of control. Cressey describes the dancers as performing 'sensual dancing' and he goes into detail in describing the backgrounds of the dancers and their life course. The young girls, mostly ranging from age fifteen to twenty-eight, were a combination of locals, immigrants, orphans and runaways. Many had difficult family backgrounds with little formal education.

The taxi-dance halls were squarely equated with modernization and commercialization. Cressey sums this up thus: 'In the last analysis the problem of the taxi-dance hall can be regarded as the problem of the modern city' (1932: 287). When the study was published in 1932, the Taxi-Dance Halls were under moral and political attack and were often the sensationalist front cover stories of newspapers, although Cressey took a more sympathetic stance on them. Salerno stresses that Cressey 'opened doors for similar researchers and made it easier for others concerned with so-called bad subjects' (2007: 141).

Hong and Duff (1977) explored the process of becoming a taxi-dancer in Los Angeles over a four-year period using semi-covert methods. They refer to Cressey's work throughout and describe it as 'pioneering research'. More recently, Colosi (2010a) semi-covertly explores the distinctive occupational subculture of the contemporary lap dancer for her doctorate. She draws explicit parallels to Cressey and stresses that 'his was one of the first studies to emphasize the need of the researcher to speak the same 'language' as those being studied' (2010a: 3).

Case study 3: Leon Festinger, Henry W. Riecken and Stanley Schacter (1956) *When Prophecy Fails: A Social and Psychological Study of a Modern Group that Predicted the Destruction of the World*

The study was supported by the Laboratory for Research in Social Relations. The work was seminal in the study of religious cults, despite being criticized by several in the field. Festinger et al.'s popular psychological theory of cognitive dissonance was applied to the study, to culturally manage failed expectations and delusions. Thus, put simply, they found that when prophecies failed or were disconfirmed, it was followed by an increase, not a decrease, in conviction and hence heightened efforts to recruit new followers by the cult members. Festinger et al. (1956) did not use gate-keeping arrangements and it is hence a rarer, more purist example of covert research.

Marian Keech, a housewife, was a key figure who had mysteriously been given messages from aliens that the world would end in a great flood. She had previously been involved with Ron Hubbard's controversial Scientology cult. The group of believers, headed by Keech, displayed their commitment by leaving jobs, college and spouses, and had given away money and possessions to prepare for their rescue by flying saucers and alien life forms. The group was eventually disbanded as police scrutiny increased and large mobs regularly gathered by their houses. The group was headline news nationally and aroused mass interest for a short period of time.

In a methodological appendix, Festinger et al. (1956) stated: 'Our observers posed as ordinary members who believed as the others did. ... We tried to be nondirective, sympathetic listeners, passive participants who were inquisitive and eager to learn whatever others might want to tell us' (1956: 237).

The data was gathered by trained male and female observers, all of whom were staff or students of sociology or psychology with some methodological knowledge. Festinger et al. stress the fatiguing nature of these observational roles, which included all night meetings and opportunistic note taking in bathrooms and outdoor spaces. Group data was also supplemented by the covert work of the authors. On one occasion, two of the authors telephoned and then visited Mrs Keech, the cult leader, on the pretence of being travelling businessmen, and interviewed her and a friend. They refer to their procedures as unorthodox due to 'the complete novelty and unpredictability of the movement' (Festinger et al., 1956: 252) and argue that their work was 'as much a job of detective work as of observation' (Festinger et al., 1956: 252).

Festinger's theory of cognitive dissonance has been the standard paradigm for understanding reactions to failed prophecy (Balch et al., 1983; Hardyck and Braden, 1962). This theory, however, has been criticized by scholars of religion, on both methodological and theoretical grounds (Bainbridge, 1997; Batson and Ventis, 1982; Melton, 1985). Balch et al. (1983) replicated the classic Festinger et al. study with an ethnographic exploration of a millennial Baha'i sect for eight months. Balch et al. (1983), contrary to Festinger et al., argue that reactions to prophetic failure are shaped less by psychological forces than by social circumstances. More recently, Tumminia (1988), in her study of reasoning in a Flying Saucer cult group, refers to the Festinger et al. study as a 'classic', as do many others in the field.

Case study 4: Melville Dalton (1959) *Men Who Manage: Fusions of Feeling and Theory in Administration*

The use of Dalton's work and its impact, unlike the other exemplars, has been more restricted to organizational sociology and is, regrettably, less cited in the wider social science literatures. What is utterly extraordinary is the length of time Dalton spent in a sustained covert role within an organization. The opportunity to provide comparative and longitudinal data from this is quite remarkable and there are few covert research projects that can measure up to this length of time in the field. It is rather surprising that its legacy has not been more far-reaching.

Melville Dalton held a post as Associate Professor of Sociology in the Department of Anthropology and Sociology and an Associate Research Sociologist at the Institute of Industrial Relations, both at the University of California, Los Angeles. Dalton's work was supported by a research grant from the Committee on Human Relations in Industry and supervised by Professor Herbert Blumer, at the University of Chicago. Dalton's case study materials were drawn from four firms, consisting of three factories and one department store in Mobile Acres, central United States.

Dalton describes his role as involving 'prolonged touch-and-go relations' (1959: vii). In the introduction, Dalton clearly maps the mission of his book as:

> … a study of how managers manage, this is not an effort at muckraking, or an apology, or a guidebook in disguise, or an attempt to belittle bureau-cratic operations. Rather the aim is to get as close as possible to the world of managers and to interpret this world and its problems from the inside. (1959: 1–3)

In terms of longitudinal data, the study was very impressive as 'the period of employment, the direct fieldwork, and follow-up visits continued for over a decade' (1959: 2). Dalton's more detailed discussion on methodology is usefully contained in the last chapter of his book titled 'Appendix on Method'. Therein, Dalton stresses 'in no case did I make a formal approach to the top management of any of the firms to get approval or support for the research' (1959: 275).

His justification of his covert stance centres on his critique that the typical results of many overt studies are 'controlled experiments which are not suited to my purpose' (1959: 275). Dalton used an extensive network of key informants, or what he describes as '*intimates*'. It is difficult enough to manage single cases of covert research, but this amount of information flow seems extraordinary. Dalton was aware of the controversial and unorthodox stance he was adopt-ing, what he calls a 'masquerading researcher' (1959: 284), but, for him, such arrangements were legitimate. Thus: 'It seems no more unethical than the use of "visiting shoppers" in business or "projective techniques" in psychological research' (1959: 277).

Dalton also utilized work diaries for recording events, including gossip, joking remarks, threats and accusations in arguments and overheard remarks. Dalton commonly used opportunistic strategies in what he refers to as 'conversational interviewing' (1959: 280). Part of this opportunism also extended to socializing outside the plant gates at the local Yacht club, although he provides scant detail on this.

Schein, in an interesting review essay titled 'A Social Psychologist Discovers Chicago Sociology', refers to the positive impact of the pioneering work of E. C. Hughes and his students Dalton and Goffman. On Dalton, he remarks on how well he 'infiltrated the hallowed halls of an economic enterprise' (Schein, 1989: 103).

For me, Dalton's longitudinal covert stance was pioneering, if somewhat complicated. What seems extraordinary is the size of the covert community that was implicated in his study and, in certain ways, manipulated over a lengthy period of time. Such a role would have been clearly very demanding to sustain. How one manages, never mind controls, the behaviours, interactions and information flows of a large number of informants is puzzling and does lead to a reasonable level of scepticism over some of Dalton's claims. Is his account a rather sentimental, glamorized or heroic one, where informants tolerated his intrusions and were more knowledgeable about his true motives than he claimed?

2.7 Learning exercise

1. List what you understand from each of the four early pioneering covert research case studies above as regards the motivation of the author, the key concepts of the study, potential impact and critiques.

2. In your opinion, could any of these studies be regarded as, and hence added to, the list of classic exemplars in Chapter 4?

3. Are these covert studies still relevant today?

3

DEBATES ABOUT COVERT RESEARCH

3.1 Introduction

This chapter has two broad purposes. First, to historically chart and scope the key debates and controversies surrounding covert research, which have been ongoing for some time. Hence, it is important to critically historicize these debates, which removes one from the botched assumption that the controversy around covert research is only current and contemporary and hence has no roots, which would be erroneous and trivialize the issues involved. Second, to review the current ethical regimentation and bureaucracy in which covert research is saturated, and which effectively fetters and stifles the development of creative and imaginative covert research.

There is an extensive and well-established generalized literature on ethics in the research process, which I do not aim to review in this chapter. Rather, the focus is on the impact of such debates on the specific shape of covert research. The debates about covert research are typically embedded in long-standing debates about the role, place and management of ethics and ethical dilemmas in social research. Although such debates have occupied the central ground for a number of years, they can act as a gloss for the specific, rich and diverse debates about covert research. I do not wish to provide another rehearsal of the familiar tropes on general research ethics, but I have adopted, if you will, more of a covert optic and gaze.

3.2 Early comments on covert research

Some very early general comments on deception in scientific research are worth noting. In 1830, Charles Babbage, the founder of the modern computer, in his book *Reflections on the Decline of Science in England, and on Some of its Causes*, describes four classes of 'fraud', including hoaxing, forging, trimming and cooking. In 1919, under the controversial heading 'Scientists as Spies', Franz Boas, one of the founding fathers of academic anthropology, published a letter in *The Nation* which claimed that four anthropologists, whom he did not name, had abused their professional research positions by conducting espionage in Central America during the First World War. Boas, despite some organizations trying to censor him, strongly condemned their actions, writing that they had prostituted science by using it as a cover for their activities as spies. For Boas, anthropologists spying for their country severely betrayed their science and damaged the credibility of all anthropological research.

The early sentiments of Boas find some resonance in the debates over Project Camelot (Horowitz, 1967), which basically centred on covert espionage about Latin America initiated by the CIA, which did not come to fruition. More recently, the Network of Concerned Anthropologists (NCA), an independent ad hoc network of anthropologists working in the USA, Canada and the UK, was established to seek to promote an ethical anthropology. The NCA was formed in 2008 in opposition to what they view as unethical anthropology.

An early statement about experimental research was *The Nuremberg Code* of 1945, which is still commonly quoted by most textbooks on ethics. Pimple argues that 'the Nuremberg Code was probably the first major internationally influential code of research ethics' (2008: xvi). The Nuremberg Code was followed historically by numerous others that collectively reflect a medical model of ethics, which has a rather protectionist mentality to the subject in terms of harm and responsibility. Such a mentality is still very prevalent today in the social sciences, as articulated in the concept of informed consent. In some rare instances, belligerent social research can result in litigation, but surely it cannot serve as a model for the majority of cases.

There have been some infamous horror stories from research over the years, which have resulted in a generalized and extreme reaction to covert research. One of the most notorious cases of belligerent unethical research was the *Tuskegee Study of Untreated Syphilis in the Negro Male*, also known popularly as the

Tuskegee Syphilis Study and the *Tuskegee Syphilis Experiment*, published in 1972 by the Tuskegee Institute in the USA. This was longitudinal research, which took place over forty years from 1932 to 1972, and followed the medical history of 600 participants, all poor black male farm workers in Alabama. The subjects were not fully aware of their disease and the nature of the controlled research by the Public Health Service and the Tuskegee Institute and so informed consent was not gained. Researchers also actively deceived the participants by not treating the disease, which they termed 'bad blood', when they could have by using penicillin. It resulted in suffering and eventual death. This was met with widespread outrage and condemnation and instigated processes to try to protect human subjects from such treatment. The compensation cases and legal trials are still ongoing in the United States. Several researchers have viewed this research as displaying forms of early institutionalized racism (Brandt, 1978; Jones, 1981; Littlewood, 1993). Patton describes this as: 'a past littered with scientific horrors for which those of us engaging in research today may still owe penance' (2002: 271).

3.3 Some key debates about covert research

It is useful to historically chart some, but not all, of the key debates around covert research in some more detail. Edward Shils (1959) opposed all forms of covert research without explicit and fully informed consent as dishonest. Hence, all research projects should fully disclose their intentions and purposes. For Shils (1959), social science activity should be disciplined by careful attention to the problems of privacy. Julius Roth, in opposition, argued that secrecy was effectively institutionalized in sociological research as, for him, all research had elements of secrecy and hence trying to regulate this would 'perpetuate current moral biases and restrict rather than aid further ethical development' (1962: 284).

In many ways, the much quoted essay by Kia Erikson (1967) continues the traditional stance against what was generally described then as 'disguised observation' and 'secret observation'. Erikson argues that 'It is unethical for a sociologist to deliberately misrepresent the character of the research in which he is engaged' (1967: 373). For Erikson, covert strategies may be appropriate for espionage and journalism, but he argues that sociology has different rules of engagement. Erikson maintains four objections to disguised observation that include: harming the actors in the social scene under study; damaging the reputation of sociology in society and spoiling future investigation of a field; exposing students to difficult ethical dilemmas; and betraying the complexity and subtlety of the social structure under observation.

Denzin (1968) recognized that most of the comments made regarding the ethics of what he characterizes as disguised observation had broadly followed the path of condemnation that Shils (1959) had previously laid out. Barnes (1963), in a British context, had followed a similar line of condemnation and viewed covert research as ultimately dishonest. Denzin (1968) sensibly argued that the use of disguise by sociologists was not always unethical and could be justified in certain circumstances.

In *Unobtrusive Measures: Nonreactive Research in the Social Sciences* (1966), Webb et al. present what they considered to be novel methods, which included physical traces, archive records, and simple and contrived observations. They 'purposely avoided consideration of the ethical issues which they raise' (Webb et al., 1966: v). Unobtrusive measures are basically the research procedures used to avoid what Webb et al. viewed as reactivity or artificial behaviour by the respondents to the presence of the researcher that could distort data in some way. Namely, the classic '*Hawthorne Effect*' previously highlighted in the pioneering research experiments of Mayo (1933) and others on the relationship between workplace conditions and production levels.

Webb et al. do have a chapter on 'contrived observations; hidden hardware and control' in the original book, but do not discuss covert research in any detailed way, despite a brief discussion of entrapment. Webb et al. argue that generally research techniques should 'avoid the problems of invasion of privacy' (1966: vii) and permit 'ethically scrupulous social scientists to do their work effectively and to sleep better at night' (1966: vii).

In the revised and updated version of the original book, edited by Eugene Webb, entitled *Nonreactive Measures in the Social Sciences* (1981), two new chapters were added on 'overt ethics for covert measurement' and 'limitations on the use of nonreactive measures', which discuss informed consent and ethical issues in more detail but not covert research in a dedicated way. Lee (2000) calls for an increased use of unobtrusive methods in social research and usefully explored its use in the social sciences, including in internet research. Lee claims that it can 'encourage playful and creative approaches to data' (2000: 15).

In opposition to more conventional views on deception at the time, Douglas (1976) argues that deceptive methods are essential to do good social science research as they mirror the social world, which has elements of deceitfulness, evasiveness and secrecy. For Douglas, investigative methods have their place in the social sciences and can ultimately be justified as a reasonable means to richer research ends. Douglas argues that most methods are 'still genteel and certainly harmless' (1976: xiv). Douglas proposes that we should use fieldwork techniques and procedures modelled on professional investigative occupations such as journalism and security services. Accordingly, Douglas argues that for the fieldworker, 'rather than seeking entrée, we infiltrate the setting' (1976: 167). For Douglas, investigative social research is necessary because conventional anthropological field methods have been based on a flawed consensus view of society. Hence, Douglas stresses that 'conflict is the reality of life; suspicion is the guiding principle' (1976: 55).

Hilbert (1980) argues that covert participant observation is an 'unstudied phenomenona', which is comparatively still the case. Hilbert suggests that not all covert participant observation is necessarily unethical. For Hilbert, the covert role translates practically into 'what it takes to sustain competent membership' (1980: 53). Indeed, Hilbert argues that 'covert participant observation is participation *par excellence*' (1980: 53).

Hilbert (1980) usefully bases his discussion partly on his own covert investigations for his doctorate on an elementary teaching credentials programme, over a one-year period. Hilbert also discusses the classic case of Agnes, an intersexed person who collaborated with Harold Garfinkel (1967). Agnes actively maintained various secrets from Garfinkel about her sexual identity. Interestingly, Hilbert creatively likens the covert condition to the blurring problem of Agnes, who guarded her projected identity and engineered past and had to credibly 'pass' in the setting as a female, despite being male.

Bulmer (1982a), in his useful review of alternatives to covert participant observation, asks the pertinent question 'When is Disguise Justified?' Bulmer stresses the need to recognize a wider variety of observational research strategies that are not captured by the naïve and crude polarized either/or dichotomy around covert and overt research. Such simplistic reasoning, which does not recognize complexity, for Bulmer, 'stultifies debate and hinders methodological innovation' (1982a: 252).

Barnes argues that lies play a ubiquitous part in social life, stressing that: 'most people accept that in everyday life we often encounter lies … lying has been a human activity for a long time, and it is not merely a recent and regrettable innovation' (1983: 152). For Barnes, lying is an expected part of our culture, learnt in childhood and normalized in various adult contexts. Barnes describes his approach as developing a 'sociology of lying' (1994).

Homan (1991) argues that the dissident stance against covert research is akin to a 'professional consensus'. He sums up the standard and familiar 'case against covert methods' in his popularized thirteen objections. These respectively include: flouting the principle of informed consent, eroding personal liberty, betraying trust, polluting the research environment, damaging the reputation of social research, discriminating against the defenceless and powerless, damaging the behaviour or interests of subjects, when deception becomes habitual for the researcher, when deception spreads to other spheres of human interaction, when covert methods are invisibly reactive, when covert methods are seldom necessary, when covert methods confine the scope of research, and finally, when the covert researcher suffers excessive strain in maintaining the cover.

For Mitchell, secrecy is a fundamental part of qualitative research. Mitchell opens his very interesting yet neglected book *Secrecy and Fieldwork* (1993) claiming that 'secrets are an integral part of social science research and are by no means limited to covert inquiry' (1993: 2). Mitchell disagrees with crude debates about deception and concludes that: 'Secrecy in research is a risky but necessary business. If the social sciences are to continue to provide substantive, enduring insights into human experience, timid inquiry will not do' (1993: 54).

Miller (1995) more assertively argues that social science has 'virtually ignored' covert research and, moreover, 'this disregard has made covert observation the truly least used of all the qualitative research methods' (1995: 97). Miller cautions that 'new generations of researchers therefore remain unfamiliar with a potentially valuable research option' (1995: 97). For Miller, 'covert designs tender opportunities to reach relatively unstudied topics' (1995: 103). Miller is more optimistic for the future, proposing that 'covert participant observation may well become more commonplace' (1995: 104). Miller argues for a reconsideration of covert methodology, claiming that 'the study of crime invites and sometimes requires the covert method as does examination of the clandestine nature of many faces of the formal social control apparatus' (1995: 103).

Adler and Adler, in *Ethnography at the Edge* (1998), an edited collection of researchers concerned with risk and danger in fieldwork settings, cogently sum up some of the effects of the stricter ethical regimentation on covert research: 'Potentially gone, then, is any ethnographic research involving a covert role for the investigator (thus removing hidden populations further from view)' (1998: xiv–xv).

Herrera (2003) proposes that the clash with undercover research is effectively between methods and morals. Herrera argues 'there does not seem to be a way that covert research can meet ethical guidelines unless we adjust our conceptions of research, ethics, or both' (2003: 351). For Herrera, covert studies appear to be in an 'ethical and methodological limbo' (2003: 354) but a robust space for covert research should be found.

Lugosi appeals for a sensible approach to field ethics stating: 'Instead of labelling "covert" research and dismissing it on the grounds of ethical irresponsibility, it is more useful to consider how the nature of the study, the character of the fieldwork context, and the relationships between informants and ethnographer determine overtness or covertness in the field' (2006: 542).

Ferdinand et al. (2007), draw on four different ethnographic 'tales', some of which were covert, from their respective fields to examine the ethical and moral dilemmas they have faced in the field, particularly illegality and wrongdoing. They call for an appreciation of 'a different kind of ethics', rather than crude dualities. They sensibly conclude that: 'Our responsibility as ethical researchers we believe lies with finding resolutions to the situated dilemmas we encounter throughout the course of research. ... This does not mean that we live in a fragmented post-modern world where anything goes' (2007: 540).

Spicker adds that covert research is 'often muddled with deception and condemned as intrinsically unethical' (2011: 118). For Spicker, the debates about covert research are hampered by 'widespread confusion about the duties that researchers owe to their subjects' (2011: 131). Spicker is critical of the misconceived, restrictive and stereotypical view of research by ethical boards, which constructs an ideal type ethics. Spicker stresses that 'the rules which are being applied to covert research are based in concerns about a marginal set of special cases' (2011: 131).

Barrera and Simpson argue that the 'norms governing the use of deception are now firmly entrenched along disciplinary lines' (2012: 383). They suggest that researchers should not adopt dogmatic ideological positions about deception but 'instead adopt a pragmatic, evidence-based approach to the question of when deception is advisable' (2012: 406). For them, deception does have a role in research and its appropriate use has to be evaluated around potential costs and benefits.

Shilling and Mellor (2015) call for a sociology of deceit, which, building on Simmel's classic early paper 'The Sociology of Secrecy and of Secret Societies' (1906), explores doubled identities, interested actions and situational logics of opportunity. For them, sociology can play a robust role in the interrogation of deceit as a political, cultural and intellectual strategy. Shilling and Mellor cogently argue that: 'a sociological re-engagement with deceit is overdue. This, as we have suggested, needs to be attentive to the possibility that sociology can be implicated in the deceit it seeks to comprehend' (2015: 618).

3.4 The mantra of informed consent: a dynamic process

The standard contemporary ethics debates, which have structured much discussion on covert research, have been centred on informed consent in various guises. It is informed consent that drives standard research practice. Professional codes typically inform and guide various social science disciplines. Most take a standard view on covert research, wherein it is frowned upon and the object of disapproval, in different ways. It is commonly characterized as what I term a 'last resort methodology' (Calvey, 2008).

The standard position, then, views covert research as violating the principle of informed consent by using deception. The rationalizing tendencies of the ethical review boards deny ambiguity in the research relationship, which is problematic in ethnographic real-world research. Most sensible researches are not against informed consent *per se*, but are sceptical of the pervasive 'one size fits all' mentality.

As you would expect, there is a dedicated critical literature on informed consent in the social sciences (Corrigan, 2003; Librett and Perrone, 2010; Marzano, 2007; Sin, 2005; Wiles et al., 2007), with many researchers viewing informed consent as ultimately partial, contingent, dynamic and shifting, particularly when dealing with vulnerable groups and sensitive topics. Indeed, for Punch, absolute consent is an impracticable ideal and forcing it 'will kill many a research project stone dead' (1986: 36). Homan (2001) sensibly argues that informed consent more realistically 'lapses' into assumed consent in many research settings. Shilling and Mellor argue that: 'The phenomenon of "informed consent", for example, is a cornerstone of empirical research, but research involves transformations unrevealed to those involved' (2015: 617–618).

Let us turn to some varied cases from the social sciences for a more detailed look in order to display informed consent as a dynamic, contingent and complex research process.

Adler (1985), in her famous study of street cannabis dealers, states: 'With many of these people, then, we took a covert posture in the research setting. ... Confronted with secrecy, danger, hidden alliances, misrepresentations and unpredictable changes of intent, I had to use a delicate combination of overt and covert roles' (1985: 17/27).

Paterniti (2000) investigated the micro-politics of identity in a chronic care home. Her study was conducted over a four-month period where she worked full-time as a nursing aide. This was a private, long-term care facility for the aged and mentally ill, and one that she characterized as a *total institution*. She informed both staff and patients about the study, but aspects of it became covert due to the specific dynamics and practical realities of the setting.

Lawton (2001) similarly reflects on the process of gaining and maintaining consent and the ethical concerns in her ten-month participant observation of dying patients in an inpatient hospice in the UK. The project had strict ethical gate-keeping arrangements with medical staff, but the embedded choice of going native as an active volunteer was one encouraged by the hospice staff. As Lawton states: 'By becoming a part of the hospice culture, it was possible to collect data by means of direct observation rather than by a heavy-handed use of interviews' (2001: 696–697). In this volunteer role, Lawton sat with distressed and dying patients, sometimes helping to feed weaker patients. In this sense, 'participant observation constituted a viable and ethical approach' (2001: 697), although she warns against 'any complacency that may accompany such an approach' (2001: 703).

Patients were told of the research on admission and could choose to opt-out of the study, but due to the large turnover of such an unbounded community with two hundred deaths over the study period, not all patients could practically be informed or were aware of the research. This insider role in this setting was then profoundly emergent. As Lawton states: 'Because a role was adopted in the hospice that allowed me to go native and to become part of the furniture as it were, the very real dilemma had to be confronted that patients could forget very quickly that research was actually taking place' (2001: 699).

Consent with dying people is clearly a very controversial and emotive area, particularly when dealing with complex forms of dementia. Hence, Lawton poses the complex question of 'how informed can informed consent be?' Such extreme cases clearly disrupt any generalized and crude blanket statements about methodological strategies and models, although most research settings are clearly not as sensitive and particularistic as these ones.

Murphy and Dingwall (2001, 2003, 2007) explore the application of informed consent to ethnographic research into various health care settings. They cogently argue that anticipatory regulatory regimes operating in Canada, the USA and the UK are inimical to ethnographic research and hence threaten the valuable contribution ethnographic research makes to the health care field. For Murphy and Dingwall, such regulatory regimes were developed for the governance of clinical and biomedical research and are 'ill-suited' to assessing ethnographic worth, value and relevancy. However, this does not lead to an abandonment of informed consent by Murphy and Dingwall. Indeed, they fully agree with the principle of informed consent but question its standard operationalization to research settings, which ignores variability.

Griffiths (2008) reflects on the ethical conduct of being both a nurse ethnographer and practising nurse in an Acute Medical Admissions Unit in Swansea, Wales. She stresses that informed consent was not obtained from some patient informants despite research proposals to various committees ensuring informed consent. Griffiths passionately states: 'The ethical judgement was made that not to seek informed consent was in the best interests of patients who were very ill or distressed and that to insist on informed consent would have been potentially harmful to these patients' (2008: 350).

For Griffiths, her contextual moral judgement enhanced her ethical decision-making rather than impoverished it. Indeed, 'rigid adherence to formal bio-medical guidance can lead to inappropriate ethical actions' (2008: 350). Griffiths argues that despite the complexity of dealing with patients in acute pain, sometimes resulting in death, researchers should operate with an 'ethic of care' (Gilligan, 1993) that is 'bound to the particulars of time and place' (Gilligan, 1993: 59).

Librett and Perrone (2010), based on their research work on undercover police officers and recreational drug users in dance club settings in the United States, argue that there is a 'fundamental disconnect' between what the typical ethical review boards perceive as protecting privacy and the ethnographers' practical view of trust and partnership with their research participants. For Librett and Perrone, such a disconnect has 'greatly affected contemporary ethnographic research' (2010: 729).

Perez-y-Perez and Stanley (2011) reflect on what they refer to as 'ethnographic intimacy' in their studies of two distinct sex worlds. They consider their 'hybrid selves' in conducting fieldwork on sensitive topics and how they negotiated various ethical dilemmas. They also stress the lack of fit between ethical guidelines and the practical reality of fieldwork. Stanley conducted overt research on male sexual negotiation, risk and HIV and Perez-y-Perez conducted research on massage parlours in New Zealand, which was part of her previous doctoral research. To embed her understanding of this sex work world, Perez-y-Perez got a job as a paid shift manager in a massage parlour. Management and staff knew of the research. However, typical of such real-time commercial research settings, clients often believed or were led to believe that she was a shift manager or receptionist and not a researcher. Therefore, she was part of an interactional deceit in not letting them know her real research role.

Menih (2013), in her ethnographic research on vulnerable homeless women in Brisbane, found that managing informed consent involved continual improvisation as many of the participants had ongoing mental health problems and some comprehension problems when consent was given. On some occasions, the participants were under the influence of drugs and on other occasions, age became an issue in terms of being involved in the study. For Menih, applying ethical principles with a vulnerable population is deeply problematic and is symptomatic of the disconnect that can emerge between the textbook theory on ethics and the fieldwork reality.

The popular urban street ethnography *On the Run: Fugitive Life in an American City* (2014) by Alice Goffman, which was based on her doctoral thesis, was a controversial one. It presented a host of ethical dilemmas for Goffman as she witnessed daily drug dealing and police raids and, more specifically, she willingly gave a lift in her car to a friend who was carrying a firearm explicitly to carry out a revenge attack, which did not happen.

The project is impressive in longitudinal terms, with Goffman spending six years conducting the fieldwork in a lower-income black neighbourhood in Philadelphia. Goffman argues at the outset that 'it is an account of a community on the run' (2014: xii). The project is methodologically similar to the famous *Street Corner Society: The Social Structure of an Italian Slum* (1943) by William Foot-Whyte in terms of its sustained community immersion and the use of key informants. In his case, this was a slum area of Boston for three and a half years, exploring Italian migration patterns and gang-based street racketeering. Goffman asked various key informants and their families for permission to conduct the research, but some aspects of her study must have been covert because not everyone she came into contact with over such a lengthy period of time would have been universally informed about her project.

Goffman states: 'I stumbled into the project as a student at the University of Pennsylvania' (2014: xii) while doing a community volunteer project as an undergraduate. She ended up staying in this poor neighbourhood and sharing roommates with local residents in Philadelphia. She negotiated her place in the community by adopting the 'role of sidekick and adopted sister' (2014: 228) and observed 'local black young men dipping and dodging the police' (2014: 211).

Her fieldwork involved regular visits to county jails and state prisons and interview data with official figures in the criminal justice system, including two lawyers, a district attorney, three probation officers, two police officers and a judge. Goffman outlines her ethnographic drive as: 'Beyond being a fly on the wall, I wanted to be a participant observer' (2014: 240). The book has been a source of controversy and media attention, with some critics viewing it as an exaggerated account that is ethically dubious and cavalier. Lubet (2015), a stern critic, controversially titles his critique of her work 'Ethics on the Run'.

In rare cases, research can become genuinely dangerous. In 1993, Rik Scarce, while a doctoral student at Washington State University, spent five months in jail on a federal contempt of court charge rather than reveal details of his research interviews with militant animal rights and liberation activists, who were involved in significant criminal vandalism and were being investigated by the FBI. Scarce maintained that he was entitled to a 'scholar's privilege', ensuring the confidentiality of his informants, but this argument was rejected by the judge. Neither the American Sociological Association nor his institution could stop the sentencing. He still did not divulge the information to the police and was released from prison because this sanction was not effective. His case received widespread press attention.

Scarce later reflected on his experiences, including his imprisonment, as part of a growing convict autoethnography tradition, in various publications, including his book *Contempt of Court: A Scholar's Battle for Free Speech from Behind Bars* (2005). Richard Leo (1995), a leading expert in police interrogation, was also threatened with contempt of court and potential incarceration, although he did not go to jail. He testified when requested to divulge sensitive and confidential observational information on police interrogators he had gathered. However, Leo felt that he had betrayed subject confidentiality and also called for the need for 'evidentiary privilege for academic researchers' (1995: 113).

Parker and Crabtree (2014) argue that covert research can be useful in the context of studying vulnerable groups. It does not remove robust ethical scrutiny from the process of selecting a covert approach, but it should not be seen as automatically redundant because of the topics under study. Thus, Parker and Crabree argue: 'Covert research assists in illuminating the hidden voices and lives of vulnerable people that may otherwise remain inaccessible. Such research needs to be subject to rigorous ethical standards to ensure that it is both justified and robust' (2014: 29). The argument here, then, is to relax, not remove, ethical safeguards in collaboratively researching vulnerable groups and sensitive topics. The question then of whether a covert approach can be used or not in sensitive cases should then be sensibly reviewed on a case by case basis rather than apply a type of risk averse motivated blanket refusal or avoidance.

It is little wonder, therefore, that many of the standard contemporary debates, which have structured much of the current discussion on covert research, have been centred on informed consent in various guises. It is not to say that informed consent does not have a valuable role to play in social research, but it is my contention, despite the dissident literature on it by some, that we effectively still have a 'fetish' for informed consent and a sort of blind faith belief in it that becomes a ritualistic research mantra (Calvey, 2008, 2013) to many in the social science community.

Atkinson, in his recent exploration of ethnography, sensibly points to the complexity in gaining and maintaining informed consent:

Ethnographers would find it especially difficult to establish the boundaries of informed consent in any case. This is not because we wish, in most cases, to engage in covert research, but because the nature of the research itself is so profoundly an emergent property of the processes of data collection and research design. (2015: 179)

3.5 Ethical governance and regimentation

Professional codes and associations regulate, inform and guide various social science disciplines with their statements and guidelines. Most take a standard view on covert research, wherein it is frowned upon and the object of disapproval, in different ways. An example of this standard view is that taken by the British Sociological Association (BSA) and other associations. Thus, covert research is effectively designed out of, or at best marginalized by, the ethics review process. Concerns about the restrictive regimentation of research are not new. What we have in the current regime is a distinct increase in ethical regulation.

Clearly, there is relevant and appropriate legislation, and sensitivities to vulnerable groups and resulting codes of practice on dealing with the Mental Capacity Act 2005 and Safeguarding Vulnerable Groups Act 2006 that precludes covert research in certain areas. However, these are very particular contexts and settings, with specific rules that the vast majority of sensible researchers would ordinarily comply with. Moreover, the majority of research would not typically be undertaken in such settings. Hence, it is not an ethical 'one size fits all' situation. There are also more recent codes and protocols that have been developed for visual methodology and internet ethics because of their specific challenges and contexts.

In the UK, a common source of public funding for social science research is the Economic and Social Research Council (ESRC). In 2010 it published *The Framework for Research Ethics* (FRE), which was updated in January 2015. It effectively exerts a type of bounded censorship on ethical practice. When outlining its 'principles and expectations for ethical research', what it refers to as 'justified deception' 'should only be used as a last resort when no other approach is possible' (2015: 43). As a result, *Research Ethics Committees* (RECs) exert a stronger influence and remit on practice through ethical scrutiny and review, which extends throughout a project's life and not just at the proposal stage, as before. For those seeking funding from the ESRC, which is a common source for social sciences research in the UK, it becomes mandatory to follow the stipulations in the FRE. Stanley and Wise (2010) argue that the ESRC's FRE is ultimately not 'fit for purpose'. Covert research under such a regime is even more marginalized.

There is a growing critical dissident literature on ethical governance and regimentation (Bosk and de Vries, 2004; Crow et al., 2006; Dingwall, 2006, 2008; Haggerty, 2004; Hammersley, 2009, 2010; Hammersley and Traianou, 2011, 2012; Hedgecoe, 2016; Hunter, 2008; Israel, 2004; Reed, 2007; Richardson and McMullan, 2007; Wiles et al., 2007). Various writers here flag that researchers are effectively faced with both ethics and audit creeps, which are often abstracted and disconnected from the complexities of real-world research.

Previously, Wax (1977) classically warned that the expansion of university administration and bureaucracy restricted academic freedom and autonomy and were out of touch with fieldwork realities. Fine argues that 'illusions are essential for maintaining occupational reputation' (Fine, 1993: 267). For Fine, part of this is the methodological illusion of idealized ethical standards, with ethnographers: 'caught in a web of demands that compel them to deviate from formal and idealistic rules' (1993: 269). For Fine, ethnographers routinely develop a 'body of conceits' (1993: 289), hence his suggestion is to: 'let us open our conceits to ourselves and our readers' (1993: 290). For me, part of this 'body of conceit' is, among other issues, covert tactics and moves.

For Katz (2006), many fieldworkers risk becoming IRB (Institutional Review Board) outlaws and 'underground ethnographers' under overly strict ethical regimes. Katz argues that: 'the very rationale for fieldwork is often unpredictability' (2006: 500). For Katz, 'the requirement for preauthorization condemns most participant-observation fieldwork to an underground existence' (2006: 500).

For Murphy and Dingwall, professional ethical regulation is necessary but it needs to be more sensitive and fit for purpose. They argue that: 'it is time to reclaim research ethics from the bureaucrats' (Murphy and Dingwall, 2007: 2231). For them, the anticipatory regulatory regimes developed for the governance of clinical and biomedical experimental research: 'threaten the survival of ethnographic research with little gain in protecting research participants' (Murphy and Dingwall, 2007: 2224).

Murphy and Dingwall also stress that covert research has been effectively usurped by investigative journalists, writers and commentators working with different motives, often appealing to the public interest, and relatively free of ethical regulation. For them, ethical regulation cannot be ignored nor tinkered with in its current paradigm. They argue: 'It requires a root and branch re-thinking of ethical regulation, and a reassertion of the continuing value of professional self-regulation and mutual accountability' (Murphy and Dingwall, 2007: 2232).

Schrag (2010) provides a historical analysis of the development of research governance through IRBs, which are broadly similar to the UK's 'Research Ethics Committees' (RECs). He argues that the biomedical model of research governance, which has traditionally framed and bounded the debates, has spread and is not well suited to social scientific research. Similarly, Stark (2012) reminds us that modern IRBs have been defensively conceived.

Van Den Hoonaard outlines the inappropriate imposition of the medical model on the social sciences as part of the current ethics regime in what he describes as 'the coming defeat of the social sciences by the imposition of medical ethics' (2011: xii). Van Den Hoonaard, based on his own professional experience and interview data with various members of ethics review boards from forty-nine Universities in Australia, Canada, England, South Africa and the United States, attempts to develop a pragmatic and alternative 'system of ethics that speaks to the needs of social researchers' (Van Den Hoonaard, 2011: xii).

Van Den Hoonaard makes reference to the opposing and disconnected cultures and communities of the bureaucratic research ethics committees and the researchers, and for the need to have strategic and sensible dialogue, and a willingness to adapt rather than adopt either full compliance or total avoidance. Van Den Hoonaard usefully argues that many ethics review boards and committees are restricted by 'institutional display'. Van Den Hoonaard and others have recently called for an 'ethics rupture', which would open up thinking about alternative ethical praxis and frameworks.

Emmerich (2013, 2016) sensibly calls for a reframing of research ethics and the development of a type of internal professional ethics in the social sciences, which is not based on the prior orthodox biomedical models but respects the diversity of the disciplines and importantly is not always 'entirely aligned'. For Emmerich, the Clinical Ethics Committee, which operates successfully on the principles of flexibility, robust dialogue and the specificity of cases, could be a more appropriate model for the social sciences to adopt. Hopefully, covert research would be recognized and supported in such a reframing.

Some universities are encouraging more flexibility in ethical research governance by constituting discipline-specific ethics committees rather than institution-wide IRBs and RECs. Accordingly, Fistein and Quilligan (2011) argue that more social scientists need to directly and actively engage in the 'lion's den' of ethics committees and in doing so shape the future. We certainly cannot apply a simple 'checklist mentality' (Gawande, 2010; Iphofen, 2009, 2011) to complex ethical decision-making. As Iphofen sensibly argues: 'Qualitative researchers cannot argue for immunity from the growth of formal ethical scrutiny. But novice, particularly postgraduate, researchers need all the constructive support they can get' (2011: 445).

Hedgecoe (2016) argues that ethics review committees and boards, both in the UK and USA, exhibit behaviour that ultimately 'prioritises the reputational protection of their host institution over and above academic freedom and the protection of research subjects' (2016: 486). Such reputational risk and brand management by universities, in an increasingly pragmatic and competitive climate, will no doubt intensify and in turn make it more problematic for covert research to prosper.

3.6 Conclusions

What we find with some of these ethical debates, despite the new context of governance, is that it points to the deeply recursive and repetitious nature of sociological knowledge. Problems with covert research are not new. Research governance needs to be realistically relaxed, not removed, for in-depth research into a range of topics. Some topics, like the study of crowd behaviour and public disorder, are often difficult to achieve in standard overt ways and require types of flexible covert 'bystander' approach. Also, when studying cyber-space and social media, including cloaked extremist sites, covert lurking often seems more appropriate. In various opportunistic circumstances, gaining informed consent is impractical and hence it is rather naïve to formally adhere to it in any dogmatic sense.

Hopefully, this chapter has placed the debates about covert research into a reasonable historical perspective, which attempts to display the grounding of reactions, many being exaggerated, to covert research. In short, covert research is often treated as an antithesis to open and overt research, which is a very simplistic duality. Many authors have recognized that there is not a clear and polarized divide between overt and covert research. The debates about covert research are then philosophically embedded in long-standing debates about the role, place and management of ethics and ethical dilemmas in social research. It can also be seen that the increasing ethical regimentation plays some complex part in stifling covert research.

It seems as if the adverse, and for some hysterical and exaggerated, reactions to covert research is based on research extremity. As if, to put it bluntly, all covert research results in the harm and brutalization of both the researcher and the researched. Therefore, by definition, for some, covert research is always unethical and an inevitable act of wilful ethical transgression and moral trespass. I ultimately take a type of 'situated' approach (Calvey, 2008; Fletcher, 1966) to ethics in practice, in opposition to any sort of universalism. Within that stance, covert research can be justified and ethical dilemmas are typically managed in the setting and not resolved. Clearly, the debates over covert research are far from settled. More discussion is to be expected, and indeed welcomed.

In my conception, covert research is not a belligerent, heroic or cavalier 'anything goes' business. It is a case of sensibly working out the boundaries of ethics in practice. Most social scientists are not independent professionals governed by their own personal code of ethics, but most commonly employees of university bureaucracies and hence, as researchers, acting as representatives of those organizations and often under their legal protection. Much of what covert research wants to access is more mundane activity, in both public and private realms, rather than that which is necessarily surreptitious, concealed or transgressive.

The ethical issues, and particularly those about harm, seem inflated because, as the previous diverse catalogue of covert studies shows, the issues involved in most cases are typically not very serious and are more mundane. Ultimately, the demand for informed consent has rather more of a ceremonial role than forming a protection against significant or seriously harmful infringements of people's actual rights. The protectionist preoccupation with ethics does, in some ways, for me, point to an exaggerated sense of the status, importance and influence of the academic role in research settings. Additionally, the fixation on some ethical dilemmas is often self-centred on the researcher's sense of well-being and can become a mask of self-regard.

It is not to say that there is not a role for ethical committees and there is no need for or value in ethical scrutiny. Clearly, we need appropriate ethical boundaries and sensitivities, particularly for vulnerable groups and sensitive topics. Indeed, in some research cases, ethical restrictions are often utterly necessary and required. Ethical regulation is concerned with the entitlements of those being researched, with informed consent becoming akin to a right to often safeguard privacy. This is neither to be treated frivolously or casually, as if it does not matter. Researchers also do need to engage with research ethics bodies in a sensible way rather than pompously distance themselves as privileged participants.

3.7 Learning exercise

1. What are the purposes of ethics boards and committees? Who are such boards protecting and why?

2. What do you understand informed consent to mean?

3. Is there too much ethical regimentation now? Can it stifle the development of covert research?

4. Is there a disconnect between the reality of fieldwork and the ethical code, statements and obligations of various professional bodies? Should we be more relaxed with the ethical scrutiny of research proposals? Ask these questions in a group context, with students being divided into different sides. A sort of 'for' and 'against' covert research debate.

To assist you in this task, you can reflect on the 'statement of ethical practice' (March 2002) of the British Sociological Association (BSA) below (31–33). It acknowledges the ethical codes and statements of the Social Research Association, the American Sociological Association and the Association of Social Anthropologists of the UK and the Commonwealth. Many other professional bodies follow this standard stance on covert research.

31) There are serious ethical and legal issues in the use of covert research but the use of covert methods may be justified in certain circumstances. For example, difficulties arise when research participants change their behaviour because they know they are being studied. Researchers may also face problems when access to spheres of social life is closed to social scientists by powerful or secretive interests.

32) However, covert methods violate the principles of informed consent and may invade the privacy of those being studied. Covert researchers might need to take into account the emerging legal frameworks surrounding the right to privacy. Participant or non-participant observation in non-public spaces or experimental manipulation of research participants without their knowledge should be resorted to only where it is impossible to use other methods to obtain essential data.

33) In such studies it is important to safeguard the anonymity of research participants. Ideally, where informed consent has not been obtained prior to the research it should be obtained post-hoc.

You also might want to explore some controversial but instructive examples of covert fieldwork to assist in your ethical debate. The following three suggestions are from different settings:

Buckingham, R. W., Lack, S. A., Mount, B. M. and MacLean, L. D. (1976) 'Living with the dying: use of the technique of participant observation', *Canadian Medical Association Journal*, 115 (18 December): 1211–1215.

Pearson, G. (2009) 'The researcher as hooligan: where "participant" observation means breaking the law', *International Journal of Social Research Methodology*, 12(3): 243–255.

Scheper-Hughes, N. (2004) 'Parts unknown: undercover ethnography of the organs-trafficking underworld', *Ethnography*, 5(1): 29–73.

4

THE CLASSIC EXEMPLARS IN COVERT RESEARCH

4.1 Introduction

This is not a definitive or exhaustive list of classic covert exemplars but a collection of popular, recognizable and commonly identified ones in the covert literature. There is a type of 'conventional wisdom' found in ethics and research methodology genres around what the covert classics are. If routinely quizzed, most of the social science community would have at least some, if not all, of these standard exemplars of covert research in mind, or what I call the 'usual suspects'.

Clearly, each study has a different part to play in the history and legacies of their individual field. What I hope to do in this chapter is to summarize and make sense of the key covert aspects of these various studies, including their context, motivation, key themes, responses and influence. What I refer to broadly as their 'covert condition'. The classic exemplars offer instructive scenarios on which to reflect as part of developing a methodological covert imagination. It is important to make sense of these exemplars and gain an adequate picture of these studies from a detailed reading in order to avoid mis-characterizations, botches and mythologies. They are listed chronologically and not ranked in order of significance. Also, it is important to recognize that these exemplars are not in an incremental relationship to each other but rather come from different contexts.

4.2 Erving Goffman (1961): *Asylums: Essays on the Social Situation of Mental Patients and Other Inmates*

The study

There is a vast literature and scholarship generally on Goffman (1922–1982). My specific concerns here are with *Asylums* and its covert aspects. Goffman is clearly an iconic figure in the social science community, whose influence extended beyond sociology, his parent discipline. His text, *Asylums* (1961), which is his most academically cited work and was probably his most well-known book out-side sociology, was to have a major impact on the social science community, including health care fields and the anti-psychiatry movement.

Goffman's methodological reflections are brief in comparison to his concep-tual theorizing, which centred on the process of mortification and the features of total institutions. Clearly, such a setting was a credible place to see the effect of stigma. Most of his limited methodological reflections can be found in the pref-ace and in some footnotes. In particular, Goffman refers to Dalton's *Men Who Manage* (1959) as a 'very remarkable study' (1961: 190).

Goffman spent a year doing fieldwork, between 1955 and 1956, at St Elizabeth's Hospital, Washington, DC. This federal institution held over seven thousand inmates. This research was funded by a grant from the National Institute of Mental Health (NIMH) and was written up at the University of California at Berkeley. Goffman describes his covert fieldwork role in the opening page of the preface as:

My immediate object in doing work at St. Elizabeth's was to try to learn about the social world of the hospital inmate, as this world is subjectively experienced by him. I started out in the role of an assistant to the athletic director, when pressed avowing to be a student of recreation and community life, and I passed the day with patients, avoiding sociable contact with the staff and the carrying of a key. I did not sleep in the wards, and the top hos-pital management know what my aims were. (1961: ix)

An obvious alternative role would have been for Goffman to become a pseudo-patient himself and hence gained a type of 'patient's perspective'. On this Goffman stresses 'had I done so my range of movements and roles, and hence my data, would have been restricted even more than they were' (1961: x). What is very interesting here at the outset is the semi-covert nature of the study and, in particular, the nature and impact of his specific gate-keeping arrangements with senior medical staff. Goffman reminds the reader that he was actively encouraged to 'look at the hospital with sociology in mind, not junior psychiatry' (1961: xi).

In the introduction to the book, Goffman articulates his conceptual concerns as: 'This volume deals with total institutions in general and one example, mental hospitals, in particular. The main focus is on the world of the inmate, not the world of the staff. A chief concern is to develop a sociological version of the self' (1961: xiii).

In more detail, *Asylums* consists of four essays. First, 'On the Characteristics of Total Institutions', which is a general examination of the 'involuntary membership' of mental hospitals and prisons. Second, 'The Moral Career of the Mental Patient', which is an analysis of institutionalization. Third, 'The Underlife of a Public Institution: A Study of Ways of Making Out in a Mental Hospital', which is concerned with attachment, adjustment, insubordination and distancing. Lastly, 'The Medical Model and Mental Hospitalization: Some Notes on the Vicissitudes of the Tinkering Trades', which is mainly concerned with the application of the medical perspective of the professional staff in the setting.

Goffman concludes the book with a passionate statement:

> Medical patients can find themselves in a special bind. To get out of the hospital, or to ease their life within it, they must show acceptance of the place accorded them, and the place accorded them is to support the occupational role of those who appear to force this bargain. ... Mental patients can find themselves crushed by the weight of a service ideal that eases life for the rest of us. (1961: 386)

Critiques and legacy

On his more general reflections of fieldwork, which are very sparse, taken from a 1974 talk on method, later transcribed and published from a bootlegged tape, Goffman remarks that he tried to be more an 'observant participant than a participating observer' (Goffman, in Smith, 2006: 115). For Goffman, the fieldwork role was primarily akin to being a witness in most observational settings.

Goffman had a rather blurred fieldwork role as he attempted to avoid identification with staff yet had freedom to explore the organization without sleeping in the wards or being involved in patient therapy. Thus, it was a sort of free-floating role, which he does not fully unpack for the reader. As a result, several readers have questioned the rather sketchy, fragmented and somewhat de-contextualized details Goffman provides of his fieldwork practices and experiences. Fine and Martin describe Goffman's ethnography as 'a literary experiment' (1990: 112) and find Goffman's brief descriptions of his research role rather vague and glossed. Greg Smith usefully summarizes the methodological puzzlement as: 'Goffman, as it were, absents himself from his own acute and astute observations of patient life' (2006: 81).

Nugent and Abolafia (2007) view *Asylums* as a type of critical ethnography where Goffman routinely uses rhetoric throughout his narrative. Nugent and Abolafia claim:

The reader has probably never been in an Asylum; however, the reader likely has experienced anxiety in controlling situations. The reader imagines what the 'inmates' are going through and by reading those accounts is invited to experience sympathetic feelings toward these characters. (2007: 207)

On Goffman's methodological strategy, Manning sums this up succinctly:

... he took a marginal position as 'assistant to the athletics director'. In this capacity he could freely observe hospital life and move at will from ward to ward. In addition, his lowly institutional position meant that no-one expected much of him and no-one tried to influence him either. (2009: 767)

You are ultimately left conceptually satisfied yet methodologically frustrated by *Asylums*. Charmaz argues that 'Goffman shared his views of methods privately with his closest students and colleagues but provided little concrete advice for his readers' (2004: 977). Similarly, Howard Becker said of Goffman: 'He felt very strongly that you could not elaborate any useful rules of procedure for doing field research' (2003: 660). Ironically, after Goffman had lived through his wife's mental illness and suicide, he stated that 'had he been writing *Asylums* at that point, it would have been a very different book' (Mechanic, in Smith, 2006: 81).

More generally, Fine and Manning accurately stress 'Erving Goffman has a hold on the sociological imagination. ... The dramaturgical metaphor has become sociology's second skin' (2003: 34). Pierre Bourdieu, a seminal figure himself, passionately argues: 'The work of Erving Goffman is the product of one of the most original and rarest methods of doing sociology' (1983: 112). Bourdieu describes Goffman as the 'discoverer of the infinitely small' and describes *Asylums* as 'probably his most important work, and stands quite apart among his writings' (1983: 112).

More specifically, MacSuibhre, while reflecting on fifty years since the publication of *Asylums*, argues that it is a 'key text in the sociology of mental illness. … Goffman's key role was in humanising patients' (2011: 1). In many ways, *Asylums* can be seen, along with other texts, as an applied exploration of the interaction order, which was Goffman's primary concern. Despite Goffman having a complex and contradictory stance on anti-psychiatry himself, some have linked *Asylums* directly to the anti-psychiatry movement (Sedgwick, 1974). Katz sums up the irony of the influence of *Asylums* stating: 'In most of his writings, Goffman was not demonstrably concerned with policy or practical consequentiality and yet *Asylums* has been directly relevant to policy formulation' (2004: 284).

4.3 Laud Humphreys (1970): *Tearoom Trade: Impersonal Sex in Public Places*

The study

The legendary saga of the book involves a failed attempt to revoke the doctorate of Laud Humphreys (1930–1988), the loss of his teaching and grant work, the polarization and resignation of university colleagues and the eventual award of the prestigious C. Wright Mills Award of the Society for the Study of Social Problems. The Humphreys story forms part of sociological folklore and is the stock-in-trade trope in set texts on fieldwork ethics.

As with the other exemplars, it requires close and careful reading to make reasonable sense of it. In the acknowledgements, after thanking various academics, including Lee Rainwater, his doctoral adviser in the Sociology Department at Washington University in St Louis, as well as Goffman and Becker, Humphreys states: 'From most of my respondents, I can only beg pardon for intrusion into their secret lives. I have tried to be as protective and unobtrusive as possible and trust that none will be worse off for the experience' (1970: xx). Humphreys outlines his goal at the outset 'to describe for the reader the social structure of impersonal sex, the mechanisms that make it possible' (1970: 14).

Some readers might assume that this famous study was a purist covert one but this was not the case. The study, which was semi-covert, ran from 1965 to 1968 in two stages. The first stage was covert participant observation over two years on a part-time basis followed by twenty-seven interviews and survey data from more than one hundred respondents over a six-month period, where he was assisted by two trained graduate students. Indeed, he extends his personal gratitude to his 'intensive dozen' of key informants throughout the book. On this Humphreys states: 'After the initial contacts with this intensive dozen, I told them of my research, disclosing my real purpose for being in the tearoom' (1970: 36).

Because of the popular emphasis on the controversial ethically transgressive character of the research, the overt interview-based components of the project are rather overlooked. His concern with sampling and representation runs throughout the book. The latter data collection methods, which are quite quantitatively sophisticated, are generally ignored or, worse, not known, in cruder reviews and accounts of *Tearoom Trade.*

It is immediately obvious that it is gendered research exploring the male experience to the exclusion of females. He claims to have made fifty systematic observations of tearoom encounters, spent close to sixty hours in them, observed one hundred and twenty sexual acts in nineteen different men's rooms in five parks of the one city, as well as informal observations of various other cities. The tearooms are 'market places of the one-night stand variety' (Humphreys, 1970: 10), which are mainly carried out quickly in silent interaction to 'assure the impersonality of the sexual liaison' (1970: 13). Humphreys is keen to point out that tearooms serve a variety of heterosexual men's sexual needs and not just the homosexual community.

In a chapter on methods entitled 'The Sociologist as Voyeur', Humphreys explores entering the field: 'From the beginning, my decision was to continue the practice of the field study in passing as deviant. … I am convinced that there is only one way to watch highly discreditable behaviour and that is to pretend to be in the same boat with those engaging in it' (1970: 24–25).

For Humphreys, the 'real methodological breakthrough of the research' (1970: 27) was in serving as a watch queen or voyeur-lookout, which meant he actively rather than passively participated in the setting but without actually committing a criminal sexual act. Much of the controversy centred on the latter phases of the research where he traced one hundred and thirty-four licence plates of cars that tearoom participants drove. He proceeded to interview fifty of the participants, many of whom were married, under the auspices of a social health survey, which he was previously involved in. He undertook the interviews with the assistance of a trusted graduate student.

On his wilful deception in the latter stages, Humphreys states: 'I was careful to change my appearance, dress, and automobile from the days when I had passed as deviant. I also allowed at least a year's time to lapse between the original sampling procedure and the interviews' (1970: 42).

In his later life, Humphreys (1970), who was a gay man trapped in a heterosexual marriage, founded a network to support academics with alternative sexual orientations. He is keen to challenge the stigma attached to the tearoom trade and vigorously questions public policy and police activity around it. The activism of Humphreys, which was intimately related to his own biography, is evident throughout his study, as he states: 'If there is any threat to society from tearoom action, my data do not indicate it. The only harmful effects of these encounters, either direct or indirect, result from police activity' (1970: 163–166).

Were the home interviews an ethical step too far? Many in the social science community felt that it was transgressive. Humphreys was himself arrested for 'loitering' in a public park, so his devotion to his academic study transgressed normal bounds. He was clearly committed to safeguarding his respondents and was willing to run the risk of prosecution. It is important to remember the context of the study. It was a time when such public activities were seen as sexually deviant, when there were arrests and attempted convictions by the police on the grounds of sodomy and a general atmosphere of homophobia. The decriminalization of homosexuality has been a protracted process of liberalization in the United States, starting in 1962 in Illinois through to a Supreme Court ruling in 2003.

The study is a partisan account, and is now commonly celebrated as such. Simplistic readings of the book have omitted the ethical sensitivity he displays in a sustained manner throughout the book and in contrast presents a more cavalier image of his work and sentiments. An enlarged edition of the book, including a retrospective on ethical issues, was published in 1975, but many of the more basic commentaries omit to mention this. In this later book, interestingly he includes certain essays written by other people, some of which are critical of the approach he took. Humphreys ends the retrospective with his personal and biographical account of ethical issues in social research. He passionately states: 'There was no question in my mind that I would go to prison rather than betray the subjects of my research' (1975: 230). And he stresses: 'My greatest pleasure came from the consistently favourable reaction of the gay press' (1975: 225).

On the legal objections to his study, which resulted in a failed attempt by the Chancellor of Washington University to take legal action against him, he had to seek independent legal advice after being temporarily suspended from his university teaching post. Additionally, Alvin Gouldner, a famous sociology department staff member at Washington University, physically assaulted him in 1968 over his supposed unethical conduct.

Humphreys did regret the tracing of licence plates and the interviewing of respondents at home, stating 'I now think my reasoning was faulty' (1975: 230). If the study was repeated, Humphreys claims:

… although I remain convinced that it is ethical to observe interaction in public places and to interview willing and informed respondents, I direct my students to inform research subjects before interviewing them. Were I to repeat the tearoom study, I would spend another year or so in cultivating and expanding the category of willing respondents into which the 'intensive dozen' fall. (1975: 231)

In a very brief letter published in the journal *Science*, in response to some inaccuracies about his study, Humphreys describes his cruder critics as 'Ayatollahs of Research Ethics' (1980: 714) and stresses that 'the moral entrepreneurs fail to note that, in the mid-1960's, the sociologists had no Code of Ethics mentioning "informed consent"' (1980: 714).

Critiques and legacy

Several early book reviews of *Tearoom Trade* (Hoffman, 1971; Reiss, 1971; Rosen, 1972; Wiens, 1971) took a standard line in being very critical of Humphreys' ethical approach as belligerent. The study caused widespread controversy and press coverage. Journalist Nicholas Von Hoffman from *The Washington Post* described the study as an indifferent form of 'sociological snooping' (1970), displaying the indifference of academics to real-world realities.

Warwick (1982) was his sternest and most popularly quoted critic. For Warwick, his key objections were that Humphreys took a relatively powerless group that could not challenge the work, that such deceptive tactics would spread a negative image of sociology and spoil the field for future research, and that such disreputable research behaviour could spread to other parts of society. Warwick zealously claims: 'Humphreys' research provides a unique case study of deception. The concatenation of misrepresentation and disguises in this effort must surely hold the world record for field research' (1982: 46).

For many, there are ethical question marks about Humphreys' approach and his work still consistently provides case study material for the 'means/end' discussion about ethics and the boundaries of ethical transgression. However, it is also apparent that Humphreys inspired a whole paradigm of diverse sex/sexuality and gay studies research, often from standpoint, insider and partisan perspectives. Not all of these studies are covert, but many have taken broadly voyeuristic forms in exploring what has been commonly termed the 'erotic oases' (Delph, 1978; Tewksbury, 1995, 2010), which often involves anonymous sexual encounters in different spaces.

Edward Delph (1978) was influenced by Humphreys and wanted to extend the analysis to various forms of public sexual activities by homosexual and bisexual male eroticists. The settings analysed were much more varied than Humphreys' and included streets, park benches, beaches, public restrooms, movie theatres, and gay bars and baths. His observations, which took place in New York City over a two-year period, were mostly covert but also involved him simulating availability as most of the symbolic movements and behavioural cues were done in silence.

Desroches (1990) replicated the Humphreys study by exploring tearoom activity using data gathered from police case materials and interviews with law enforcement agencies in five Canadian urban areas. Desroches argues: 'Although shopping malls have usurped public parks as the favourite locale of tearoom participants, the basic rules of the game and profile of the players – as Humphreys contends – remain the same over time and place' (1990: 60).

Groombridge (1999) argues that Humphreys' work adds to the knowledge base of the sociology of deviance and sexualities, and positively contributes to a potential 'queering' of criminology, which represents a return of the repressed sociology of deviance. Bell sums up much of the contemporary sentiment around Humphreys: 'While incredibly controversial in terms of research ethics, Humphreys' research has been to some extent reclaimed as pioneering in its focus; it certainly inspired a whole raft of ethnographic investigations into particular scenes – highway rest areas, bathhouses, porn cinemas, beaches, bookstore backrooms and so on' (2001: 133).

Tewksbury's (2002) study of two gay bathhouses involved what he describes as a 'potential participant role', which included wide-ranging covert observations but not full participation in sexual activities. Namely, a type of voyeuristic methodology similar to what Humphreys proposed. For many, *Tearoom Trade* was the beginning of 'a new world of research methodologies and questions' (Douglas and Tewksbury, 2008: 1) in which to study alternative sexualities and intimate-yet-anonymous interpersonal relations. Hence, 'although the full scope of his work would not be understood for decades, the ramifications were immense' (Douglas and Tewksbury, 2008: 2).

Babbie neatly argues that Humphreys and the debate over his research ethics are still relevant today: 'Laud Humphreys' willingness to work in the shadows of right and wrong, all the while committed to being ethical in those endeavors, forces students to think about ethics rather than swearing allegiance to an established code' (2004: 18).

Mowlabocus (2008) explores virtual cottaging, sexual acts in public lavatories, by gay men online. Cottaging is illegal so there were obvious sensitivities here. Mowlabocus lurked online on cybercottage, the virtual space based at a university, for several months. The site acted as an information source and a way for gay men to safely share a queer space and, if necessary, meet up in person. Mowlabocus states: 'Today, postgraduate students are often shown Humphreys' book as an example of how not to carry out ethnographic fieldwork, though interestingly the question of how to better conduct this type of research rarely seems to get answered' (2008: 423).

Albert (2011) sensibly adds that the erotic oases have been primarily conducted within a masculine paradigm, and there has been a lack of studies about public sex between women. An early and prophetic book review by Hackler states: 'Occasionally a book is published in criminology that has all the earmarks of becoming a classic. *Tea room Trade* is such a book' (1971: 119). Love it or loathe it, *Tearoom Trade* is a classic and likely to remain so.

4.4 David L. Rosenhan (1973): 'On Being Sane in Insane Places'

The study

The Rosenhan experiment was an influential covert study which had a considerable impact on the anti-psychiatric movement and future studies of pseudo-patients. David Rosenhan (1929–2012), a Professor of Psychology and Law at Stanford University at the time of publication, opens his brief but polemical article, asking 'If sanity and insanity exist, how shall we know them?' (Rosenhan, 1973: 250).

Rosenhan wanted to question the accuracy, validity and reliability of psychiatric diagnosis as he passionately states: 'psychological categorization of mental illness is useless at best and downright harmful, misleading, and pejorative at worst. Psychiatric diagnoses, in this view, are in the minds of the observers and are not valid summaries of characteristics displayed by the observed' (1973: 251).

Rosenhan briefly discusses Goffman's (1961) and Caudill et al.'s (1952) work. He claims that the hospital administrator and chief psychologist, as gate-keepers, knew of his presence, but none of the staff knew of the pseudo-patients or the research. Rosenhan also claims that he had legal advice about the project beforehand and an attorney was kept 'on call' during every hospitalization. In a footnote, Rosenhan justifies his covert stance in more detail: 'However distasteful such concealment is, it was a necessary first step to examining these questions. Without concealment, there would have been no way to know how valid these experiences were' (1973: 258).

To effectively 'test' the robustness of psychiatric diagnosis in the field experiment, eight 'sane people' gained secret admission to twelve different hospitals across five states by feigning that they 'had been hearing voices'. Immediately upon gaining entry to the admissions ward, they ceased simulating any symptoms of abnormality and took the prescribed medication, which was not swallowed. Field notes were kept by the pseudo-patients throughout the period. The pseudo-patients comprised three women and five men from varied class backgrounds, including Rosenhan himself as the first pseudo-patient. All of the pseudo-patients used pseudonyms, and those who worked in the mental health field were given false jobs to avoid invoking any special treatment.

The pseudo-patients were never detected nor seen as suspect by staff, although other psychiatric patients voiced their suspicions. Each pseudo-patient was discharged with a diagnosis of 'schizophrenia in remission'. Their stays ranged from seven to fifty-two days, with an average of nineteen days. Despite constantly and openly taking extensive notes on the behaviour of the staff and other patients, none of the pseudo-patients were identified as imposters. Indeed, some of the staff saw the note-taking as a pathological symptom of their 'writing behaviour'.

The pseudo-patients were required to get out of the hospital on their own by getting the hospital to release them, which could be problematic. Rosenhan claims that a 'psychiatric label has a life and an influence of its own' (1973: 253) that endures beyond the hospital gates as a type of 'self-fulfilling prophecy'. What Rosenhan describes as the 'stickiness of psycho-diagnostic labels' (1973: 252).

Data were also gathered on patient interactions with psychiatrists, nurses and attendants, throughout the experiments, along with data important to patient care and management. Issues like eye contact and verbal conversations were part of the analysis of the powerlessness and depersonalization of the patient in the psychiatric setting. Rosenhan stresses that there was a clear reliance upon psychotropic medication, and the average contact time with staff was estimated to be a very lowly six to eight minutes per day.

Rosenhan also reports on incidents of brutality, detail that would have been more difficult to gain by standard means. Rosenhan controversially claims: 'Occasionally, punishment meted out to patients for misdemeanors seemed so excessive that it could not be justified by the most radical interpretations of psychiatric canon' (1973: 255–256).

In his conclusion, Rosenhan states in a humanistic manner:

> It is clear that we cannot distinguish the sane from the insane in psychiatric hospitals. The hospital itself imposes a special environment in which the meanings of behaviour can easily be misunderstood. The consequences to patients hospitalized in such an environment – the powerlessness, depersonalization, segregation, mortification, and self-labelling – seem undoubtedly counter-therapeutic. (1973: 257)

Rosenhan is aware of the limitations of his experiment, stating 'We do not pretend to describe the subjective experiences of true patients' (1973: 257). He attempts to make some practical recommendations on refraining from quick institutionalization. He is also sympathetic to staff constraints, claiming: 'our overwhelming impression of them was of people who really cared, who were committed and who were uncommonly intelligent' (1973: 257).

Critiques and legacy

The Rosenhan experiment caused obvious controversy and outrage, not least in the professional psychiatric community. A number of early methodological criticisms were typically made about bias, sample size and representation (Crown, 1975; Davis, 1976; Farber, 1975; Millon, 1975; Weiner, 1975). Spitzer was part of that dissident literature, stressing that the Rosenhan experiment is 'pseudoscience presented as science' (1975: 442). For Spitzer, contrary to Rosenhan: 'In the setting of a psychiatric hospital, psychiatrists are remarkably able to distinguish the "sane" from the "insane"' (1975: 451).

Pattison (1974) is one of the sterner critics. Pattison feels that Rosenhan subverts scientific research as propaganda for trenchant social criticism about mental health, which deeply discredits all concerned. Rosenhan (1975) replies to some of the early criticisms stressing that psychiatric diagnoses are contextually based and can be professionally sanctioned justification of diagnostic error.

In her controversial book *Lying: A Metaphorical Memoir* (2001), psychologist Lauren Slater reported her attempt to replicate Rosenhan's hypothesis on an individual rather than a group basis and in a generally more therapeutic modern context. Over eight days Slater presented herself to different psychiatric emergency rooms with the lone complaint of an isolated auditory hallucination. In almost all cases, she reported receiving the diagnosis of depression with psychotic features and was prescribed antidepressants and antipsychotics. Slater concludes, similar to Rosenhan, that psychiatric diagnoses are largely arbitrary and driven by a zeal to prescribe. Slater describes her experiment as: 'It's a little fun, going into ERs and playing this game' (2001: 88–89).

Herrera claims that the Rosenhan experiment is 'as exciting and romantic as social science can get' (2003: 352), but ultimately, he is sceptical of the data stating: 'we should accept stories like Rosenhan's only on sufficient evidence' (2003: 352).

Some of the exemplars have entered into popular culture and have been engaged with in different ways. *How Mad Are You?* was a British two-part BBC Horizon/Discovery Channel co-production television programme (2008) that was clearly inspired by the Rosenhan experiment. The programme explores the relationship between character traits and mental illness and considers the social implications of inaccurate diagnosis. Ten volunteers, five of whom had been previously diagnosed with psychiatric disorders, were observed and interviewed by a panel of three mental health experts, including a psychiatrist, a professor of clinical psychology and a psychiatric nurse. The volunteers and experts had no prior knowledge of one another and were brought together for this one-week study. There were some accurate diagnoses but also some significant misdiagnoses by the panel. In a series of follow-up interviews, a few of the volunteers appeared to feel vindicated by the inability of the experts to diagnose their psychiatric disorders.

4.5 Stanley Milgram (1974):
Obedience to Authority: An Experimental View

The study

One of the most famous exemplars, in that it has crossed disciplinary boundaries and fields, is Stanley Milgram's (1933–1984) experimental work in social psychology. Milgram's career also produced other creative, though much less controversial research, with the small-world method, the lost-letter technique, mental maps of cities, the familiar stranger and the effects of televised antisocial behaviour. His supposed 'ethical transgression' with the obedience to authority experiments reached a very broad audience both inside and outside academia. Indeed, his experiments became part of much wider populist discussions about conformity, with some commonly referring to his work as the *pain* or *torture* experiments. As with the other exemplars I have discussed, there is a recognized scholarship on Milgram. Milgram was influenced by the work of Arendt (1963) on the banality of evil. The initial experiments were undertaken at the Department of Psychology at Yale University between 1961 and 1963, and published in the early 1960s in various psychology journals before being collected in the 1974 book. He also made a film of some of the experiments, entitled *Obedience*, which was distributed in 1965 by the New York University Film Library. Before conducting the experiments, Milgram polled Yale University psychology students and colleagues to gain their views on the validity of the experiments and the likely results.

The experiments were repeated over the years and involved around 663 participants. The studies were initially advertised in the local press as a 'scientific study of memory and learning', and forty male participants between the ages of twenty and fifty from the New Haven area were recruited. They were paid $4.50 per hour and when they arrived the studies were then explained as an experiment concerned with 'the effects of punishment on learning', which is more specific but still involves concealment.

Milgram also conducted a series of experimental variations, which have not been as intensively discussed as the main one. These eighteen variations, which did not significantly change the key theoretical propositions, included an all-female respondent data set, the experimental location being shifted from a laboratory to an office block, letting the ordinary men give orders, varying the distance between learner and teacher, voice feedback levels, touch and tactility and using the teacher as a bystander. In each of these variations, Milgram found broadly similar results.

At the start of the preface of *Obedience to Authority*, Milgram outlines the centrality of the topic under study:

Obedience, because of its very ubiquitousness, is easily overlooked as a subject of inquiry in social psychology. But without an appreciation of its role in shaping human action, a wide range of significant behaviour cannot be understood. … What the present study does is to give the dilemma contemporary form by treating it as subject matter for experimental inquiry, and with the aim of understanding rather than judging it from a moral standpoint. (1974: xi)

Clearly, Nazi war crimes and atrocities provide the context for his specific worldview. As Milgram states:

The question arises as to whether there is any connection between what we have studied in the laboratory and the forms of obedience we so deplored in the Nazi epoch. The differences in the two situations are, of course, enormous, yet the difference in scale, numbers and political context may turn out to be relatively unimportant as long as certain essential features are retained. (1974: xii)

In terms of the experimental setup, Milgram had a 'teacher' (true participant), a 'learner' (confederate), and an 'experimenter', who was played by a high school biology teacher. The subjects drew slips of paper from a hat to determine who would be the teacher or learner, but the draw was rigged so that the true participant was always the teacher. The teacher and learner were then taken to a room, where the teacher observed the learner being strapped into an electric chair connected to a large shock generator in the adjacent room. The teacher was then taken to the adjacent room containing the very intimidating shock generator. The shock generator had 30 switches labelled with voltage levels, ranging from 15 to 450 volts, with verbal designations such as 'slight shock', 'moderate shock', 'danger severe shock' and 'XXX'.

When the learner gave a wrong answer in the learning test an electric shock was supposedly administered, with increasing severity as the experiment continued, provoking fake grunts, verbal protestations and agonized screams from the learner. The voltages are not decreased, even after a series of correct answers are given. The teacher communicated with the learner through a one-way intercom. The teacher was thus saturated in a series of what Milgram (1974) describes as *'situational obligations'*.

The learner gave responses after each question, until the 300-volt shock was administered. At this point pounding on the wall was heard and no response to the question was received from the learner. As you might have expected, subjects turned to the experimenter for guidance at this point. The experimenter instructed the teacher to treat the absence of a response as an incorrect answer. The learner pounded on the wall at 315 volts, and continued not to answer the questions. At higher voltages the learner gave no response whatsoever, giving the impression that he was at the very least unconscious, and at the worst dead. Naturally, the teachers in this experiment turned to the experimenter for guidance before administering shocks in excess of 300 volts. The white-coated experimenter politely but firmly gave one of four standard, scripted prods to continue with the experiment, with the reassurance that the teacher would not be held legally responsible.

On his data, which obviously serves to 'shock' the reader, Milgram boldly claims: 'Indeed, the results of the experiment are both surprising and dismaying' (1974: 5). In the original experiment with 40 subjects, no subject stopped before 300 volts. A total of fourteen subjects defied the experimenter, although none completely refused, with twenty-six of them obeying until the end, administering 450 volts to the learner. Many of the teachers routinely displayed signs of tension, with some being more visibly distressed. Milgram also observed that many subjects devalued the victim to help rationalize their actions.

Milgram (1974) ends the book in a humanistic manner:

The results, as seen and felt in the laboratory, are to this author disturbing. They raise the possibility that human nature, or more specifically, the kind of character produced in American democratic society, cannot be counted on to insulate its citizens from brutality and inhumane treatment at the direction of malevolent authority. (1974: 189)

There is an interesting appendix to Milgram's book, entitled 'Problems of Ethics in Research'. At the outset, Milgram reflects on 'theatrical staging' and 'illusions' and 'experiments being planned', which many would view as a significant underlying problem that would skew the results. Put basically, how many participants knew the experiment was faked but went along with it? It is very difficult to answer this accurately. Milgram states: 'most of what occurred in the laboratory was what had been discovered, rather than what had been planned' (1974: 193).

For some, retrospective debriefing is important in such controversial research and mediates the charge of research being unethical. In the Milgram experiments, subjects were formally debriefed as part of the protocol at the end of the experiment. Milgram highlighted his extensive debriefing or 'de-hoaxing' procedures, which he supported by citing the results of a quantitative follow-up study he undertook. This study indicated that 83.7 per cent of the participants were glad that they participated and that the majority of participants felt that more experiments of this sort should be carried out.

Milgram (1977), in an interesting later defence of his experiments, states:

A majority of the experiments carried out in social psychology use some degree of misinformation. Such practices have been denounced as 'deception' by critics, and the term 'deception experiment' has come to be used routinely, particularly in the context of discussions concerning the ethics of such procedures. But in such a context, the term 'deception' somewhat biases the issue. It is preferable to use morally neutral terms such as 'masking', 'staging', or 'technical illusions' in describing such techniques. (1977: 19)

Critiques and legacy

Milgram clearly caused controversy among many researchers, with some being sceptical about his data claims. Baumrind (1964), an early critic, argues that the laboratory is an unfamiliar setting. Therefore the rules of behaviour are ambiguous for the subject, who would be more prone to obedient behaviour compared to other environmental conditions. Also, in terms of harm, after revealing the deception, subjects may feel used, embarrassed, or distrustful of psychologists and future authority figures in their lives.

Mixon (1972) replicated the Milgram experiments with volunteers in a 'role-playing simulation' but, crucially, without deception. The persuasive role of the experimenter is highlighted by Mixon, who accuses Milgram of being delusional and suggests that his subjects would have known the deceptive game being played. Harré, in a stronger critique, argues that: 'the most morally obnoxious feature of this outrageous experiment' (1979: 106) was in fact the belligerent behaviour of Milgram and his assistants and not the participants.

Herrera, in a careful historical review of deceptive experiments in American psychology, argues:

Commentators frequently cite Stanley Milgram's work in the 1960s as a harbinger of changed attitudes towards deception, and suggest that today's psychologists abide by more enlightened ethical practices. It is difficult to find evidence to support this portrayal. (1997: 23–24)

Brannigan (2004) provides a sceptical critique on the failure of social psychology's use of the experimental method. He refers to experimental social psychology as an 'impossible science' involving decontextualized 'dramatizations' and 'theatrical simulations'. For Brannigan (2004), the popular appeal of Milgram, and others in that tradition, is effectively their pronounced and evocative moral stories and not the credibility of their empirical findings. Brannigan cogently argues:

Despite the official orthodoxy, experiments serve as platforms for the dramatization of ideas, not for the testing of hypothesis and the building of theories. And that seems unlikely to change given the centrality of the experiment in the arsenal of social psychologists. But the moral tone also explains the enormous appeal of the field to undergraduate students who get an 'ethical fix' packaged as science, and who enter the moral high ground under the guise of scientific training. (2004: 60)

Slater et al. (2006) repeated the Milgram experiments in an immersive virtual environment in what they refer to as a 'virtual reprise'. The participants were invited to give shocks to a virtual female learner on incorrect answers in a word association memory test, in the obvious knowledge that it was fake. Of the thirty-four participants, twenty-three saw and heard the learner and eleven communicated with her only through text. Despite there being no experimental deception, those who saw and heard the learner reacted more emotionally. Slater et al. conclude that their virtual obedience experiment opens the door to explore extreme social situations, which might be restricted ethically, in virtual environments.

Burger (2009) also conducted a partial replication of Milgram's obedience studies that allowed for useful comparisons with the original investigations while protecting the well-being of participants. The covert nature of the study was not the same as Milgram's and it included female participants but obedience rates in this replication were only slightly lower than those that Milgram found. Burger concludes:

Milgram's obedience studies have maintained a place in psychology classes and textbooks largely because of their implications for understanding the worst of human behaviors, such as atrocities, massacres, and genocide. ... Since Milgram's studies, concern for the well-being of participants has limited research on obedience to authority. (2009: 10)

Nicholson (2011) argues that Milgram deliberately misrepresented the extent of his debriefing and downplayed the harm done by his experiments. Drawing on archival material from the original participants and Milgram, in what he describes as 'Torture at Yale', he argues that Milgram had repressed doubts over the scientific value of the experiments. He calls for 'the need to be much more self-critical when examining the ethical justifications of human experimentation in psychology' (Nicholson, 2011: 758).

Gina Perry (2013), based on original data from the Yale archives, states that Milgram's arguments are flawed as he manipulated any data that contradicted his key ideas. She takes a sceptical position on what she calls 'the shock machine' and maintains in her 'untold story' that many participants disobeyed and needed continual prompts, with some even thinking, in their faked compliance, that it was a reality television show.

More recently, building on the Milgram archive at Yale, Brannigan et al. (2015) attempt to 'unplug the Milgram machine' by critically exploring participant resistance and trauma, Milgram's deliberate cherry-picking of findings, misrepresentations of prods and failure to debrief the vast majority of participants. They wish to vigorously challenge 'the discipline's adulation of the obedience research' and hence 'offer a more realistic assessment of Milgram's contribution to knowledge' (2015: 551).

Milgram directly influenced two field experiments in psychology, which briefly require consideration: the Stanford Prison Experiment (Haney et al., 1973), which is infamous, and the earlier Hofling Hospital Experiment (Hofling et al., 1966), which is less well known.

The Hofling Hospital Experiment

Milgram had a direct influence on the Hofling Hospital Experiment, which was designed partly in response to early criticisms of Milgram's work that it was undertaken under unique, and hence potentially distortive, laboratory conditions. Some feel that this field experiment, led by Charles K. Hofling, a professional psychiatrist, had created a less staged and much more realistic obedience experiment than Milgram's, although it is much less quoted and not as infamous in the field.

Hofling et al. (1966) created a study of obedience in the nurse–physician relationship in a psychiatric hospital setting by carrying out field studies on twenty-two on-duty night nurses who were unaware that they were involved in an experiment. Three psychiatric hospitals in the American Midwest took part in the study. Hofling et al. successfully demonstrated that medical staff in this context are very unwilling to question supposed 'authority', even when they might have good reason to do so. The procedure involved a fake doctor, in a rush, phoning a nurse and asking her to administer a high dosage (twice the maximum) of a fictitious drug, Astroten, to a patient, stating that the paperwork would be completed later. A placebo bottle of Astroten was placed in the cabinet with dosage instructions. The responses of the nurses were observed and they were stopped at the patient's door when they tried to administer what would have been an overdose. Twenty-one of the twenty-two nurses followed the instructions despite the clear violation of both hospital policy and professional standards. The nurses were debriefed about the experiment and several expressed feelings of both personal and professional guilt and embarrassment.

Rank and Jacobson (1977) queried the facts that the nurses had no knowledge of the drug involved and that they had no opportunity to seek advice from any-one of equal or higher status. They replicated Hofling's experiment, but this time the instruction was to administer *Valium* at three times the recommended level. The telephoned instruction came from a real and known doctor on the hospital staff and the nurses were able to consult with other nurses before proceeding. Under these conditions, only two out of eighteen nurses prepared the medication as requested. Rank and Jacobson (1977) argued that most nurses had a more developed sense of professional discretion than Hofling et al. (1966) suggest.

The Stanford Prison Experiment

Milgram's work also had a direct influence on the infamous Stanford Prison Experiment (SPE), undertaken by social psychologist Philip G. Zimbardo and others (Haney et al., 1973). This started out as a mock prison study and simula-tion study on the psychology of imprisonment in 1971, but went wrong in terms of the unforeseen psychological harm to and brutalization of the participants. The cruelty of the guards, under the implicit instructions of Zimbardo, included sleep deprivation, sexual humiliation, solitary confinement and constant surveillance.

The SPE lasted six days instead of the intended two weeks, and was not com-pleted as a research project. Indeed, one participant left after thirty-six hours. It is popularly raised as the standard example of unethical research, although it was not covertly done as each of the twenty-four male student participants, randomly allocated guard and prisoner roles after interview screening, willingly and overtly took on their role in the research. However, there were staged and dramatized covert elements in the experiment. The student prisoners were not informed about their arrest by a real police officer in their homes, being handcuffed and charged with theft or robbery, which was televised locally, or about the fictitious parole board hearings, administered by a real former prison inmate.

Zimbardo candidly reflects on the prison experiment:

The research represents one of the most extreme experimental demonstra-tions of the power of situational determinants in both shaping behaviour and predominating over personality, attitudes and individual values. As such, it extends the conclusions from Stanley Milgram's research on obedience to authority. (1973: 243)

There is a specific literature on the SPE, although, unlike Milgram, its full details came out much later on, rather than at the time. It received, like Milgram's experi-mental work, much media coverage and attention. For our specific purposes here,

I want to recognize the link between them. Zimbardo explicitly viewed Milgram as a progressive pioneer and extended his psychological situationist research into evil, cruelty, obedience and authority in an institutional context of a mock prison, which was constructed in the basement of the psychology department at Stanford University.

Indeed, the Stanford Prison Experiment was revisited in the popular press as an explanation of the abuse of Iraqi prisoners by military guards at the Abu Ghraib Prison in 2004 (Carnahan and McFarland, 2007). In fact, Zimbardo acted as an expert witness in legal prosecution proceedings at the latter prison. A successful Hollywood film has also been made about the SPE, with the same title and released in 2015, to further embed it into popular culture and the popular imagination.

Brannigan (2009), rather sceptically, comments that the SPE was 'Zimbardo's singular, memorable contribution to the annals of social psychology' (2009: 698) and, moreover, that 'a good moral tale trumps the fact any day of the week in social psychology' (2009: 700).

Despite the critiques, many see Milgram's experiment as a landmark study in social psychology. Miller argues that his work is 'perhaps the most widely cited and provocative set of experiments in social science' (1986: 1). Russell and Gregory describe this as experimental innovation, 'making the undoable doable' (2005: 327). In many ways, his impact is captured by Thomas Blass, a leading authority on Milgram, in his book entitled *The Man Who Shocked the World: The Life and Legacy of Stanley Milgram* (2004). In an earlier article, Blass usefully comments:

> We didn't need Milgram to tell us we have a tendency to obey orders. What we didn't know before Milgram's experiments is just how powerful this tendency is. And having been enlightened about our extreme readiness to obey authorities, we can try to take steps to guard ourselves against unwelcome or reprehensible commands. (2002: 73)

4.6 Conclusions

The four classic exemplar studies in covert research, or what I call the 'usual suspects', have had a significant and varied impact, sometimes going beyond academia and into the popular cultural imagination. It is therefore important to understand their milieu, motivation and specific reasoning as they are drawn from different traditions and contexts. There are numerous lessons to be learnt from such studies.

However, it is also important to recognize that such studies also have a limiting effect on the conventional thinking and received wisdom on covert research. Namely, other interesting and useful covert studies are not considered and effectively lost to a wider audience. It is also important to recognize that the examples do not represent an incremental, integrated and cross-fertilized covert field in how the examples relate to each other.

The classic exemplars have gone beyond the realms of academia in terms of impact and have entered the public consciousness in different ways. The work is still utterly compelling for many social science students and scholars today. However, to view the field of covert research as only ever the usual suspects is limiting and overlooks a rich tradition, which we shall explore in the next chapter.

4.7 Learning exercise

Put yourself 'in the shoes' of the four key theorists in turn – Goffman, Humphreys, Rosenhan and Milgram – and reflect on the following questions:

1. What motivated them to undertake their studies?

2. What were the main points they wanted to make?

3. What are the impacts and legacy of their studies?

4. Should the studies be repeated today?

5. If repeated, would the results be the same?

6. If the theorists were alive today and still doing covert research, what topics would they be investigating and why?

5

DOING COVERT RESEARCH IN THE SOCIAL SCIENCES

5.1 Introduction

There is a rich and eclectic submerged tradition of covert studies that is not always referred to as part of the conventional wisdom on covert literature. Hence, several significant studies are not regularly discussed, indeed some are omitted. This extensive covert diaspora in the social sciences needs to be recovered, rehabilitated and shared.

What I hope to highlight here is the serious glossing problem with covert research. Namely, there is a constant problem of circumspection in that many researchers describe their role in various ethnographies as participant observation, in continued, direct or prolonged forms, as unobtrusive research, field study, or fieldwork, which may involve covert work, wittingly or otherwise, but this is not always made explicit and can be somewhat obscured in some studies.

'Participant observation' and 'ethnography' are common methodological grouping terms and umbrella words used in the social sciences to describe a wide variety of social research styles. The early classic taxonomies and typologies include Schwartz and Schwartz (1955), Gold (1958) and Gans (1968), which are useful in certain analytic respects but they offer little nuanced and specific detail on the covert condition. Thus, with many studies it takes detailed granulation, often through footnotes, as to what actual fieldwork role the researcher performed. With some semi-covert research, it is often a challenge to locate the phase and timing of the covert aspects in the overall fieldwork process. Moreover, while I might strongly suspect a covert approach, if it is sanitized out in the writing stage, it is clearly problematic to attach a distinct covert label.

I have explored a diverse range of studies that have been described as covert in a number of social science fields, many of which are pioneering and radical in different ways. It has been the typical archival 'can of worms' in that both the range and size of this covert diaspora is far more extensive and diverse than anticipated.

Many of the studies certainly deserve more than a passing reference or fleeting footnote, when acknowledged. Often these studies have, albeit controversially, played an integral part in shaping the sensibilities of their respective fields and communities. Hence, it is a rich diaspora in need of recovery and rehabilitation. I will make sense of this covert diaspora under the seven broad categories of crime, education, health, leisure, politics, religion and work, listed alphabetically. Each category has a range of relevant settings and studies that are briefly reviewed. These categories incorporate different academic traditions and are complex fields in themselves. The purpose here is to articulate and display both the diversity and depth of this submerged covert diaspora.

This diaspora is not united by simply using a purely covert stance. It is more akin to a covert continuum, where some covert dimensions can be seen. Neither is this diaspora systematically incremental or cross-referenced. Such a diaspora can never be exhaustive or definitive and is constantly on going, but we can at least recover and rehabilitate a reasonable amount of covert work for consideration.

5.2 Crime

Juvenile delinquency

A broad range of studies come under the label 'juvenile delinquency', with much of it from the fields of the sociology of deviance and youth studies. I will focus on two classic exemplars from the UK context. James Patrick, later revealed to be a fictitious name, in *A Glasgow Gang Observed* (1973), provides a rich, covert participant observation account of a juvenile gang, the Young Team, in Glasgow, over a four-month period from October 1966 to January 1967. In terms of entrée and gate-keeping, Patrick had been both invited and challenged to see 'whit the score wis' by Tim, a gang leader whom he had known from his days as a teacher at an approved school in Scotland, which was a detention centre for youth offenders, and whom he had befriended.

The book has numerous incidents of Patrick's secret liaisons with Tim. Patrick claims: 'within a short time it was established that I was an approved school boy, a fellow inmate of Tim's and a housebreaker' (1973: 27). His passing as a gang member, particularly the issue of blurring any age differences, was deliberately and artfully done. On this Patrick states: 'I began to concentrate on making my physical appearance acceptable to the group. I was prepared to give my age as seventeen, although this point was never questioned ... my exact age remained indeterminate but apparently acceptable' (1973: 15).

Fortunately, in terms of body capital, Patrick was the youngest member of the teaching staff and could pass in this way. He also shared common recreational interests with the gang members, such as football, swimming and pop music, which helped to build rapport. Patrick's key informant, Tim, actively colluded in the ongoing deception. On this Patrick states: 'Tim and I came to an understanding that, whatever happened, nothing would be disclosed by either of us to other members of the staff or to anybody else. This was seen by both of us as a necessary precaution for our own protection' (1973: 16).

Patrick makes clear reference to both data censorship and topic sensitivity in the preface:

> I have deliberately allowed some years to pass between the completion of the fieldwork and publication. The main reasons for the delay have been my interest in self-preservation, my desire to protect the members of the gang, and my fear of exacerbating the gang situation in Glasgow which was receiving nationwide attention in 1968 and 1969. (1973: 9)

Patrick resolved to be a 'passive participant' but this still presented him with a complex set of ethical dilemmas in terms of what he witnessed during his fieldwork. Ultimately, for Patrick: 'In fact it was the internal struggle between identification with the boys and abhorrence of their violence that finally forced me to quit' (1973: 14).

Patrick was constantly in fear of his cover being blown because a relative or friend of one of the gang members was sent to the approved school where he taught but this did not happen. Patrick recounts that his exit was a result of a gang member threatening him for not turning up at a big fight and because he had concealed a dangerous weapon, a hatchet, for the gang. Gang fighting, as well as petty theft, was important to the status of and respect for the Young Team. Patrick felt his days in the gang were numbered and his exit story was that he was leaving quickly for England. Gang-related violence, murders and imprisonment were reported in the press since Patrick's departure.

Patrick concludes the book passionately, stressing his attempt at a naturalistic insider approach:

> I have sought to describe, and to a lesser extent to interpret, the activities of one Glasgow gang in their terms and in their territory. It is only a beginning and not an end in itself. ... This book has been an attempt to present the daily lives of a group of adolescent delinquents with appreciation and empathy. (1973: 229)

Patrick's account was to receive critical acclaim. It is a commonly referenced milestone in studies of juvenile delinquency, youth culture and youth gangs. For Hallsworth and Young (2008), Patrick's book stands out as a rare early study of British gangs among the more commonplace studies on youth culture at the time. Indeed, McAra (2008) claims that Patrick's work provides a picture of the 'Glasgow hardmen', which is important in the development of a distinctive Scottish criminology. Deuchar and Holligan (2010), in their Glasgow-based study of gangs, sectarianism and social capital, claim that many of their findings 'echo' those of Patrick. In 2013, forty years after its original publication, the third revised edition of Patrick's book was published, with a new short preface. Surprisingly, both his real name and his whereabouts are still unknown, except to the publishers.

Howard Parker, in *View from the Boys: A Sociology of Down-Town Adolescents* (1974), provides another classic covert account of juvenile delinquency from the participant's perspective. The study took place in Liverpool over a three-year period and was to have a significant impact on the sociology of deviance. Parker references Patrick (1973) on several occasions, although he does not discuss the work in detail. Parker (1974) wanted to dispel some of the myths, stereotypes and prejudices around juvenile delinquency. The parameters and goals of the study are outlined in his preface: 'This study is not, nor does it claim to be, anything approaching a definitive statement about delinquency. It is an exploratory and groping affair. The participant observer who knocks around with a group of adolescents can only look in some corners' (1974: 8).

Parker initially met the adolescent boys while working as a young residential community youth worker at a country holiday centre for Liverpool 'street kids'. The study evolved from him being accepted by the group as an 'OK outsider' who could hang around with them for long periods. As he later took up a research post at the University of Liverpool, his initial acquaintances and friendships evolved into a more formal research project.

Parker (1974) goes into more methodological detail in an appendix entitled 'The Fieldwork Approach'. A few of the boys knew about his generalized research interests in the police and courts, but none knew that their lives were his specific focus. Thirty taped group interviews were also conducted by Parker later on in the fieldwork stage. Thus Parker became a 'regular face', who reassured them he was always 'on their side'. As the fieldwork continued, this translated into regular court visits with them as he became a reliable and trustworthy source of legal advice and guidance.

Part of this embedded participant observation role was a clear involvement in criminality although not actively taking part. On this, Parker states: 'I was a drinker, a hanger-arounder, and had been tested in illegal "business" matters and could be relied on to say nothing, "I knew the score". ... My position in relation to theft was well established. I would receive "knock off" and "say nothing"' (1974: 215–219).

Parker discusses 'blending in' and 'fitting into the scene', which involved funding drinking bouts, a dress code, using the local argot, playing and following their football team and participating in some camping trips. Thus, Parker argues that the project succeeded because of the 'match' in personality and style between him and the Boys. Parker reflects on the ethical problems of publication and censorship as some material he never published for fear of incriminating the Boys. Parker concludes the book reflecting: 'I am still satisfied the project was worth undertaking. It has impressed upon me and I hope it will on others how easy it is for sociological research to do grievous bodily harm to reality' (1974: 224).

Both studies by Patrick and Parker became classics within youth studies. Winlow and Hall (2009) describe both Patrick and Parker as providing rich analyses of working-class youth that uncovered a profound sense of kinship between the youths, which influenced their study of youth identity and the consumption of the night-time economy in northeast England.

Police studies

Jonathan Rubinstein, in his landmark study *City Police* (1973), elegantly portrays the everyday rhythm of police work 'on the street' as the police routinely deal with suspects, criminals, other police professionals and the public. Rubenstein, based on his study, also calls for greater accountability of the police to the public. After working for a year as a police reporter on a Philadelphia newspaper, Rubenstein negotiated with the director of the Philadelphia Police Department, as a gate-keeper, that he actually work with police on the street.

In September 1969, he entered the Philadelphia Police Academy, going through the full training of a police officer. On graduation he worked with different units full-time for one year until September 1970 and at weekends for a further year until September 1971. Rubinstein was attached to the University of Pennsylvania and supervised by Erving Goffman.

Although the study was primarily overt and needed open permission and ongoing co-operation with the Police force, covert dimensions emerged in the field. Rubenstein reflects:

> Many of the men I worked with knew that I was not a policeman (though some believed I was a federal agent or an undercover police operative), but policemen from other units and districts whom we encountered in the course of work did not. Only on a few occasions did my companions inform these men of my identity. On no occasion did any policeman I worked with inform a private citizen of my status in my presence, and only once did anyone question whether I was a police officer. (Rubinstein, 1973: xii–xiii)

Simon Holdaway's (1983) *Inside the British Police: A Force at Work* was based on the author's eleven years' service with the police force. While still in uniform, he was a sergeant based in a busy urban police sub-division of the London Metropolitan Police. He retired in 1975 so there was a reasonable time-span before publication for sensitivity reasons. After gaining a first class degree in sociology at Lancaster University while on secondment, Holdaway returned to the police force. He was encouraged by his postgraduate supervisor to conduct covert work on the occupational police culture in a 'unique manner', as a covert insider account over a two-year period, which could add to the limited body of knowledge of police studies.

For Holdaway, it was crucial to investigate the police, which is clearly a powerful, secretive and protective institution in society. He considered that much of the previous standard police criticism was bias and lacked credibility. As Holdaway states: 'I was not a sociology lecturer masquerading as a schizophrenic, alcoholic, millenarianist, pentecostalist or factory worker; I actually was a police officer who had no idea of when or if he would leave the field setting for other work. That, as will be seen, was the cause of considerable personal stress' (1982: 65).

Holdaway reflects on the limits of his tolerance, attitudes towards other officers and a range of ethical dilemmas that he encountered while on duty. He was unsure of what to document and found the covert role demanding. Holdaway states that his study 'was a balancing of personal ethical limits with the aims of sociological research and my duty as a police officer' (1982: 71).

Holdaway argues that covert research resembles the interactional process of 'masking' but with a heightened fear of 'unmasking'. He was very aware of the possible sensationalist press coverage that his work could attract and had to manage that post field. Holdaway stresses that 'we should avoid the impression that research ethics are a clear-cut matter' (1982: 79). His study was an early and insightful insider account of the police force. According to Heslop, he was a 'police research pioneer' (2012: 525). Holdaway has since become a successful academic and has influenced police practice and policy on various issues over the years.

Malcolm Young, in *An Inside Job: Policing and Police Culture* (1991), similarly provides an insider covert account as a serving police officer in Newcastle and Northumbria. He started his career as a uniformed police constable in the mid-1950s and, over a career spanning thirty-three years, covered a number of roles in the police force before latterly doing a doctorate in anthropology at Durham University. Interestingly, he has witnessed changes to police culture, increasing bureaucracy and political agendas. As with Holdaway, his data represents a combination of retrospective autoethnography and participant observation as a liminal and ambivalent insider role.

Prison studies

Covert work in this area is rarer to find, due to obvious access problems and the sensitivity of the topic. An innovative practitioner piece of covert work was done in this area by William Cahn, a district attorney, due to reports of brutality, corruption and unrest, at Nassau County Jail in San Francisco in 1970. Complaints were being raised about prison life generally across penal institutions in the United States. After necessary gate-keeping arrangements were made with senior staff, Cahn sent in fifteen undercover agents, pooled from a private detective company rather than academics, as inmates, without the knowledge of correctional staff. The agents were male and female and were black and white.

Cumulatively, the agents spent more than a year in jail. Overall, the report painted a fair picture of the running of the prison, with the major problem being overcrowding. They also reported guard corruption and brutality in a minority of cases, which resulted in some prosecutions. This rather radical covert method would be continued as a way of 'gathering unbiased information so that standards may be maintained and improved' (Cahn, 1973: 13–14).

Fleisher (1989), an anthropologist, spent a year at the maximum security Federal Penitentiary at Lompoc, California, after training and becoming a certified Federal corrections officer. The participant observation study explored the prison's typical culture of violence. Fleisher argues that the institutional culture rewards obedience and fosters a work ethic and attempts to avoid a profit-led factory culture. In the long term, Fleisher stresses that imprisonment costs are reduced by encouraging an employment-based system of social control and a more open management style.

The timely context of Fleisher's ethnographic study of prison life is an over-crowded prison system – a warehouse – with more inmates classified as violent and, with some hardened cases, perceived as beyond parole and rehabilitation. Hence, throughout the study Fleisher had to cope with an ever-present threat of violence.

Fleisher argues that his covert role gained him the respect of fellow officers, when he revealed this, which later led to him training correctional officers in the prison. His embedded role gave him the purchase to describe the daily routines of the prison in rich detail. He discusses his personal trust relationships with inmates in a chapter titled 'Rapport with Inmates'.

Shoplifting

Shoplifting is a typical 'hidden crime' that has most often been studied using official, secondary statistical data provided by either retail security personnel or law enforcement officers, with obvious problems of bias. Buckle and Farrington (1984), from a criminology background, conducted a pioneering study of shop-lifting by covertly observing shoppers in a department chain store in a city in the Southeast of England over a three-week period, with the co-operation of staff in the store and the company. The observation team was one male and one female, who communicated via hand signals. They were trained psychologists, experi-enced at making observations, and one of the researchers had been mentored by a store detective for five months.

Buckle and Farrington state: 'direct, systematic observation has rarely been used, and should be used more. The challenge to criminologists is to overcome the difficulties and develop it as a method of studying offending' (1984: 72). This pioneering study of shoplifting was replicated by Buckle and Farrington (1994) in a different part of the country ten years on, with broadly similar results in terms of the main motivations to shoplift.

More recently, Dabney et al. (2004) examined shoplifting by covert observa-tion using an unobtrusive CCTV system installed in a typical retail drug store chain in Atlanta, in the United States. The store gave gate-keeping permission. By this method, which removes researchers from directly following suspects, a significant number of shoppers were observed shoplifting over a year. The researcher team of ten observers were trained on camera use and analysis. Dabney et al. conclude: 'We hope that these new methodological directions inform future researchers seeking to better understand the dynamics of offenders, criminal offending, and crime control within natural settings' (2004: 722).

Workplace resistance

This category includes the complex and broad topics of workplace sabotage, theft, pilferage and misbehaviour, which are typically difficult to measure and chart. One of the classic early studies is Jason Ditton's *Part-time Crime: An Ethnography of Fiddling and Pilferage* (1977). It explored a medium-sized factory-production bakery in the southeast of England and was the basis of the author's doctoral studies. Ditton had some familiarity with the setting and the participants as he had previously worked there during undergraduate vacations. Thus, he had no access problems, gate-keeping arrangements or rapport issues.

Ditton describes how he worked initially 'as a plant worker, né undercover participant observer' (1977: 5). However, his covert stance was not sustained, which is typical of the shifting roles in research, due to the practicality of carrying out such a role. So it was the start of the ethnography that was covert and not the whole two-year period of the study as his methodology also involved interviews and questionnaires, while working as a despatch operative and then as a bread salesman.

Ditton explores the process of learning to become a fiddler as a recruit salesman, the normalization of fiddling and pilferage in the industry and fiddling as a subterranean subculture of business. For the majority of participants, 'the fiddle' was a way of making out, a sort of acceptable fringe benefit. Management performed occasional enforcement, resulting in some symbolic sackings, but most of the fiddling and pilferage was expected and not systematically challenged. It was not deviant but a case of widespread, and hence normal, occupational crime found in various industries and workplaces.

British anthropologist Gerald Mars, who has written extensively on workplace crime and deviance (1982, 2013), which includes forms of pilferage, sabotage, cheating and theft, primarily based his influential cultural theory on his retrospective covert experiences in a range of ordinary jobs in the ten years after leaving school and before he started his university career. Around thirty job experiences covered shop, hotel, pub, fairground, café, office and factory settings, much of it in Blackpool, a popular tourist resort in the Northwest of England, as well as two years as a storeman in the Royal Air Force. Workplace fiddling for Mars was primarily over cash, goods and time. It was not crudely anarchic but operated according to understood and shared rules and was invariably subject to moral imperatives, restraints and justifications. A type of normalized deviance in the workplace (Mars, 2013) that many actors in a range of ordinary work settings would be familiar with.

Van Maanen (1991), based on his three years' covert experience as a part-time ride operator in the late 1960s, gives a critical account of Disneyland, in Anaheim, California. Van Maanen characterizes Disneyland, which is a global entertainment brand, as 'the smile factory' and outlines the oppressive and conformist organizational culture that a 'well screened bunch' (1991: 59) of employees are socialized into. This is displayed in their strict dress code, adherence to service scripts and corporate manuals, and intense surveillance culture. Van Maanen details how he was publicly fired and escorted from the park grounds, in what he calls 'status degradation', by growing his hair too long, which broke the rules on personal appearance. Van Maanen's account is a typical retrospective one, which also involved informal interviews with some ride operators much later, after his original covert fieldwork.

Analoui (1995) spent six years exploring workplace sabotage or 'unconventional practices' in a global entertainment organization. These practices include destruction, inaction and wastage and occur across both management and worker groups. After a gradual process of vetting by his co-workers, he became 'accepted as a fully-fledged member of the community' (Analoui, 1995: 51) and was then included in their secrets and gossip. Analoui reflects on the dynamics of his prolonged fieldwork: 'Dismissal, being laid-off and the chance that his cover might be blown were constant and potential threats to the research' (1995: 52).

Sosteric (1996), in his four-year ethnography of workplace autonomy, de-skilling and resistance to management control in a Canadian nightclub, started off covertly as a complete participant. Most of the data was gained through his covert participant observation but his shift to an overt position in the latter parts of the fieldwork was to acquire missing information from interviews about strategy from management as there had been significant organizational change. Sosteric does not go into detail about the dynamics and consequences of managing the revelation and shift but the logic of the shift makes sense.

Richards and Marks (2007) explored social identity and resistance in restaurant teams, with the first author gaining paid employment for a twelve-week period within the catering facility of a global hotel chain, mainly working with waiting staff. They call for further research into organizational resistance and misbehaviour by exploring different team settings. On their covert methodological strategy, they argue: 'Observations are efficient because it reveals behaviour that people usually prefer not to report' (Richards and Marks, 2007: 47).

Brannan (2016) in his ethnographic study of malpractice and mis-selling in a new retail financial services call centre, adopts a covert position as a part-time sales adviser/agent for a three month period. On his covert stance he states: 'A covert approach to fieldwork was necessary because the practices that were common in the organization were not disclosed to customers and, as outlined above, involved embedded structural deceit' (2016: 7). Brannan wanted to explore mis-selling in situ as a ritualized part of the sales culture in the organization in both a nuanced and evocative way.

The very interesting deception dynamic here was that Brannan disclosed his true research identity to only fellow employees that he worked closely with in a team, many of whom were initially recruited with him. This has the advantage of gaining their comparative perspectives as key informants but clearly heightens the risk of exposure. His narrative was also fact checked by a former and experienced employee of the organization, which is another interesting dimension of the study involving a type of collaborative deception. Brannan concludes his paper by calling for: 'a more finely grained analysis of our notions of culture as they pertain to organizational contexts' (2016: 22), which by implication firmly includes covert methodology.

5.3 Education

Children

Researching children is clearly a highly sensitive area and is covered by certain legalities. These researchers discuss and justify their reasons for the use of deceptive techniques and the 'ethical safeguards' they used in actively debriefing all participants after the study and obtaining parental consent prior to the study.

Underwood (2005) used deception in the analysis of how older pre-adolescent children manage anger in response to peer provocation. One control group played a competitive game with a provoking child actor, and the other group involved a pair of close friends responding to a child actor posing as a difficult play partner. Peer maltreatment and bullying was observed throughout the experiments. Hubbard (2005) also used deception in his experimental study of measuring children's anger and emotional competence as a way of guiding intervention efforts by psychologists. Child actors, who were given extensive and standardized training, were again used to provoke anger in an arranged game. Hinshaw (2005) explored children's antisocial behaviour in response to children being tempted to steal objects and small amounts of money and to deface property.

School cultures

Richard Hilbert (1980), for his doctoral dissertation, enrolled on a year-long elementary teaching programme, where he secured certification, 'with a decided preference for not revealing my research interests' (Hilbert, 1980: 52), although some programme personnel knew of his identity as a sociology graduate. Hilbert was simultaneously doing research on teacher training while getting qualified. Hilbert formally debriefed key personnel during the last eight weeks of the programme, with most being mildly interested and not offended.

Burgess (1983), in his research on a comprehensive secondary school, informed the teachers that he was doing research, but the students were deceived and told that he was a new part-time teacher, although they eventually found out about the research by quizzing him. Atkinson's (1981, 1997b) doctoral research on the bedside teaching of medical students in hospital took place with the consent of the medical specialists but not the students or patients observed.

University life

Rebekah Nathan, in *My Freshman Year: What a Professor Learned by Becoming a Student* (2005), posed as a freshman, or first-year student, and lived in a student dormitory hoping to learn about the behaviours and attitudes of today's college students. Even before the book was released, she and her home university were exposed by a journalist as Cathy A. Small, an anthropology professor at Northern Arizona University (NAU). The Institutional Research Board (IRB) at her university approved the research. A few days later Small and NAU publicly acknowledged their roles. Indeed, the front-page story of the *New York Sun* in August 2005, a month before the book's official release, was headlined 'On the Trail of an Undercover Professor'.

Small spent a year trying to understand undergraduate culture, such was her distance from it. Small argues that she worked to *be* 'as anonymous as I could' (2005: 168). Small took a range of undergraduate courses and stayed on campus most of the time, as she attempted to credibly pass as a student. Small describes this as: 'learning the ropes, meeting other students, getting acclimated to the dorm, trying out student clubs, and discovering what it took to do my academic work' (2005: 16).

In addition to using covert methods, Small also used overt methods, such as conducting forty formal interviews with American and international students, leading two focus groups and asking students to complete activity diaries. Small challenges the myth of student-centred education and argues that the student–teacher relationship plays a relatively minor role in the experience of undergraduate life. Most students are much more pragmatically driven and have to work to fund their education.

5.4 Health

Alcohol addiction

Lofland and Lejeune conducted what they describe as an 'exploratory field experiment' (1960: 102) into thirty-five Alcoholics Anonymous (AA) groups in

New York City, the main organization dealing with alcohol addiction. They were specifically interested in how 'first contact' is organized between AA members and newcomers via social class symbols such as clothes, postural behaviour and conversation. The six researchers attended open meetings, with hidden recording equipment, and 'posed as alcoholic newcomers' (1960: 103).

Fertility

Martin (2010) investigated anticipated infertility, a sensitive and stigmatized topic, through a mixture of overt and covert approaches. She was conceptually interested in the growing and affluent fertility industry and related debates around fertility, choice, risk, ageing, illness, wealth and reproduction in American society.

Martin conducted qualitative content analysis of textual materials such as scientific, mainstream and marketing literature about egg freezing for two contrasting groups, healthy young women and cancer patients. This was combined with field notes from unobtrusive participant observation at free public events, sponsored by fertility clinics, pharmaceutical companies and non-profit advocacy organizations, in New York City and the San Francisco Bay area in the United States. Moreover, at the paid conferences, she gained admission by being a volunteer.

This opportunistic strategy by Martin seems sensible and productive in the situation, as her approach might have been deemed unethical by medical ethics committees. Martin describes her concealed role as: 'because I wanted my presence to be as unobtrusive as possible, for the most part I did not disclose my role as a researcher. ... As a participant, my goal was to experience the seminars in the same way as the strangers sitting next to me' (2010: 532).

Nursing homes

Hochschild (1973), who became famous for her work on the theory of emotional labour, conducted her doctoral fieldwork on a lower class special housing project in California, which mainly housed elderly women, many of whom were widows on the poverty line. Hochschild's initial entry was covert, as a paid employee of the city department of recreation and parks for a prolonged period. She revealed her true identity as a researcher in the latter stages of the project, which she claims did not offend them. Hochschild found a strong and developed sense of community rather than a stereotypical picture of isolation and alienation in her 'portrait of an old-age subculture'.

Smithers (1977) explored the institutional dimensions of senility by working as a volunteer for two days a week over eight months in a convalescent home. For Smithers, such places 'operate as depositories for aged persons who are deemed incapable of returning to a viable role in community life' (1977: 274–275). Smithers describes her volunteer role as highly advantageous: 'Because I was unsalaried, I occupied a marginal status in which I was someone who could be safely utilized as a sounding board for the airing of complaints, without fear of retaliation' (1977: 275).

Diamond, an American medical sociologist, was curious about the lack of detailed knowledge from the professional literature about nursing homes and the related work of nursing assistants, which is the largest single category of health care workers, the work mainly being done by women. He had some chance encounters with nursing assistants over a period of months while he was teaching at a university, and this had initially stimulated his interest. Moreover, the growing commercialization of the medical care of the elderly, which ran counter to a historic care philosophy, was a key and perturbing question for Diamond.

Diamond reflects on his methodological rationale: 'I would go inside to experience the work myself. I became a nursing assistant' (1992: 5). In order to do this, he went to college for six months to get the relevant certificate. Ethnographically, he worked in three different nursing homes in Chicago, one mostly private and the other two mostly state-supported. The fieldwork was for three to four months in each setting, followed by overt visits to other nursing homes across the United States and, briefly, some in Canada, England, France and Switzerland. Diamond reflects on the opportunistic nature of his field research and methods of data collection: 'While I was getting to know nursing assistants and residents and experiencing aspects of their daily routines, I would surreptitiously take notes on scraps of paper, in the bathroom or otherwise out of sight, jotting down what someone had said or done' (1992: 6–7).

Diamond's study was not a purist covert one. He informed some nursing assistants and residents of his dual role during the fieldwork, but not all. Indeed, when he informed some of the participants they did not believe him and thought he was delusional. The project was not deliberately planned as covert but rather emerged as a partially covert study. Diamond states: 'as the study proceeded it was forced increasingly to become a piece of undercover research' (1992: 8).

Diamond's study was to be influential to future studies of health care work. Charmaz and Olesen argue that: 'Diamond's covert approach to research allowed him to study the structure of the nursing home in ways that otherwise would have been inaccessible to him' (1997: 473). Frank adds 'he puts his body in the nursing home, changing dirty linen and diapers' (2004: 435). In more recent reflections, Diamond refers to the impositions of the current research context: 'Researchers now have to explore creative ways to pose an investigation that does not involve overt deceit' (2006: 60–61).

Organ trafficking

Scheper-Hughes, a professor of medical anthropology, conducted a controversial study of organ trafficking that was to have an impact on policy and resulted in a considerable amount of media coverage. Her study, which involved collaborating with activists, investigative journalists and political documentary filmmakers, fed into wider medical human rights issues and an establishment of an innovative organ watch project. For her, the topic is clearly: 'a hidden and taboo subject, as forbidden a topic as witchcraft, incest or paedophilia' (Scheper-Hughes, 2004: 31).

The organ trafficking economy is a global underworld network of buyers, sellers, brokers and surgeons trading between poorer third world and wealthy western countries. It is important to recognize here that she used multiple methods, including key informant interviews with a wide range of collaborators, questionnaires by local research assistants and observational work with some transplant surgeons. In this ethnography, the driving principle was always to 'follow the bodies' (Scheper-Hughes, 2004: 32), which took her to twelve countries. She describes her politicized work as an 'engaged and enraged ethnography' (Scheper-Hughes, 2004: 35) and 'a militant anthropology' (2004: 58).

However, vitally, she also took on several important faked roles in what she describes as an 'undercover ethnography' to access delicate information. Hence, she briefly posed as a kidney buyer in a suitcase market in Istanbul and also travelled incognito with a private detective from Argentina investigating organ theft from inmates in a locked state facility for the profoundly mentally retarded. She also posed as the relative of a patient looking to purchase or broker a kidney with sellers and brokers in person and over the telephone. Observationally, she sometimes visited transplant units and hospital wards unannounced, posing, if anyone inquired, as a confused friend or family member looking for another part of the hospital. She mixed this with introducing herself to medical staff as a doctor doing international research, but not stating the nature of the research or her field of expertise.

On previous covert studies she briefly mentions Goffman and Humphreys adding: 'but such deceptions are no longer permissible for researchers operating under the strict guidelines of human subjects protection committees. But there are times when one must ask just whom the codes are protecting' (Scheper-Hughes, 2004: 44). She asked for the project to be given exceptional dispensation akin to a human rights investigative reporter, which was granted.

Access to 'the secret world of transplant' (Scheper-Hughes, 2004: 37) was challenging. As Scheper-Hughes emotionally stresses: 'Transplant surgeons vie only with the Vatican and its cardinals with respect to their assumption of privilege, irrefutability and of a kind of "divine election" that seems to place them above (or outside) the mundane laws that govern ordinary mortals' (2004: 37).

The project findings, unlike other academic studies, had to be made public as quickly as possible, which meant the direct involvement of the press early in the project rather than at the end. Another radical move was to report some of the findings to the relevant government officials, criminal investigators and agencies across the world. Such moves resulted in her collaboration with the South African Police in a round-up of organ traffickers.

Scheper-Hughes argues that transplant tourism is a euphemism for the dark underbelly of human trafficking in spare body parts, which has been legitimated by both buyers and sellers. For her, 'organ selling has become a hidden "body tax" on the world's poor' (Scheper-Hughes, 2011: 85). She claims that organized and extensive criminal networks of brokers and traffickers are involved in global 'transplant tours'. Her work has seminally influenced international researchers and policy makers concerned with organ sale in the Islamic Republic of Iran (Tober, 2007), organ transplants in Egypt (Budiani, 2007), trafficking in the Philippines (Yea, 2010), commerce in cadavers in the United States (Anteby, 2010) and biological relatedness in China and India (Cohen, 2011).

Pseudo-patient studies

Bulmer, in a useful review of pseudo-patient studies, defines them as 'studies in which a medical sociologist or anthropologist masquerades as a patient' (1982b: 65). A number of radical studies have emerged from this tradition.

Caudill et al. (1952) studied a mental hospital from the 'patient's point of view'. This early pseudo-patient approach, particularly for the time, was very innovative. William Caudill, an American anthropologist at the University of Chicago was invited by Yale Medical School to take part in a study of interpersonal relationships among psychiatric patients at the Chestnut Lodge Asylum in 1950.

Caudill was admitted to the 'less disturbed' ward of the hospital, and on being assigned to one of the psychiatrists, he was treated as an in-patient there for a period of two months. He was a resident on the ward and took part in the daily routine and interacted with the other patients as if he was, put simply, one of them. After the first week, Caudill had going-out privileges each afternoon which enabled him to leave the ward for a few hours each day to write up his material. Neither the other patients nor the medical staff with whom he was in daily contact knew that he was a researcher. His status as a pseudo-patient was a secret known only to two senior medical personnel. In reflecting later on his experience, Caudill reported that his covert study: 'provided a rich body of data concerning many problems, hitherto only incompletely recognized, which were faced by the patients as a social group in their life on the ward' (1952: 315). Interestingly,

Caudill was also frustrated by the limitations of his concealed approach which led him to conduct a more intensive study of the setting between 1952 and 1953 as an overt researcher.

Based on this data, Caudill wrote his book about his experiences entitled *The Psychiatric Hospital as a Small Society* (1958). Rosenhan, in his famous pseudo-patient experiment (1973), references the Caudill et al. study. Addington, in her introduction to the influential text *Hearing Voices*, claims that 'Qualitative research is not new to psychiatry' (2012: 5). She lists both Goffman's *Asylums* (1961) and Caudill's 1958 book as 'classical textbooks' (2012: 6) in the field.

Falling under the pseudo-patient tradition is Buckingham et al.'s controversial and greatly under-utilized 'Living with the Dying' (1976). This study was conducted by medical anthropologists who used covert participation observation to explore methods of treating terminal cancer patients in a hospital in Montreal, Canada. In terms of other covert studies, Buckingham et al. reference Rosenhan (1973), although they do not discuss it in detail.

Such were the serious medical risks of life-threatening infection, senior medical staff were part of the necessary gate-keeping arrangements. Buckingham passionately committed himself to an embedded covert role as he assumed the role of a patient with terminal pancreatic cancer. A second medical anthropologist acted as his cousin and was his key contact during the hospitalization period.

Buckingham et al. describe his detailed and somewhat extreme preparations: 'Puncture sites from intravenous infusion needles on the hands and arms, a 10-kg weight loss induced by a six month diet, patchy beard alopecia related to the stress of preparation, and abstinence of several days from washing or shaving completed the picture' (1976: 1211–1212).

Buckingham spent a total of nine days in the hospital. On his opportunistic note-taking, Buckingham et al. state: 'Throughout the hospitalization M made notes and kept records of quantitative data, with the explanation that he wished to finish writing a book before he died' (1976: 1212). Buckingham et al. stress the emotional angst over his disguised role and his feelings of going physically and emotionally native: 'he identified closely with these sick people and became weaker and more exhausted. He was anorexic and routinely refused food. He felt ill' (1976: 1212).

Their results showed that, although the needs of the dying and their families are widely recognized, the patient perspective still needs emphasizing. Health care staff, the dying and their families display varied coping and adjustment mechanisms but this can result in inappropriate distancing by staff, which can lead to feelings of isolation and abandonment for the dying. They argued that support for dying patients came from other patients, patients' own families and adopted families, volunteers and student nurses, as much as from nursing staff or physicians. In particular, the inappropriateness of doctors travelling in groups, avoiding eye contact with the patient and not speaking to the patient by name was regularly observed.

Buckingham et al. humanely conclude:

> There is a need for comfort, both physical and mental, for others to see them as individuals rather than as hosts for their disease, and for someone to breach the loneliness and help them come to terms with the end. These needs may be better met by a unit specifically designed for this purpose. … It is in this situation, where there are such limited methods of gathering information, that participant observation can give significant insights into the subcultural behaviour and values of this group and those who care for them. (1976: 1215)

The interesting question here is that many would zealously view this study as an ethical step too far because of the vulnerable groups studied and the clear topic sensitivity, yet it compassionately reveals issues about a subject still saturated in taboo. Do the means, albeit controversial, justify the ends? For me, they do and it was ultimately worth undertaking the study. It would be very difficult to imagine such a covert study being funded in the present climate.

As expected, there was an initially strong reaction and response to this controversial study from several medical professionals as belligerent and extreme, but it would later be seen by many as a landmark study in medical anthropology and sociology. In a much later comparative study of cancer hospice care in London, using overt interview data, Seale and Kelly (1997) comment on the similarities of key findings: 'Buckingham et al.'s observation of the considerable extent of mutual help and support between relatives and patients is supported by this study' (1997: 105). In discussing the history of hospice research, Kovacs similarly stresses that the Buckingham et al. study 'helped substantiate the need for hospice care' (1998: 296). So, the policy implications could be seen as part of the positive consequences of this study, despite its controversial methodology.

Van der Geest and Sarkodie (1998) continued the pseudo-patient tradition in their study of being a 'fake patient' in a rural Ghanaian hospital. Under restricted gate-keeping, most of the staff knew about their purpose but patients did not. They conducted a hospital ethnography, which is comparatively rare in non-western medical settings. Namely, one of the authors was admitted as a patient. The experiment was a short one, lasting only three days. Although they argue that rich data could also have been gained by standard overt methods, covert methodology gave them a distinctive and sustained patient point of view. If repeated, interestingly,

Van der Geest and Sarkodie (1998) add that it should be conducted over a longer period of time and should deceive patients but not staff.

Hester Parr (2000), from a human geography perspective, conducted a covert study of five months' duration in an inner-city drop-in centre in Nottingham, England for people with mental health problems. Parr is interested in how exclusion and inclusion operate in a semi-institutional location, which the drop-in centre was. The covert study, with Parr acting as a drop-in client, had gate-keeping permission and indeed was encouraged to adopt a concealed role by staff. As Parr reflects: 'they were eventually supportive of my aims to undertake the work covertly. It was agreed that I might understand more about how the drop-in worked if I took a more participant role' (2000: 228).

For Parr, such 'deinstitutionalized landscapes' as the drop-in centre and similar places need to be further explored from a faked patient point of view. Parr argues: 'post-asylum geographies are complicated landscapes of inclusion and exclusion, and we are only just beginning to understand the processes, relations and spaces at stake here' (2000: 236).

A contemporary extension, although not a simple repetition, of the pseudo-patient tradition is the simulated client method (SCM) used by health care researchers. Here, researchers pose with fictitious case scenarios and then later report on their visit. In some cases, providers might know that a study is to be conducted. On the value of this method, Madden et al. state:

> The situated client method (SCM) has been used for over 20 years to study health care provider behaviour in a first-hand way while minimizing observation bias. In developing countries, it has proven useful in the study of physicians, drug retailers, and family planning services … [T]he information gathered through the use of simulated clients is unique and valuable for managers, intervention planners and evaluators, social scientists, regulators and others. (1997: 1465)

Secure psychiatric unit

In Clarke's controversial study of a secure psychiatric unit, where offender residents were often locked up, deceptive strategies were clearly embraced to 'attain as uncontaminated a picture of the unit as possible' (1996: 431). Although, people were generally aware of research being done, Clarke is adamant that: 'to attain even a measure of social alignment with subjects, it is necessary that the researcher's identity is kept vague and/or marginal' (1996: 433). Throughout the study, covert eavesdropping was regularly used, particularly in the guise of faked newspaper reading. Interviewing was also used but 'conducted in as casual a fashion as possible' (1996: 432). Note taking was done in the toilet using a miniature dicta phone. Clarke used participant observation over a period of six weeks while working part-time as a nursing auxiliary. He states: 'In this study the researcher's role was played down and a "one of the lads" stance was adopted in order to gain their confidence and thus elicit less guarded accounts' (1996: 432).

For Clarke, the rhetoric made by a mental health secure unit to be a therapeutic community was explored. The findings revealed unresolved conflicts between two groups of staff known as 'carers', who saw their role as therapeutic, and 'controllers', who saw their role as being custodial. Clarke aimed to display that these conflicts compromised the unit's aim of being a therapeutic community. The backdrop to the study was concerns about the excessive use of restraint in such units and the growing 'macho' nursing culture. Various complaints were made to Clarke's university as a result of this study and he thus had to cut his ties with the secure unit.

His sternest critic, Johnson (2004), argues that the covert aspects of Clarke's study were unnecessary and akin to crude 'television journalism'. In response, Clarke reflects rather honestly:

> I broadly endorse anti-psychiatry, and if it results in work that smacks of 'journalese' then so be it. … My paper contributed to a growing disenchantment surrounding the uses of control and restraint. It led to the beginning of a lot of soul searching on the part of those involved. … Finally, I confess that, in the tradition of Goffman and Rosenhan, I set out to expose what I suspected would be bad practice. (Clarke, 2004: 390–391)

Smoking ban

Petticrew et al. (2007), a team of public health researchers, covertly explored the effects of the prohibition on smoking legislation, in operation since March 2006, in public bars and other enclosed public spaces in Scotland. The large research team reported a range of problems in sustaining their concealment, including emotional fears and various risk scenarios, the most extreme being intervention dilemmas when witnessing criminal and antisocial behaviour. The observations were lengthy, starting six months before the ban and extending nine months after the ban. Despite the challenges, many of which revolved are being misperceived as local government regulatory officials, the team felt that the benefits of such covert observational data outweighed the numerous risks, and contributed to key debates about smoking-related health inequalities.

Weight loss

Darmon (2012) explored a commercial weight-loss group in France over a fourteen-month period from 2005 to 2007. Darmon was interested in how this organization used surveillance and transforming apparatus to control body discipline. She used covert participant observation and attended weekly meetings as an ordinary group member. Darmon reflects: 'I chose to go undercover because I was actually participating in the program, because it seemed to me it was difficult to be totally and always overt for everyone' (2012: 379).

5.5 Leisure

Football

In studying football crowd behaviour, typically, sports researchers use covert participant observation, along with audio-recordings of chants, archival data, press reports, field interviews and self-reports from supporters to analyse collective crowd behaviour. Early use of ethnographic research into football hooligans in the 1970s was often about the fans on the terraces and their social dynamics. This was very much classical ethnography of the public crowd and mob from a distance rather than getting 'among the thugs' (Buford, 1991).

John Sugden explores a different aspect of the football industry in *Scum Airways: Inside Football's Underground Economy* (2002). As football has commercially and globally expanded so has its unofficial hidden economy of ticket touts, fake goods, and the independent travel business. Sugden's study is of a deviant group of 'grafters' at Manchester United Football Club. Sugden, inspired by the investigative tradition (Douglas, 1976), describes his style broadly as 'new journalism'.

Sugden developed rapport with the gate-keeper, Big Tommy, who had direct links with the hooligan element of Manchester United's fan base, the lads of the Red Army. Big Tommy has achieved wealth and status through his entrepreneurial grafting and is now the legitimate owner of a large independent football travel business. Sugden reflects on his covert stance:

> In this particular study, when required, the author adopted a role as courier in a travel operation that was central to the black and grey economic activities of the gang. Although the key gatekeeper and a few close associates were aware of this researcher role, the majority of people who inhabited or passed through this world necessarily did not know this and could not be told. (2007: 244)

Millward (2009) conducted participant observation of Glasgow Rangers football supporters in Manchester city centre, where they were playing Zenit St Petersburg in the UEFA Cup Final. The 'fan party' degenerated into a 'hooligan riot' when fans clashed violently with the police. Reflecting on his mixed methodological stance, Millward states: 'The research was neither definitively overt nor covert, but readily switched between the two codes' (2009: 386). Millward readily informed fans of his research role but this changed, according to the practicality of the situation. Hence: 'Once the disturbances began, I did not tell those people I spoke to that I was carrying out research, but merely tried to offer support and help' (2009: 386).

Hylander and Granstrom (2010) researched crowd violence in the particular case of a football match in Dortmund, Germany, between Germany and Poland during the World Championship in June 2006, which was considered high risk by the police and media. The research was supported by the Swedish Emergency Management Agency and clearly had policy implications for policing strategy. Part of their multiple methods approach, along with interview data, was covert fieldwork observations where three pairs of observers followed the crowds at strategic locations as well as mingling with them throughout. This was a sort of bystander method, which the authors described as 'multi-point observations'. Photographs were also opportunistically taken throughout the observation period. For them, such mixed methodology can be usefully applied to various crowd events as well as political protests and social movements.

Geoff Pearson has been forthright about his covert role in researching crowd behaviour and football hooligan subcultures since the mid-1990s. Indeed, a 2009 journal article was provocatively entitled 'The Researcher as Hooligan: Where "Participant Observation" Means Breaking the Law'. The study required the researcher to become involved in pitch invasions and be regarded and treated as a fellow hooligan by the participants. Pearson defines his proxy hooligan role as a form of 'intensive participant observation' (2011: 5).

Part of the reason for adopting covert methodology, for Pearson, 'despite severe practical and ethical difficulties' (2011: 6), centred on the problems of gathering accurate interview data from fans who either exaggerated or down-played their involvement in violence, which is equally problematic. Pearson stresses: 'If you are genuinely interested in "who did what to whom and when", there is still no substitute for getting out there into the field and being a bit naughty' (2011: 14). Pearson, like others in this field, walked a risky legal tight-rope throughout his study.

Gambling

Chambliss (1975) explored the work of illegal gambling and racketeering and in turn organized crime and police collusion in Seattle, USA, through his ini-tial covert approach of playing in the illegal card games at various late-night venues for a couple of months. He states: 'I had discovered the broad outlines of organized crime in Seattle, but how it worked at the higher level was still a mystery. I decided it was time to "blow my cover"' (Chambliss, 1975: 36–38). The research project turned into a protracted longitudinal one over a ten-year period as Chambliss, as a known researcher into the area, became a trusted person to talk to about a variety of illegal rackets in Seattle.

For two years Oldham (1974, 1978) worked part-time as a croupier in a casino, while still holding a teaching appointment in Brighton, UK. His initial study was about the role of chance, skill and calculation by roulette players, which then broadened into the wider study on compulsive gamblers and gambling as a form of addiction.

Sallaz (2002) conducted a covert study of legal gambling by becoming a croupier in a corporate casino in Nevada over a four-month period. Sallaz is interested in how dealers develop their autonomy and offer resistance to strict casino management control and intense surveillance. Before taking up a job as a blackjack dealer in a strategically chosen corporate casino, Sallaz enrolled in a state-licensed vocational school offering standardized courses in dealing, which was an occupational requirement. On his covert research role, Sallaz states: 'During my tenure as a croupier, I kept my status as researcher hidden from both management and co-workers. When asked about myself on job applications or by other workers in the casino, I would reply that I was between jobs or looking for a new line of work' (2002: 399).

Getting tips is an essential part of the subculture of croupiers. As the policy is that tips are evenly shared, new dealers are socialized into tip-making tactics by veteran dealers, including helping tippers win and forcing off non-tippers. Thus, the tipping system is a way that workers negotiate management control and cope with an increasing lack of work autonomy. Sallaz was aware of the ethical problems associated with covert research but felt that the participants were not put in any danger or harmed. He justifies his approach in terms of his observational access to illicit workplace behaviour. Sallaz argues that his work can be usefully extended to the analysis of other tipped employees in the large and growing service sector, such as taxi drivers, food servers, valets and bartenders.

Jun Li (2008) studied female gambling culture as part of a postdoctoral fellowship supported by the Ontario Problem Gambling Research Centre in Canada. Li views gambling as a sensitive topic since many of the participants are from vulnerable backgrounds. She argues that she was 'psychologically unprepared for the ethical challenges embedded in ethnography' (2008: 104).

Li made around forty field trips to the three largest casinos in southeast Ontario, Canada, regularly taking shuttle buses with casino-goers. She played slot machines with the fixed budget of research money and interacted with female gamblers whenever possible. She recorded notes discretely when alone.

She played the deliberate role of a 'beginning player who was curious about recreational gambling entertainment' (Li, 2008: 104).

Jun Li experienced emotional discomfort in sustaining a concealed covert research role, which prompted her to shift from covert participant observation to overt, in-depth interviewing with seven regular female gamblers from different cultural backgrounds. The respondents were drawn from public research advertisements in local community centres and grocery stores and vetted over the telephone. Li stresses: 'I contend that in sensitive studies research ethics must go beyond the simple avoidance of research covertness to a mindful consideration of the well-being of marginalized individuals and communities' (2008: 112).

Mystery shoppers

The use of mystery shoppers is akin in some ways to the pseudo-patient tradition and is a popular method in the fields of marketing and travel and tourism. This simulated method has been variously described as surrogate patients, standardized patients, confederates, mystery clients and simulated purchase survey, according to the clinical or commercial setting. Interestingly, the level of ethical scrutiny and reflection is very variable and dependent on the tradition in which the method is used.

Walden et al. (1974), within a social work tradition, describe an experimental 'immersion' whereby graduate social work students posed as clients in a variety of agencies for the purpose of learning first-hand about service delivery and identifying with the client role. Miller (1998) claims that mystery shoppers, or what he calls 'undercover shoppers', methodologically stem from cultural anthropology and have become a mainstream technique in market research. It has been applied extensively in the study of customer service encounters and exchanges (Grove and Fisk, 1992; Wilson, 1998) and retail banking (Morrall, 1994).

Hudson et al. (2001) used mystery shoppers to test travel agent recommendations with the three largest travel agency chains in the UK. Fifty-two agencies in total were sampled through a mixture of thirty-six actual visits and one hundred and twenty telephone calls. Hudson et al. state that this method was 'used to get an insight into what happens when potential holiday makers call or walk into a travel agent to book a holiday' (2001: 150). They were particularly concerned with the strength of recommendations by the travel agents or what they describe as 'directional selling'.

Mystery shopping was used by Van Hoof et al. (2009) to investigate compliance rates about underage drinking. Four underage students, two boys and two girls, visited fifty-eight alcohol sales points, consisting of eight bars and fifty supermarkets in October 2008 around the city centre of Pitesti in Romania. All of the purchase attempts were successful. Only one cashier at a supermarket questioned their age, but still sold to them after they lied about it, based on a provided script. Hence, alcohol sales to underage youths turns out to be a major point of concern which, Van Hoof et al. (2009) stress, requires stronger intervention by local licensing and control bodies.

Recreational cultures

The public context of night-time spaces, including clubs, pubs and bars, provides a rich source of covert research. More recently, some of these spaces have also been settings for the study of recreational drug cultures, with many of the earlier studies concentrating on alcohol consumption.

From a sociological interactionist tradition, an early study was Sherri Cavan's *Liquor License: An Ethnography of Bar Behaviour* (1966). It provides a rich account of recreational culture, which involved observing a wide variety of public drinking places. Humphreys (1970) makes a footnote reference to this work in his classic *Tearoom Trade*. Cavan's ethnography was undertaken from 1962 to 1965, with data gained from approximately one hundred bars in San Francisco. The observational periods varied in time as some places were visited only once and others as many as ten or twelve times.

Her research involved covert participant observation. Cavan discusses this briefly at the outset of the book as: 'I visited all establishments in the guise of a "typical patron," attempting to be indistinguishable from other patrons present' (1966: 15). This covert role involved her in what she calls 'conversational encounters' with patrons, prompted by sociability overtures by patrons or initiated by herself, as well as generalized eavesdropping. In addition, two male field workers, 'posing as out of town patrons' (1966: 21), asked the bartenders about the 'availability of female companionship' (1966: 21). Follow-up focused interviews with some key informants were also undertaken.

Roebuck and Frese were interested in the 'after-hours club' as unlicensed and illegal social organizations that catered to a 'potpourri of deviants' (1976: 131–132). After-hour clubs were semi-secret establishments where drinks were sold during the hours when other clubs had closed. Roebuck and Frese following gate-keeping with the owner-manager and assistant manager, primarily used covert participation over two years. They also conducted extensive interviews at the end stage of the study. They describe their empirical approach as being similar to Goffman's, whom they acknowledge as making critical comments on the paper. For Roebuck and Frese, the club served as a 'respectable' interaction place between organized criminals and non-criminal clients over the sale of illegal goods and services.

Snow et al. (1991) were concerned with the survival strategies of women in singles bars and nightclubs. Their three-month participant observation phase involved two of the female authors visiting nine different nightclubs and drinking establishments, including singles bars, discos, rock bars, country and western bars and a topless bar. Snow et al. stressed that the researchers positioned themselves strategically so they could covertly 'simultaneously eavesdrop and observe' (1991: 429) and do 'interviewing by comment' (1991: 430) as a way to elicit focused information.

Slavin (2004) explored drugs, space and sociality in a gay nightclub in Sydney, Australia. He gives a nuanced account of a night out which covers recreational drug use and casual sex, which are normalized aspects of the nightlife scene he investigated. Slavin's wider research explored injecting drug use and HIV health awareness for the gay community and was conducted over a two-year period. Although he used a range of overt key informants, his strategy was intentionally blurred by others. Slavin states 'sometimes, key participants chose to make my role covert *vis-à-vis* their friends and acquaintances' (2004: 269). Slavin, biographically, is a gay man with ten years' insider knowledge of the gay scene, in terms of the obvious sensitivities surrounding a range of illicit substances which typically included ecstasy, ketamine, speed and amyl nitrate. Slavin opportunistically took advantage of what he describes as 'degrees of membership of particular groups' (2004: 270), some of which knew of his research, while others did not.

Lugosi (2006) made exploratory visits to various bars, restaurants and clubs. He eventually focused on a single case study over twenty-seven months as a consumer and worker. This was a bar in a suburban town in England which was largely patronized by the gay and gay-friendly community. Lugosi started the study as a frequent customer but, as he felt this was limiting, opted to get a barman's job initially, which ended up in him jointly managing the bar.

He delayed disclosing his true research role until the second week when trust and rapport had developed. Despite his disclosure, concealment was pervasive throughout the study. Lugosi describes how he 'continually appropriated idle gossip, conversations and comments' (2006: 549), without formal consent. Lugosi sensibly asserts: 'I maintain that while these techniques contain elements of covertness, it is wrong to suggest that they are unethical' (2006: 550). Lugosi describes his negotiated disclosure as 'the research never became completely overt … and disclosure was always incomplete' (2006: 554) as some customers remained unaware of the study whereas others were partially informed. This is to be expected with a fragmented and transitory community of customers who visited the bar.

For her doctoral research, which formed the basis of her book *Flashback: Drugs and Dealing in the Golden Age of the London Rave Scene* (2010), Jennifer Ward explored drug users and sellers in the rave dance scene in London over a five-year period in a range of public and private settings, including nightclubs, dance parties, pubs and houses. Her reflexive and experiential research was semi-covert and heavily utilized a friendship network to explore this sensitive and illegal subculture. As this friendship network organically grew, it was difficult to maintain any sort of standard informed consent approach, particularly when the participants were clearly under the influence of various substances. For Ward, the complex nature of the friend/researcher relationship turned out to be ethically ambivalent on several occasions, in terms of witnessing cases of addiction, drug dealing and, in some instances, prosecution by the police.

Similarly, Bhardwa (2013) reflects on the challenges of conducting fieldwork in various dance settings and her shift from a dance consumer to field researcher. She dynamically uses a mixture of overt and covert strategies, some using gate-keeping and key informants, some purely covert and some within friendship networks. Trading on the notion of being a *'partial insider'* (Measham and Moore, 2006: 16), she actively called on multiple identities in her fieldwork.

Sexual practices

Varni (1972) investigates swinging, or in his early context married spouse-swapping, through first-hand experience and knowledge, not by participating in or observing actual sexual interaction, but rather by socializing with them to better understand their subculture. At the time he was writing, this was a 'new social phenomena' (1972: 522). Varni reflects on his method of entry:

> In order to gain entrance into the world of swinging, my wife and I presented ourselves as a couple favorably disposed to the idea of swinging, who wanted to meet with swingers in order to get a better idea of what it was all about. ... I did not divulge my researcher role to any of the couples. (1972: 507–508)

Varni put advertisements in a local underground newspaper and met with sixteen swinging married couples, usually in their home, under the disguise of being 'novice swingers' (1972: 508). Notes were taken immediately after the meetings, which averaged about three hours. Varni, within a symbolic interactionist stance, attempts to classify and describe different types of swinging and the process of becoming a swinger, which for many in mainstream society would be viewed as deviant.

Karp (1973) was interested in the nature of urban anonymity in public contexts, in particular hiding behaviour in pornographic bookstores, which was part of his doctoral study of the Times Square sexual community. Karp makes references to both Humphreys and Goffman in his analysis. Karp spent over a year and a half frequenting pornographic bookstores and movie theatres, despite feeling awkward. He states: 'I was the sociologist documenting others' behaviour in this setting' (1973: 435).

Sundholm (1973), building on Goffman, provides an early study of the moral order of the pornographic arcade, which he views as a semi-public leisure setting. He contrasts his work to Cavan's (1966) earlier ethnography on bar behaviour and references Humphrey's (1970) classic work. His covert observations of various patrons were made over a three-month period.

Corzine and Kirby (1977) investigate sexual cruising among truckers in high-way rest areas. Combined with gate-keeping information from key informants and follow-up interviews and conversations, they conducted forty separate covert observations, averaging three hours, of cruising over a six-month period from their parked car or picnic tables in the rest areas. They also took a more active role by riding with co-operating individuals while cruising but this proved to be too disruptive. Crozine and Kirby (1977), who reference Humphreys (1970), argue that this type of sexual marketplace is widespread but hidden in American society.

Styles, as a 'gay man committed to gay studies' (1979: 135), covertly researched gay baths for nine months, taking the role of a customer. Rather than view the promiscuous and impersonal sex rumoured to occur there as deviant, it aroused his curiosity. On his voyeuristic role, Styles states: 'As a nonparticipating insider, I felt that I could retain my sympathy, my claim to sociological objectivity' (1979: 137). Styles encountered regular sexual offers and, after some trepidation, shifted his stance and took on a full participant role, stating: 'I simply gave up observing without sexual intent and plunged fully into the sex life of the baths. ... After all, I was now a "real" insider' (1979: 142).

Weatherford, in *Porn Row* (1986), conducted an ethnography of the red light district of Washington DC, in the United States. He took a job covertly as a night operator of a pornography store, which sold magazines, sex products and had sixteen 'peep booths'. Such a place was open to a series of illegal activities, such as gambling, masturbation, prostitution, homosexual pickups, drugs sales and fencing stolen goods. The store operator gave tacit approval of such criminal activities to increase revenue. The space had to be discreetly managed in terms of obvious police suspicion and investigation.

Prior to the current explosion of online dating, Goode (1996) explored the topic of courtship in personal advertisements. Goode argues clearly for the use of covert research:

Certain kinds of deception are necessary to gather certain data in certain settings. I placed bogus ads in a personal column to obtain and analyse responses. The data would have remained inaccessible – indeed, many of the responses would not have existed in the first place – without some measure of deception. (1996: 11)

Frustrated by the limitations of overt research techniques in this field, Goode placed four bogus ads, two male and two female, all heterosexual, in the personal columns of four different publications in different parts of the country in the United States. Written responses, rather than verbal ones, were stipulated in the bogus personal ads and then analysed by a panel of twenty judges, of mixed gender and professions. The panel, who knew the ads were fraudulent, judged the likely success of the respondents as dates. They also maintained that the research method used was not 'especially unethical' (Goode, 1996: 11). Goode, from this study, argues that there is a strong place for covert research: 'I do not wish to close down my research endeavours because they may object to my violating an article of ethics they believe in but I don't' (1996: 32).

Berkowitz (2006) explores the consumption of eroticism via gendered performances and presentations in pornographic establishments. She argues that there is a dearth of research in this area. The data collection involved participant observation in the evenings over a six-month period as a customer in an adult bookstore in a Southeastern college town in the United States, with field notes being taken in the car after visits. Berkowitz describes her role as: 'I was a covert participant in that I wandered around the store pretending to be a patron, carefully observing the actions of the other patrons' (2006: 590).

Similarly, Hefley (2007) explored the stigma management of male and female customers in a non-urban adult bookstore in a college town in the Southwest of the United States. She argues that most of the research in this area has focused geographically on urban localities and on masculine usage rather than female usage, which is increasing. For her, therefore, the gendered differences in the consumption of pornography are neglected. In her covert study, she worked as a sales clerk for nine months on weekend evenings, the busiest times for an adult store. This embedded working role involved her in close interaction with the customers, as Hefley states:

As a sales clerk, one of my duties included regulating customer behavior. I was expected to sense when customers needed help, to prevent patrons from opening product boxes or otherwise being destructive, stealing merchandise, or harassing other customers. This required close observation of the patrons of the store, which aided my research purpose. (2007: 85)

McCleary and Tewksbury (2010) similarly explored the gendered consumption of pornography by observing customers entering thirty-three stores for 162 hours over a two-year period, which includes all weekdays and times. The comparative study was conducted across Los Angeles, Orange and San Diego counties in the United States. The covert observations were conducted by nine trained graduate researchers observing customers from a distance as well as them entering the stores and posing as customers. They conclude that men and women experience, use and prefer different types of adult stores.

Sports

Tomlinson and Yorganci (1997) explore gender and power relations between female athletes and male coaches in competitive athletics. In particular, the vulnerability of the young female athletes in coaching situations is identified. The control and domination by the coach is manifested in various forms of sexist practice and sexual harassment. Mixed methods are used, with interviews and a questionnaire survey complementing a covert participant observation phase.

The fieldwork was undertaken by Yorganci, an experienced and competitive runner, and focused on two sprint groups. She was present, as an athlete, at training sessions, competitive meets and some informal social gatherings. Field notes were taken after club sessions on the different attitudes shown to male and female athletes by the coaches. Tomlinson and Yorganci stress: 'the integrity of the observational project was valued above any ethically driven openness. In revealing her researcher role, the field-worker would have encountered the most counterproductive of Hawthorne effects, and the context of everyday coach–athlete relationships would have been changed' (1997: 140).

Wheaton and Tomlinson (1998) explore the gendered nature of windsurfing culture on the south coast of England. Interestingly, the research into this 'macho' subculture was done covertly by Wheaton, a female researcher who was both an active member of a local club and a journalist working for a windsurfing magazine. The research project used mixed methods, combining interviewing, media analysis and an initial covert eighteen-month participant observation period. Wheaton and Tomlinson argue: 'So the field-worker adopted a covert role based on her established role within the group, and her familiarity with the main setting under observation' (1998: 255).

Tourism

Seaton (2002) used unobtrusive participant observation for three days while studying a conducted coach party touring the First Wold War battlefields of the Somme, France and Flanders. For him, the conducted tour represented a 'travelling laboratory'. Seaton refers to three simultaneous participant modes in his ethnographic role: 'as passenger note-taker and log-book recorder during the tour; as conversational eavesdropper at stops; and as social participant at lunch, at night etc.' (2002: 311).

Seaton reflects on group infiltration: 'This induction problem may be called the "mole under cover" syndrome that confronts plain-clothes policemen penetrating criminal groups' (2002: 312). Seaton argues that the covert role: 'is one that effectively offers the researcher a travelling laboratory which can be readily accessed, studied and reported in ways that are more difficult under open field conditions, or using other methodologies' (2002: 317). Covert methodology is one that Seaton (1997) had previously used to study a multi-programme Easter festival in Scotland, in combination with the main quantitative visitor study. Seaton stresses that many tourism researchers have 'theorised frequently at a distance' (Seaton, 2002: 317) and hence covert research should become part of their toolkit.

Bowie and Chang (2005) studied tourist satisfaction in a mixed nationality guided package tour of Scandinavian destinations over twelve days, with particular emphasis on the role of the tour leader. The second author, a Chinese male, undertook the research. On their covert methodological stance, Bowie and Chang state: 'He paid the same fee for joining the tour, and the tour operator and company employees were not aware of this research' (2005: 311).

Kwortnik and Thompson (2009) use a mixed methods approach to exploring service experience on a leading cruise line company. Part of this was covert participant observation conducted by two students from a research team of five over a ninth-month period, totalling eleven days of onsite field research. Chang (2009) explored Taiwanese tourists' perceptions of service quality on outbound package tours. After gaining gate-keeper access, Chang decided to use covert methodology in his observations to 'gain deeper views of travellers' perceptions of service quality' (2009: 1970). The observational data was then enhanced by semi-structured telephone interviews conducted after the tour had finished.

Charters et al. (2009) used a modified mystery-shopping approach to explore the winery tasting rooms in two large vineyards in Australia and one in New Zealand. Wine tourism has become increasingly popular. Participants were recruited from the nearby areas to the vineyards. Teams were debriefed beforehand and then sent into the winery tasting rooms. The project covered twenty-eight winery visits by twenty-eight participants, in teams of six. Post-visit questionnaires and focus group data also supported the analysis of the hospitality service encounter and brand loyalty.

Andriotis (2010) used a covert ethnographic approach to explore transgressive behaviour on an unofficial gay nudist beach in Crete, a Greek holiday island, which functioned as an erotic oasis for tourist makers and some locals. What

Andriotis describes as 'deviant beach use' (2010: 1076), which, for him, could not have been openly and richly accessed by standard methods.

Thurnell-Read's (2011) investigation of Eastern European stag tourism, which explored masculinity and embodiment, involved covert observations over nearly a year of fieldwork in Krakow, Poland. Informed consent was sought with some groups but a key source of data was gained from a 'more removed role' that was 'unavoidably covert' (2011: 981), which observed the public behaviour of around one hundred separate stag parties and 1,400 stag tourists in various settings.

The ethnographic work of Daniel Briggs in his book *Deviance and Risk on Holidays: An Ethnography of British Tourists in Ibiza* (2013) uses extensive interviews and focus groups with both holiday makers and various resort workers about leisure rituals and hedonistic practices within a context of global capitalism and mass consumerism. He also uses participant observation and an admission of using alcohol but not drugs in his fieldwork period. Such participant observation would have been very difficult to do with open and full informed consent due to the unbounded nature of the setting. What Briggs sensibly describes as a 'flexible but entirely serious methodology' (2013: 16). In a similar vein, Briggs and Ellis (2016) explore stag events in the UK with regard to risk, deviance and consumerism employing a similar methodology, with some aspects of a semi-covert participant observation methodology.

5.6 Politics

Begging

Hall undertook some covert begging from strangers in central London streets while he was spending some time in hostels and shelters in the early fieldwork phase for his year-long study of youth homelessness, *Better Times than This: Youth Homelessness in Britain* (Hall, 2003). This equipped him with some vital experiential and insider knowledge about the field.

Adriaenssens and Hendrickx (2011) explored the revenues and yields of begging in Brussels, Belgium. Reliable and accurate knowledge about such underground street-level informal economic activity is very limited. Linked to that is the criminalization of those involved in begging. The authors propose triangulated methodology which involved what they call 'a quasi-experimental version of participant observation' (2011: 29). What this typically meant was one hour spent in begging activities by four male and two female test subjects using a small concealed microphone, watched by an observer from a distance.

Adriaenssens and Hendrickx are aware of the vulnerable nature of the groups being researched and redistributed any moneys gained from imitating beggars. On the specific risks and dangers associated with this simulation, they state:

Although the police were informed in advance of the research, the test subjects behaved like other people who beg when chased off by the police or private security companies. In case someone was arrested, the observers did carry a letter from the chief of police clarifying the aim of the begging activities. (2011: 31)

Purdam (2014) reflects on citizen data and citizen social science in an innovative pilot observation study of begging. He used thirteen volunteers, who strictly followed a non-participatory and unobtrusive protocol to covertly gather everyday observational data from their daily routines of street begging in central London. Purdham contends that such citizen research will become much more popular and hence become central to policy-making methodology.

Community race relations

Ken Pryce explored the lifestyles of the West Indian community in Bristol in the context of neo-colonial relations. More specifically, he was concerned with the response of West Indian workers to '*slave labour*' and '*shit work*' in the contemporary British economy. Pryce, who was based in the Sociology Department at Bristol University, conducted ethnographic research over a four-year period between October 1969 and July 1974 for his doctorate. Pryce is critical of integration policies and hopes to clarify the problems of discrimination and racism that West Indian communities continually faced.

This research was an example of typical semi-covert ethnography wherein certain gate-keepers were aware of his research role while the majority of participants were unaware of it. For Pryce, this was an 'insider's view of West Indian life-styles in Bristol' (1979: xii). Pryce (1979) stresses: 'My concealment of my role as a researcher was not intended to deceive, but merely to sustain the rapport which I was developing' (1979: 280).

Pryce (1979) traded on his Jamaican heritage and constructed a partly true claim about losing his religious faith. Pryce spent twelve months in contact with the church, which played a significant role in the community. Pryce was 'on the look-out for the most appropriate opportunity to reveal my true role' (1979: 284), which led him to reveal his true identity to the church pastor who took him 'under his wings'. Ironically, the pastor then actively colluded with him to conceal his identity and interests from the rank-and-file members in return for baptism and permanent membership of his church. Consequently, he became far more involved in church life and 'the street corner crowd'. Some of the participants became aware of his 'university background' and distanced themselves while others associated themselves with it as a positive symbol of 'black power' militancy.

The book was seen as a classic in studies of race relations and racism and his work is commonly referenced in contemporary studies of black identity and culture (Gunter, 2008; Hunt, 2002).

Extremist organizations

Nigel Fielding's *The National Front* (1981) explored a politically sensitive and deviant area, an extremist right-wing political organization. Fielding, on a personal and moral level, abhorred the belief system of the National Front. This was 'a group whose ideology is wholly alien to me' (Fielding, 1981: 7). His study was semi-covert in that he negotiated access with key informants and gate-keepers at the local and national level over a two-year period. Fielding deliberately used a mixed strategy of overt interviewing and covert observations at party branch meetings, where not everyone knew of his research role. Fielding's study, for me, is akin to studying religious cults, where detailed insider knowledge is typically difficult to access, which necessitates a more embedded sympathizer role.

Fielding deliberately blurred his 'outside' academic research role with some participants as he gradually gained their trust under a 'friendly near-convert status' (Fielding, 1981: 7). So he was clearly not covertly disguised as a new National Front member, but he concealed his true feelings as he was involved in 'deliberately misleading statements of support and implanted expectations of advocacy' (Fielding, 1982: 80). By necessity, he felt compelled 'to play the part of unconverted sympathiser' (Fielding, 1982: 85).

More recently, Garland and Treadwell (2010) and Treadwell and Garland (2011) have studied the rise of the English Defence League (EDL) and its close links to football hooliganism and forms of Islamophobia. For them, the analysis of the EDL is tied up with violent masculinity, political marginalization and reactionary politics. As well as the analysis of media coverage and various internet sources, Treadwell used covert ethnography by 'gaining access to EDL networks and hence attending a number of demonstrations ostensibly as someone who sympathises with its ideas' (Garland and Treadwell, 2010: 20). Types of conversational interview data are also used with key informants, who are former members of violent football hooligan firms and now active EDL members, whom Treadwell had access to due to his previous longer-term study of football disorder.

5.7 Religion

The study of religious cults and communities, as secretive 'closed groups' and 'hard to access' sensitive areas, has been very open to immersive covert research. The seminal and acclaimed study by Roy Wallis, *The Road to Total Freedom: A Sociological Analysis of Scientology* (1977), which resulted in him being followed and investigated by the Church of Scientology, initially involved a covert participant observation study. Wallis, a doctoral student at Oxford University, initially enrolled on a 'communications course' with the Church of Scientology but left after two days because he was not willing to lie about his reactions to the course content. He then collected data by survey and interview methodology.

Balch and Taylor (1977) investigated a religious UFO cult in the United States, which had received much national press attention. The cult was a remarkable success story with 150 followers joining within seven months. They travelled around the country in small family groups living in spartan conditions, which was part of their salvation beliefs. In order to understand the point of view of the 'seeker', they joined as 'hidden observers' with several different families for seven weeks. Six months later they conducted follow-up interviews with thirty-one ex-members. On their decision to be hidden, Balch and Taylor argue in a footnote: 'We believed the only way we could get accurate data about the cult was to join it ourselves' (1977: 858–859). Indeed, they note that when they revealed their true identities to ex-members in interviews they perceived that there was little hostility. For Balch and Taylor, a religious cult, although deviant to outsiders, is classically normalized to converts.

Homan (1978), in his doctoral study of sectarian 'old time Pentecostals' over eighteen months, chose covert participation and covert interviewing, combined with some overt forms of investigation. This religious community were distrusting of both the outside world and sociology. For Homan, 'covert research is a pragmatic expedient, ideally nonreactive and giving access to secret transactions' (Homan, 1980: 46). To credibly pass in the assembly, Homan joined in prayer, song and praise phases, openly carried a bible and accepted tea invitations from members. He occasionally used a tape recorder, which was disguised in that it was allowed to help 'carry the blessing' to members who were not present, not to document their behaviour.

However, after using covert methods, he had 'serious reservations on its adoption' (Homan, 1980: 46), with it being 'potentially detrimental to the personality of the fieldworker, in whom certain traits may persist even after he has left the field' (Homan, 1980: 46). Due to this, he has since become a stern critic of covert research (Homan, 1991, 1992, 2001), who is popularly quoted in the literature.

Gini Graham Scott's (1983) covert observation study of a highly secretive black magic group (Church of Hu) nearly resulted in painful retribution as she was discovered and confronted by hostile members in 'the tense setting of a quickly convened trial' (1983: 133). The members then banished her from the group, threatening 'you should be glad that we aren't going to do anything else' (1983: 133).

Shaffir (1985), in his fieldwork on the Hassidic Jewish communities in Canada, started his research in a covert role by working for the Tasher Jewish organization in a full-time clerical job. As he states: 'Since I suspected that members of the community would not sanction my sociological investigation, I did not inform the Tasher that I was collecting data about them' (Shaffir, 1985: 126). However, Shaffir found this role overly restrictive and stopped the research project. Years later he researched this community openly and overtly, when there was a key change in senior administration and open access was then granted.

Ponticelli conducted covert research at a conference of a fundamentalist Christian ex-gay community called Exodus. The conference was geared towards what they termed 'spiritual warfare'. This community perceived her as a convert in need of healing and as someone looking to leave her gay lifestyle, as part of their evangelical and corrective views on her sexuality. They knew she was a graduate student in sociology but not a researcher covertly researching them. Her angst, as a lesbian researcher, was severe, as she states: 'I swallowed and wondered into what I had gotten myself. Had I joined some sort of cult?' (Ponticelli, 1996: 205–206). For Ponticelli, her 'emotions took a roller coaster ride of such intensity that I was not sure I would ever be the same again' (1996: 207).

Watt and Scott Jones (2010) covertly explored the 'God's Way' community, a small group of apocalyptic fundamentalist Christians living in isolation in the Midwest of the United States, with Scott Jones undertaking that as part of her doctoral studies. Scott Jones gives a frank and insightful account of the emotional and moral challenges of her passing in a covert role as a 'seeker' and a new member from overseas, particularly as some of the group's core beliefs were racist and homophobic, which personally appalled her as a lesbian. She 'felt a sense of personality dissonance' (Watt and Scott Jones, 2010: 119).

Her forced engagement to a group member she regularly played chess with, partly as a copying mechanism, necessitated her hasty exit via a false family emergency. This was one of the unintended consequences of playing a covert role in this setting. Such was her guilt that she disclosed her identity and purpose to both the group leader and her key informant, with whom she had developed a genuine bond. They stress:

To me, covert research brings with it tremendous guilt that is hard to come to terms with: trusted friendships were built on lies and deceiving honest and decent people is not something to be proud of. Myself and most other covert researchers would make the case, however, that this form of research is vital to allow us access social worlds which might remain 'hidden'. (Watt and Scott Jones, 2010: 123)

Donnelly and Wright (2013) explore religious rituals, using Goffman's notion of 'face-work', in twelve different Protestant and Catholic church services in the Northeastern United States. They found a range of normative disruptions, sanctions and repair work in such services. This ethnographic work was undertaken covertly for six months as they performed their roles as ordinary members of the congregation without gate-keepers. They typically located themselves at the rear of the congregations, which assisted their scanning of the space and helped discrete note-taking. Their justification was that they felt any overt methods would have been intrusive and disrupt the natural flow of the rituals and interactions.

5.8 Work

Car factory

Satoshi Kamata, a freelance journalist, spent eight months undercover as a seasonal worker in a Toyota car factory making gearboxes in Japan in the early 1970s. His insider account – *Japan in the Passing Lane* – was originally published in 1973, with an English translation in 1982. Kamata's preferred and more pessimistic title was *Automobile Factory of Despair*. He describes in a diary style the repetitiveness and acceleration of the production line and the effective wage slavery. Kamata denounces the psychological toll of this work as well as showing the camaraderie between workers in keeping the line going, despite its obvious brutality.

Laurie Graham, in *On the Line at Subaru-Isuzu: The Japanese Model and the American Worker* (1995), adopted a covert role to investigate the assembly line shop-floor culture of a corporate company, based in Indiana, in the United States. The company is a non-unionized one that employs Japanese lean production management techniques, which produced a supposed 'factory utopia' of harmonious relationships between workers and management. Graham was in a covert role for six months as a production worker, after going through a six-month pre-employment screening process, including the company's orientation and training programme, prior to entry.

She found 'the line both physically demanding and emotionally draining' (Graham, 1995: 15). Graham explores the different bases of control and resistance in the workplace and views worker selection as an initial mechanism of control. For Graham, her covert role was 'the least disruptive to the natural course of events' (1995: 16).

Domestic cleaning

Judith Rollins (1985), an academic of black ethnicity, wanted to understand the lived experience of doing domestic work as a form of racialized and gendered domination in the United States. In the early phase of her study, she worked as a domestic assistant for ten different establishments, for periods which varied from one to six months. She conducted forty focused interviews in the latter stages of the study. She reflects on her undercover strategy: 'In no case did an employer know I was doing research; I told them I had been doing domestic work for a number of years in another city and showed them letters of reference (written by me) if they asked' (1985: 9).

Legal work

Pierce worked as a legal assistant in the litigation department at two corporate law firms in San Francisco, United States. She worked at one for six months, followed by nine months in the second one. She also spent a long period of time as a paralegal assistant at various legal firms previously. Pierce is interested in the emotional labour of paralegal work and the gender segregation and gender discrimination of law firms, on which there is limited work. Her methodological strategy also involved interviews with over sixty legal workers. When her initial request to overtly observe legal staff at work had been refused on confidentiality and sensitivity grounds, she was effectively forced to adopt a covert method. Pierce discovers that the sexist attitudes of legal bureaucracies are a continuing problem for women lawyers and paralegals. Male lawyers depend on women paralegals for important work, expecting them to both mother them and affirm their superior status in the office, in what Pierce describes as using 'certain feminized components of emotional labour: deference and caretaking' (1995: 102). When this is not done, they face criticism and various professional sanctions, which stifles their success and promotion. Pierce argues that this gendered division of labour benefits men politically, economically and personally. However, she also finds that women lawyers and paralegals develop creative strategies for resisting and disrupting this male-dominated status quo of what she terms 'Rambo litigators'.

Management training

Smith (2007) explored 'new capitalism' by doing covert fieldwork in a management consultancy company, referred to as the Mind Gym. The company declined to be researched when approached, so he adopted a covert role, first as a delegate but then was later assessed by the company as a potential management coach and trainer. The initial assessment was through an online questionnaire, which he faked, followed by a week-long residential course, involving group work and presentations. Smith reflects on his embedded role: 'I had become so enmeshed in the process that I was genuinely trying to pass the try out, and that I was taking the practice as seriously as anybody else there' (2007: 438).

Retail and service consumption

This is another broad category that involves studies of consumption as customers and various forms of service exchange work. An innovative covert example of this type of research is a study into consumer discrimination and the service experience of disabled customers by Kaufman-Scarborough (2001). Kaufman-Scarborough used a mixture of disabled and non-disabled students in the study so as to compare their experiences in multiple stores in several shopping districts in a major metropolitan area of the United States.

Gate-keeping was not sought from the stores and consumers were not informed. Clearly, it is a sensitive topic to have vulnerable groups participating in the study so the students could choose whether to disclose their identity and discuss their research, if appropriate, with customers. As Kaufman-Scarborough (2001) states: 'It was judged that the relaxation of strict identity concealment would reduce potential harmful effects' (2001: 443). Not all the students felt comfortable with disclosure, so it remained a semi-covert inquiry about some of the barriers faced by disabled groups in consumption spaces.

Hebl et al. (2002) explored homophobia in terms of an innovative field experiment in a retail store, from a social psychological perspective. Eight female and eight male undergraduate students from a university in Texas volunteered for the study. Each of the participants applied for work in six retail stores. In total, ninety-one stores were visited and no gate-keeping was sought. In three of the visits the participants felt stigmatized by wearing a 'Gay and Proud' hat in comparison to the other three, who wore a 'Texan and Proud' hat. Although no formal discrimination was shown, Hebl et al. argue that a range of subtle discrimination was shown to the perceived homosexual candidates in terms of time spent with them, explanation of job roles and positive encouragement to apply.

Pettinger (2005), in her dual ethnography of shop work, took on the covert role as a shopper and a part-time shop assistant. Pettinger reflects on this innovative dual covert role:

> I did not only observe, I also tried to manipulate events. I 'tested' customer service provision by demanding customer services, as any shopper might, seeing how stores had different norms and regulations … as a shopper, I had the cultural freedom to be a 'flaneur', an activity that intrinsically involves looking. (Pettinger, 2005: 356)

Bone (2006) conducted a three-year study of direct selling in two corporate stores in the home improvement industry. The research for his doctorate was centred on flexible working, risk management and performance-related pay. It involved him partaking in part-time casual vacation work as an undergraduate and postgraduate student. His employer was aware of him being a doctoral student but was not aware of the focus of his study. Bone reflects on his covert role: 'I considered that colleagues within the industry would have reacted differently around me had they been aware that I was conducting research and was not one of them' (2006: 112–113).

Miles (2006), in his study of youth identity and consumption, combined twenty group interviews with some covert participant observation in terms of working as a sales assistant (with the permission of the leading sports store). For him, such an approach enriched his analysis of consumption. Miles states:

> By working for 10 weeks as a shop assistant, it was possible to gain access to the sorts of meanings that were applied to these types of consumer goods. The researcher's role was unknown to customers, and as such it was possible to observe the shop as a site of consumption. (2006: 147)

Russell and Tyler (2002), from a sociological tradition, look at the relationship between gender, childhood, consumption and fashion. They explore a UK retail chain and its popular 'girl power' brand, called 'Girl Heaven', which was aimed at young girls aged between three and thirteen. The researchers used a range of covert strategies in different phases of the research. They conducted covert participant observation in the store as adult customers observing the young girls shopping. What is very interesting here is that although informed consent was strictly adhered to with the young girls and their parents, the store staff and other customers were not informed. Russell and Tylor state on their mixed methods: 'We observed them whilst shopping in the store and carried out a group interview immediately afterwards' (2002: 624).

Mears (2008) worked as a catwalk model for an established agency in New York for a year. She participated in the full range of modelling work, including castings, editorial shoots and runway shows. Mears is interested in how female bodily capital is transformed into a cultural commodity by having the 'right look' and body norm coupled with continual youthful obsession. Models are subject to intense surveillance and disciplining, which they typically internalize in their pursuit of 'glamour'. Access to this subculture was accidental, as Mears remarks: 'At a chance encounter in a coffee shop, an agency scout invited me to meet with the managers at Mode Model Management' (2008: 433).

Sargent (2009) explored the gendered nature of work identity and the deskilling of retail work. She collected comparative ethnographic data from nine musical instrument stores on the east coast of the United States. As well as conducting some key informant interviews, she also conducted covert participant observation as a customer. Sargent reflects: 'my presence as a customer-observer (even one with a notebook) was unobtrusive' (2009: 670). Sargent regularly expanded on her notes in the car park immediately afterwards. Interestingly, in a footnote she makes reference to the fact that she initially told staff of her presence but this resulted in artificial behaviour: 'this caused them to overreact, as they began performing loud sexualized banter for my benefit' (Sargent, 2009: 685).

Schreer et al. (2009), from a social psychology tradition, investigated racial discrimination in retail by conducting a field experiment over three months on six retail stores. Twelve college students, of equally mixed gender and race, acted as customers, or confederates, who had asked for security tags to be removed on expensive sunglasses so they could try them on. Two other students, posing as shoppers, observed and recorded the reactions of the store staff on a coding sheet. For Schreer et al. (2009) there was subtle bias shown against black customers.

In her anthropological study of Hollywood, Ortner (2010) encountered access problems in the closed and secretive Hollywood community, even though she had a range of inside contacts. As a solution, she practised what she called 'interface ethnography' by attending public events where the filmmaking and entertainment industry presents itself. Ortner recounts: 'I was getting a growing sense of how hard – and perhaps even impossible – this project might be' (2010: 217).

Ortner decided to use 'polymorphous engagement', which meant collecting data from multiple sites, including film festivals, writers' Expos, free screenings and public relations events, which are free to register for and attend. On this opportunistic data collection, Ortner reflects: 'The panellists told personal stories and anecdotes about their own experiences, which again constituted a kind of public ethnographic data; I assume they would tell much the same kinds of stories were I to succeed in getting an interview with them' (2010: 219).

Sex work

Ronai and Ellis (1989) explore the world of the female erotic table dancer and the microcosm of the dynamic interactional strategies that occurs in this world to gain and maintain control. For them, essentially, this is 'a world where women exchange titillating dances for money' (Ronai and Ellis, 1989: 271). They argue that previous pictures of exotic dancers 'led to a static description of this occupation' (Ronai and Ellis, 1989: 272). They aim to demystify the 'deviant' aspects of the occupation but explore how the sexual exchange is made 'respectable' by the participants. Full nudity was prohibited in table dancing and tips were given during the performances. Dancers spent time with customers trying to sell table dances to customers between acts, where the dances could become sexually stimulating and masturbatory for some of the clients.

The radical methodological departure of their study is the 'dancer as researcher' viewpoint because Ronai, one of the authors, had been an erotic dancer in the past. Thus, data were gained primarily from the retrospective ethnography of Ronai, who danced as 'Sabrina' in the Tampa Bay area of Florida, United States, during the mid-1980s to pay for her education. Ronai and Ellis reflect: 'With approval of bar management, but without the knowledge of other dancers, she acted in the dual capacity of researcher and dancer. This time her primary identity was that of researcher, although as a complete member-researcher she attempted to become the phenomenon' (Ronai and Ellis, 1989: 273–274).

Trading on the idea of retrospective participant observation, Ronai 'put herself mentally and emotionally back into her experiences and record what she remembered' (Ronai and Ellis, 1989: 273). The research was clearly not entirely covert throughout. Interestingly, she used her duality as a methodological tool in terms of revealing herself to some but not all of the customers: 'as a strategy to keep them interested in spending more money and to get them to talk about their own motives for being in the bar' (Ronai and Ellis, 1989: 274). In the latter stages of the research project, standard formal interviews were also extensively conducted with a range of participants, including strippers, customers, managers, owners and a law officer. The strategies of the dancers included their stage persona, choosing a customer and closing the sale. This work was distinct from prostitution so the dancers developed avoidance strategies if formally propositioned.

In *Live Sex Acts: Women Performing Erotic Labor* (1997), Wendy Chapkis examines the life histories of commercial prostitutes in both Northern California and Amsterdam. Part of her insider account involves herself becoming a certified massage therapist and participating in paying for sexual services herself and, on one occasion, selling sex to female clients. In the methodological appendix of the book, Chapkis discusses at length a workshop she covertly attended on giving and receiving sexual pleasure. Chapkis, when later reflecting on her covert role as a masseur, states: 'I once again experimented with locating myself within the narrative I was writing. ... I was curious about the experience of commodified touch' (2010: 487). Chapkis sensibly views: 'engagement, complexity, and contradiction as resources for, rather than simply impediments to, good research' (2010: 483).

Adler and Adler, in a book review of Chapkis (1997), discuss the close parallels with Humphreys' work: 'This is brave sociology. ... Agree or disagree, you will find yourself reading this book late into the night. Not since Humphreys' path breaking and equally contentious *Tearoom Trade* (1975) has a book been so forthright in its presentation of the hidden dimensions of the sex trade in society' (Adler and Adler, 1999: 409–410).

Mattley conducted a nine-month covert study of adult phone fantasy workers, as 'a first hand, involved investigation of emotional labor' (1998: 148). She informed the manager that she was an academic needing part-time work and some of the workers knew she was an academic, although they were not fully aware of her intentions of doing a study on them. The phone customers did not know her identity at all. Mattley is interested in the commodification of emotions through sexual fantasy.

In a similar vein, Amy Flowers explores *The Fantasy Factory* (1998) and provides an insider's view of the phone sex industry in a semi-covert study. She interviewed phone workers and worked as an operator herself for four months, taking around 3,200 calls. Her co-workers were aware of the research, but not the telephone customers. She is interested in the disembodiment of intimacy, in the absence of face-to-face interaction. This involves the pretence of the self, sexual role-playing, hyper-sexualized scripts, collectively resulting in the manufacture of fantasy and desire.

Brewster (2003) argues that despite the significant amount of research on strip clubs, which has mainly been focused on female dancers, 'the patrons who frequent these clubs have been virtually ignored' (2003: 221). Using covert participant observation, he collected data on patrons who frequented a small, private, strip club located in a small, rural city in the Southeastern United States. Such a geographic location is rarely examined in comparison to strip clubs in larger cities. The study describes three 'distinct methods of tipping' and explores the contexts governing their use as well as the different types of patron, regular and occasional, who visit the club.

Katherine Frank's interesting cultural anthropological work (2001, 2002, 2003, 2007) on erotic dancing includes six years' intermittent work as a nude entertainer with five different strip clubs in the USA. Her first-hand insider experiences are recounted in her *G-Strings and Sympathy: Strip club regulars and male desire* (2002), which is a popularly quoted book in the field and was based on her doctoral studies. Like several other researchers in this field, Frank helped fund her education over a long period as a student by being a nude entertainer. She combines semi-covert participant observation with interview data with thirty regular patrons and is analytically interested in the construction of desire, touristic gaze and intimacy as 'masculinizing practices'. Like Rachela Colosi in a UK context, not everyone would have known of her research role, particularly customers, when working as an actual erotic dancer in the clubs. Counter to other researchers, she points to the useful safety valve function of strip clubs, where heterosexual married men manage the tensions between sexual fantasy and their lived reality.

Trautner (2005) investigates the gendered and classed performance of sexuality in exotic dance clubs by undertaking what she describes as 'prolonged direct observation' over seven months to four exotic dance clubs in the Southwestern United States. Due to club rules, she entered with male escorts. Trautner states on her methodological strategy:

> I presented myself not only as a paying customer but also as either the girl-friend or friend of male escort(s) to observe naturally occurring interactions and club routines. ... At each site, I assumed the role of the naïve stranger to blend in with the crowd as much as possible by looking and acting much like the typical woman customer. (2005: 775)

Trautner interestingly argues that 'the drawback' of her covert position was her 'lack of insight into the club employees' thoughts and feelings toward, and expla-nations of, the routines in which they participate' (2005: 775). Trautner analyses sexuality in the strip clubs according to images of attractiveness, stage perfor-mances and tipping practices.

Egan (2006) studies the strategic use of music by dancers in two exotic dance clubs in the New England area of the United States. For her, musical choice medi-ates the interaction between the female dancers and both management and the clientele. The ethnographic research was prolonged and completed over a four-year period, which included Egan working as a dancer in one of the clubs. She did interview both dancers and customers, but her approach had clear and deliberate covert elements. On this, Egan reflects: 'My position as a researcher within both ethnographic settings was semi-covert in two respects: one, I did not inform the owners that I was a researcher; two, I did not inform every customer with whom I came into contact that I was a researcher' (2006: 204–205).

Barton (2007) made observational visits to a range of exotic dance clubs, strip bars and peep shows in San Francisco and Hawaii over a twelve-month period. Her initial challenge was gaining entry into the venues as most clubs in the United States have rules preventing unescorted females from entering. She thus had to collaboratively negotiate entry 'with the assistance of male friends and the trust of dancer informants' (2007: 575).

While covertly being in the setting, Barton was regularly approached with 'sexual interest' by customers, although she managed the situation with 'polite refusals'. Barton discusses the emotionally taxing nature of such a covert research role and her own sexual politics as a lesbian, which made her shift from covert observations to interviews in the latter parts of the fieldwork. As she states: 'My own notes attest to how intensely uneasy I was in strip clubs, how objectified I felt simply being in the space' (2007: 578). Barton wanted to understand the mechanisms used by the dancers to cope with the toll of stripping, including man-aging persona and counterfeit intimacy. She sensibly calls for further studies on a wide range of sex workers, including prostitutes, pornography actors, internet performers and phone sex workers.

Lap dancing is a growth industry in the United Kingdom, as in other parts of the world, and is now a typical feature of the night-time economy of many major cities in the western world. Despite this, the dancers are maligned occupationally, politically and publicly, which somewhat parallels the treatment of bouncers and bouncing. Rachela Colosi, in *Dirty Dancing? An Ethnography of Lap Dancing* (2010b), provides an insightful semi-covert study of this subculture. Colosi used 'extensive participant observation', supported by a small number of unstructured interviews, over a two-year period in a very popular chain-operated lap dancing club in the north of England. Observationally, most of the data was gathered inside the club, but some was also collected while socializing and living with her fellow dancers.

Colosi was already embedded in the setting and worked as a lap dancer herself as an undergraduate. Most of the dancers were aware of her research but none of the customers would have known about it. Colosi explores the distinctive social world of lap dancing via notions of occupational hierarchy, social and emotional rituals, coping mechanisms and tacit rules. On her methodological justification, Colosi adds:

> Without the intensive engagement with participant observation over such a long period of time, the intricate details of this lap-dancer subculture, which make it distinct, would have been overlooked, thus preventing me from constructing an authentic depiction of the lap dancers' distinctive social world. (2010b: 13)

Sanders (2006) stresses that, despite the use of overt gate-keeping in her studies of saunas and brothels, unwitting covert dimensions evolved that became an intrinsic part of her role-playing and research-bargaining in the setting. She discusses her management of a typical dual role: 'my role in the sauna was overt to the sex workers but, at the request of the managers, the clients were unaware of my researcher status and I was often propositioned by interested customers' (2006: 458).

5.9 Conclusions

What this survey and review of covert studies hopefully demonstrates is its variety and diversity. It is a rich and dispersed covert corpus, drawn from a range of social science fields. Clearly, the covert role adopted is not a fixed, purist one, but can be more usefully located on a complex and shifting continuum. Many of the studies required gate-keepers to secure access. Often then, covert research is a range of opportunistic possibilities in different settings. So it becomes important to decouple danger and risk from being somehow endemic to covert research. Namely, we need to robustly demystify it and remove it from the exotica with which it is often treated.

Many of the contexts of research, on close inspection, are in public places and spaces, where different rights, assumptions and rules routinely operate. For example, eavesdropping is to be expected in many public spaces and places, and comes as no great discovery or surprise. Many of the research contexts are thus mundane, such as workplaces, and not extreme or high-risk environments, as with some illegal and secretive subcultures. In this sense, the risk and danger to the covert researcher has been somewhat exaggerated and inflated.

5.10 Learning exercise

1. List the different topics and academic disciplines that have been drawn upon in the review.

2. What do you understand by the term 'covert diaspora'?

3. Do researchers in different covert studies display similar feelings and face similar challenges?

6

A COVERT CASE STUDY OF BOUNCERS IN THE MANCHESTER NIGHT-TIME ECONOMY

This chapter focuses on a covert retrospective participant observation case study of bouncers in the night-time economy of Manchester in the United Kingdom. I will discuss my case study, comparing it to the work of other researchers who have explored this specific area, as well as others who might echo my research journey.

6.1 Manchester as a case study: my biographical and experiential backyard

The location of Manchester, the UK, for the case study, which is where I live and work, is highly strategic. The city is saturated in popular culture, being named Gunchester, Gangchester and Madchester in the past, and has been well documented by a range of popular journalists and commentators (Haslam, 1999; Swanton, 1997, 1998; Walsh, 2005; Wilson, 2002). The development of club cultures in Manchester has been specifically linked to urban regeneration (Lovatt, 1996). Namely, Manchester was promoted as a chic, vibrant, hedonistic and cosmopolitan place to come to 'party'. Doing the doors in Manchester, despite the sentimentality and sensationalism in some of these accounts, was a challenging research adventure, not least as I had been studying, working and clubbing in the city since 1984. As I walked to the venue on the first night of my covert research as a fake bouncer, I was nervously filled with both apprehension and anticipation. Would I be found out within hours? Should I just not turn up? Could I pull it off? Could I sustain the deception? Was this too extreme?

Six months later, at the end of the fieldwork, after covertly passing at various venues, I had been accepted by the bouncers of the famous *Hacienda* nightclub as being in 'the firm', which is when I chose to finish the study. The Hacienda became an icon for clubbers; it was the pinnacle of the pecking order for doors. It has been the focus of attention for various journalists, academics and film-makers over the years and was the subject of the popular film *24 hour Party People* (2006). The acceptance of me by the Hacienda door team, the highest status nightclub in Manchester, was like a 'covert nirvana'. I had convinced them that I was 'one of them', had secured job offers from them, been vetted by them by doing fairground security work for them and then finished the study.

Manchester had become somewhat of a mecca, and still is, for hedonistic night-life, and thus was a very rich case study to explore. Hutton sums up the situation: 'The right ingredients appeared to have come together just at the right time' (2006: 3). It is in this context that I was 'badged up', to use the local argot, by completing my Door Safe short course in December 1995, which was jointly run by Manchester City Council and Greater Manchester Police. After this, I spent six months from January to June in 1996 doing a range of different doors in Manchester city centre covertly. I did not need to arrange gate-keeping access, retrospective debriefing or follow-up interviewing in any part of the study. This was a purist type of covert research.

As well as working on ten different doors, pubs and clubs, in my brief door career, I also actively hung around several other doors, in bouncer mode, through-out the six-month period of my nomadic ethnography, although I was not working these doors. This was artful and, at times, nerve-wrecking in terms of my cover being blown. A sort of 'hanging out and hanging about', as Kath Woodward (2008) usefully did in her overt ethnography of boxing gyms.

I kept mental notes and wrote up my field notes as I went along, aided by a hidden micro tape recorder taped inside my jacket for recording relevant conver-sations. This technology greatly intensified my fear of being caught. Afterall, the discovery of this was clear and unequivocal evidence of doing undercover work. The ethnographic push was always to capture naturally occurring data as best I could in the setting.

This nomadic strategy of working on different doors served a dual purpose. First, it was part of my practical risk management, in terms of dispersing the risk of being found out – a classic 'getting to know them without them getting to know me' tactic. Second, it was a way of capturing comparative observational data about different doors and the ordering of their hierarchy. Therefore, I would engineer appropriate exits around wages and hours as I manoeuvred around. It was not uncommon for doormen to have floating roles with various doors, although most wanted a more permanent and settled place in the same venue for as long as possible.

I would also sometimes socialize with the bouncers I was working with by having a few drinks after our door shift had finished at other venues, typically with free entry. Again, it was an important source of data as well as being useful in terms of networking in my nomadic ethnographic role as I moved around the hierarchy of doors from pubs to clubs. I was partly trying to build a picture of the door community. Building on Foot-Whyte's (1943) famous study, it was a sort of 'door corner society'. Hence, I had a more distant knowledge of some of the door community and a more intimate relationship to others. It was a classic combina-tion of both friend and stranger roles so elegantly summed up by Agar (1980) as 'the professional stranger'.

Prior to the study, I had clubbed in various spaces, with bouncers being a con-tinued source of my sociological curiosity and imagination. This area was part of my biographical and experiential backyard, as my late father Pat Calvey had been a doorman in a Docker's club in Greenock, Scotland, in his youth. I was intrigued by his stories about this world on the odd occasion that he recounted them. Bouncers are demonized figures of folklore and the standard icons of masculinity (Calvey, 2000). For me, these mythologized and vilified figures of fear and fascination clearly required de-mystification and critical investigation. The analysis of popular culture, for me, had rightly shifted from the margins to the centre (O'Connor and Wynne, 1996).

Similar to Winlow (2001), in his covert study of bouncers in the Northeast of England, I am also 'a product of the very culture I attempt to describe' (2001: 5). For Winlow, due to his working-class upbringing, accent, age, bodily image and various biographical socializing experiences, the field was part of his cultural inheritance and not something distant and exotic. Hence, access was comparatively simple and straightforward. Winlow's ethnographic study of bouncing formed part of a much wider study of changing masculinities, entrepreneurial criminality, violence and the regulation of the night-time economy. For Winlow, contemporary bouncers usefully represent the changing nature of masculinities in a postmodern era and provide an urban career for some males who can legitimately use their bodily capital in certain ways.

I received some limited financial support in the form of teaching relief from the Sociology Department at Manchester University, where I was a temporary lecturer at the time. It is important to make clear that I did not receive formal grant funding for the project, although I received ethical approval from the department, hence I was not policy bound. Thus, this small-scale project effectively became self-funding and sustainable. More importantly, I was free to use what I considered to be an innovative methodological strategy of pure covert research.

6.2 Covert passing in a demonized subculture: body capital and interaction rituals

Doormen are simultaneously 'men of honour' when on your side and 'heavies' when not. They are a deeply demonized subculture (Calvey, 2000; Hobbs et al., 2000, 2005, 2007; Monaghan, 2003, 2004, 2006). Bouncers can make or break your night out as the club or pub effectively becomes the bouncer's monopoly. They have been elegantly described as 'tuxedo warriors', which refers to an older dress code, by Cliff Twemlow (1980), in an early gritty practitioner account of the tales of a Mancunion bouncer.

I mostly worked with male door staff as at the time, there were fewer females doing door work. The gender composition has changed currently, although not radically, as most door people are male, and there has been more related research on gendering the security gaze (O'Brien, 2009), the gendered door (Hobbs, O'Brien and Westmarland, 2007) and violence and gender (O'Brien et al., 2008).

The analytic push was to investigate the everyday world of bouncers in a faithful (Bittner, 1973) manner, using thick description (Geertz, 1973) that attempts to avoid glosses of their routine practices, practical accomplishments and mundane reasoning (Pollner, 1987; Watson, 2009). It is an attempt to explore the competent membership of bouncing through the 'lived experience' (Geertz, 1973) of doing the doors.

In terms of body capital and image, I had trained in martial arts for several years and made contact with a local door agency by openly asking local doormen at several pubs and clubs for any work in Manchester city centre. I trained regularly and was clearly part of the 'monopoly of muscle' (Hobbs et al., 2003a: 234) that made the industry work. My fabricated bouncer habitus (Bourdieu, 1977, 1984, 1990) was deliberate and wilful.

My covert role was deeply dramaturgical (Goffman, 1967) throughout and employed deliberate and sustained misrepresentations of self and a range of interaction rituals. Similar to Jacobs (1992), in his overt study of undercover narcotic agents, rehearsal, appearance manipulation, physical diversion and verbal diversion were all routinely used as tactics and moves.

A central part of the bouncer's management of the stigma and taint associated with the occupation such as violence and hyper-masculinity is the interactional mask they put on with others to practically do the job. Doing door work, for me, routinely used a series of physical and psychological deterrents. What I would characterize loosely as a form of choreographed bravado and machismo. The fear of violence, and not always the actuality of it, plays a part in this performance.

Part of my covert passing was the mimicry of their interaction rituals (Goffman, 1967), as I laughed along with racist and sexist jokes, physically horsed around on the door, made fun of some drunken customers and 'chatted up' female customers on a regular basis. I needed to fit in like any ordinary doorman doing the doors. Humour was also a distinctive way of developing bonds and dealing with the typical monotony and boredom in doing long shifts on the doors, particularly when it was quiet, much like the machine operators in Donald Roy's (1959) classic 'Banana Time' study of job satisfaction and informal interaction.

I did not find the door culture ideologically abhorrent, as say Fielding did on his study of the National Front (1981) or Schacht's survival tactics at his overwhelming feeling of self-estrangement in his study of the misogynist subculture of a male rugby club (1997), where he didn't partake in sexist songs or activities. However, I did have an ambivalent stance towards directly engaging in, as distinct from witnessing, violence on the door, which was part of their saturated occupational territory. I would do what was expected of me in supporting other doormen if there was a violent incident, but I was concerned about how far this would go, in the heat of the moment. I held a version of an active membership role where: 'researchers participate in the core activities in much the same way as the members, yet they hold back from committing themselves to the goals and values of the members' (Adler and Adler, 1987: 35).

Such covert passing was similar to a sort that Forrest (1986), in her study of spiritual mediums, terms 'apprentice participation', as a way of 'becoming experientially and emotionally involved in the activities of the setting' (1986: 436) and 'absorbing the life view of the group' (1986: 442). Hence, I had 'gone native', not accidentally but deliberately. I began to see the world like a bouncer and act accordingly. I was acutely aware of my manufactured 'bouncer self'. Thus, I could not quite turn off what my partner called my 'bouncer head' when out socially during the fieldwork period. It was psychologically intense and I had a limited immersion life due to the risks of being discovered, the type of work it could be and ongoing guilt syndromes.

My ethnographic style was the 'art of purposeful hanging around'. When doing the role, I tried to stay at the physical periphery as much as possible and typically avoid confrontations with customers. This was a very fine balancing act, as I did not want to be perceived as being an untrustworthy colleague. What they called a 'bottler' who could not be relied on to pitch in to 'watch your back' (Thompson, 1994) if it 'kicked off'.

Credible passing was clearly essential in the setting. Put crudely, I had to sound like and look like a bouncer. Indeed, a *Times Higher Education* journalist, when interviewing me after my first publication, assumed I was a mature student who used to be a bouncer and based his postgraduate studies on it, which is not the case.

One of the methodological challenges in this type of covert fieldwork was managing the tension between instigation tactics and naturally occurring data throughout the fieldwork period. The latter is ideal, where the researcher captures ordinary and mundane cultural reality and the participants' routines as they naturally occur 'in flight' rather than reconstruct an exotic, ironic and caricatured picture of them. However, the reality of covert fieldwork can also involve several instigation tactics and moves. For example, I would regularly ask bouncers to repeat certain door stories, feigning a hearing problem, and I would always attempt to get more time during the night 'fronting the door' as I continually searched for 'where the action was' and could record talk without intrusive background music. I had to stay in character and did not have the luxury of formal interviewing to verify my understanding or to seek collaborative feedback, as overt researchers would typically do. I would take field notes after a night's shift as a reconstruction of my sense making and typical fieldwork aide-mémoire.

My autoethnography of bouncing, part of which was managing my 'secret self', was an actual lived field experience for me, with my fellow bouncers being unwitting collaborators. My own self, biography and identity mediated my field experience in myriad and complex ways. My covert autoethnography presented here is deeply retrospective and experiential in character. In terms of autoethnographic authority (Buzard, 2003) and being there (Geertz, 1988), I feel that I have told an authentic tale of doing the doors, which is not romanticized, heroic or vanity-led.

6.3 The door order and door code: folklore, stories, trust, fictive kinship, masculinity, dirty work and private policing

The burgeoning nature of the night-time economy and the leisure economies (Hobbs et al., 2003a) presents interesting issues around the regulation of violence in the liminal and commodified night-time economy (Hobbs et al., 2005). More generally, the night-time economy is an arena which has witnessed an increasing regulatory architecture (Hadfield et al., 2009) centred on various moral panics about new cultures of binge intoxication (Measham and Brain, 2005) and mob disorder as a spectacle (Hayward and Hobbs, 2007).

My research was prior to the establishment of the Security Industry Authority (SIA), the organization responsible for regulating the private security industry in the UK. The SIA reports to the Home Secretary and was established in 2003 under the terms of the Private Security Industry Act 2001. Doing the doors is now simply big business. Bouncers are generally seen to be less criminalized and more professional, but there are still links to past, with many bouncers trading on that criminal legacy. They are still a somewhat demonized occupational group, although they are now currently more diverse in terms of constitution (B. Sanders, 2005). Despite some attempts, they are not unionized, due to the temporary nature of the work, which makes them vulnerable and exploitable.

In terms of the structure of this type of work at the time, most of the door staff were employed by agencies providing private security in the sector. At the time of the study, it was firmly part of the informal and hidden economy, although this is changing. It was primarily work of a part-time, casual nature, done at the weekend, although more experienced door staff would get more nights. The payment was not standardized at the time and would vary according to the venue and experience of the door team. For example, when I was 'hanging around' the famous Hacienda nightclub, I witnessed wages being distributed to the door team by the late head doorman, who was from an infamous Manchester gangster family. The thickness of the wad of cash inside a set of sealed envelopes related to a status hierarchy amongst the doormen as well as the length of shifts performed. The Hacienda was known to pay very generously amongst the door community, being the undisputed apex door in Manchester dance club land for a long time. The Hacienda is now a legendary part of club folklore.

As the night-time economy expanded and door work became more formalized, unionized and professionalized, such informal payments and practices have become a thing of the past. At the time of the study, recruitment was often by informal networking, where door staff would put forward credible friends and mates they could trust. In this way, doormen were pre-vetted. Formal recruitment processes were not part of this world.

I worked my way up the hierarchy of doors in my brief 'door career'. There was a working categorization and hierarchy of doors, from relatively 'easy' ones, such as student venues, to more 'heavy' ones, such as dance clubs, and the associated status and glamour that accompanied this. Thus, the doors worked, and hence door modes encountered, were diverse. Some generic features of door work can still be discerned but some aspects of door work were occasioned and hence related to the status of the specific 'door' you worked on.

The door hierarchy was commonly linked to several factors. First, the level and nature of any gang activity connected to the door and hence your depth of working knowledge of them and your relationship to them. Second, the level of 'recreational dance drug' use at the club and your local knowledge of the dealers. Third, the image and reputation of the venue, although this was often a fast-moving issue of fashion. Fourth, the nature of typical incidents encountered. Fifth, the geographic location of the door, with the city centre being more prestigious. Finally, who was working on the door team and their track record, that is, who was 'fronting' it. Thus, several status designations and distinctions were made between doors. Nightclubs had more status and prestige than pubs. Thus, it was rare for initial door work to be at a club rather than pub, which was the case with my fieldwork.

For me, door work is a collaborative and collective accomplishment, a sort of ecology of door labour wherein tasks and associated roles and responsibilities are co-ordinated in and through a team. As a door person you knew the door code and geared towards it in an implicit way (Wieder, 1974). Namely, membership of the community equates to some sort of understanding of the door trade and requires no lengthy explanations of it (Rubenstein, 1973).

The strength of the collective bonds and camaraderie on the door was very clear. Sticking together as a form of fictive kinship (Dodson and Zincavage, 2007; Woodward and Jenkings, 2011) was part of a coping mechanism when doing the doors. There was also internal rivalry, disputes and clashes between the door team, particularly over the job of head doorperson, which was a supervisory role and paid more. To ignore this would paint an overly romantic picture of door work.

Similar to Colosi (2010b) in her ethnography of lap dancers, the strength of camaraderie and the specific 'codes of conduct' among the dancers parallels ideas of the bouncer code and membership of the door community. Colosi argues that economic needs do not fully explain the dancer's motivation. For her, lap dancing is also emotionally driven and dancers, like bouncers, enjoy the excitement, adventure and thrill-seeking it brings. Many dancers return to it, and leaving it is, as Colosi states, 'reminiscent of the emotional reactions produced after the breakdown of a close personal relationship' (2010b: 143). Lap dancers, like bouncers, are also a stigmatized and demonized group. Colosi is motivated to challenge the myth that portrays lap dancers as 'victim or villain, lost in a dark, shameful and dangerous world' (2010b: 6).

'Having a laugh', to adopt a common work phrase, in doing door work was an essential component of galvanizing group identity as well as being a coping mechanism for such emotional labour (Hochschild, 1979, 1983). As Colosi cogently states: 'Having fun takes priority in the lap-dancing club, fuelling motivation, helping build social relationships, improving dancer status, and also how it plays an important role in dancer resistance, helping to shape lap-dancing as a form of anti-work' (2010b: 182).

Bill Sanders similarly captures the routinized character of door work in dealing with boredom:

> The majority of the time working as a bouncer was spent standing around 'doing nothing' except watching the punters. Boredom was certainly a prominent feature of being a club security guard. … While these guardians of club land might be seen as glamorous by punters, the job was marked by its routine banality, sparingly interrupted by unpleasantness. (2005: 243)

Various types of risk and danger formed part of the routine occupational territory that I was embedded in. Doing this type of work came with certain expectations and obligations. In this sense, and without turning door work into exotica, the research process and setting had a type of ambient danger (Brewer, 1993; Lee, 1995; Sluka, 1990; Yancey and Rainwater, 1970). For example, if the police inquired about any incidents, loyalty to a bouncer code (Wieder, 1974) was assumed and it was expected that I would not 'grass' to them and disclose any incriminating information. We stuck together, in a classic 'them and us' relationship. Although, we represented the pub or club, the door was our territory, our remit of control, our ghetto.

Although violence was not commonplace, it was an accepted and thus ambient part of the environment. The fear of violence rather than the actuality of it could then mediate the typical behaviour of door staff, which was mainly concerned with deterrent work and the persona or mask required to do such deterrent work. Most of the violence I witnessed during the fieldwork was between customers, with bouncers often adjudicating between disputes and dispersing and de-escalating potential violence. Hence, the focus on conflict between bouncers and customers, for me, can be exaggerated and misplaced.

The bouncer subculture was very strongly a code that was demonstrated and displayed routinely in a telling and showing manner (Wieder, 1974). There was no written rule book but a set of relevancies and schemas, practical and symbolic, that I had to gear into and enact quickly. To a certain extent the setting was self-explicating (Pollner, 1979), but I had to learn the occupational ropes and rules on the job.

The collectivity of the door team is primary and honorific articulated in the cardinal door principle of 'watch my back'. On my first night on the door, the head doorman said to me 'Whatever you do, don't bottle it and run'. Accordingly, the door team is biographically discerned in terms of personalities, characteristics and bodily types which are translated into the broad categories of 'talkers' and 'fighters'. The overwhelming logic of door work worked on deterrent and needed both former categories to operate. Accordingly, Hobbs et al. (2003a) refer to their 'gambit of skills', including talking nicely, looking the part and fighting. Similarly, Rigakos (2008) refers to a combination of verbal skills as 'talking down' and physical skills as 'taking down', when necessary.

The door staff are the first people customers meet in pub and club land and hence initially represent the ethos of the setting. More specifically, they mediate the composition of the club by enforcing and controlling a door policy based on appearance, gender, age and ethnicity. This is a secondary and less influential type of selection as such settings are partly self-selecting (Thornton, 1995). The composition and hence type of 'night' were known, designated and oriented to by the door staff according to various factors. These included the location in the week, alcohol promotion, music policy and the expected level of recreational drug use in the venue. The night could clearly still hold surprises, but for most of the time it was utterly routine.

Door work was thus profoundly about trust (Watson, 2009). The mundane tasks and troubles (Zimmerman, 1969) in doing door work were embedded in such trust relationships. Despite individual diversity, a decisive working unity of purpose must underlie the door team. The implicit and cardinal rule was to 'stick together' and 'watch my back', to use the argot, in such high-risk work. Simultaneously, so as not to view this over romantically, the door team was fragmented by friendships bonds, past working relationships and, often, competition for the head doorman position, which had authority and status. To run or bottle it, or not get involved, could involve the natural justice of the door team by giving the individual(s) concerned retributive punishment, namely, a 'good kicking'. I had not witnessed this but had been told by several doormen that it did occasionally occur.

While patrolling inside the premises you are routinely sensitized to both group interactions and spatial arrangements (exit doors, empty bottles, large groups of young men and women) via vantage points as well as general patrols. The idea is simultaneously to be seen and have a clear presence but not to continually intrude or intimidate. In that sense, the work is pro-active and reactive to situations wherein you learn, by experience, both when and how to enter a dispute.

Much of this work is vitally about, when necessary, controlling your own fear and adrenaline, particularly in confrontational situations. Therein, peripheral vision becomes an occupational prerequisite. Bouncers are thus involved in a particular type of surveillance, which requires both visibility and invisibility. You learn when to be seen and when not to be seen. Remembering that the optic of the nightclub is an interesting one, where people are watching each other for different purposes. Bouncers are clearly the few watching the many as well as the many watching them. What Rigakos (2008), in his three-year research on bouncers in four Canadian cities, elegantly calls a 'synoptic frenzy' and 'optic violence'. For Rigakos, bouncers are the vigilant and sometimes repressive 'central policing agents' (2008: 8) in the nightclub space. Many of the doormen here are either former or aspiring policeman, which is quite the opposite from the moral distancing from the police typically found in the United Kingdom.

The door code is oriented to in a taken-for-granted manner by competent members in that setting. Namely, the legitimation of the exercise of authority on the door by bouncers. The bouncer's sense of self is intimately tied up with such authority. Door work also has status, a type of street kudos; it is a way of giving privileges to certain customers, although this is changing as doors becomes more deskilled and doormen lose their autonomy and status.

A sedimented and tacit corpus of routine and mundane methods, procedures, rules and competencies are built up as part of the everyday work of bouncers. In many senses, it was a specific stock of knowledge (Schutz, 1973) that was gained in the doing of the work. Door work was deeply proactive rather than reactive in the sense that potential trouble is minimalized by managing the door. Hence, the preferred solution was that trouble was sorted out at the door and not inside the venue. Generally, more status was gained and importance attached to the front-stage rather than back-stage work. Fronting the door was the priority. If confrontation was to happen, it was more likely to be at the door rather than inside, although both could happen. The logic ran 'run the door and run the club or pub'.

The entrance game and dealing with the barred becomes part of the everyday occupational toolkit of the door staff. This typically involves identifying customer groups or types as troublesome or not and the consequent strategies one adopts on the door. The door team becomes very competent at reading people and situations so that incidents do not escalate too quickly. What I refer to as 'reading the queue', particularly when there are drunken customers or large gangs of males or females on stag or hen nights. The greeter on the door, if used, can play a supportive vetting role in this process. However, the door team could and would over-rule the greeter if they snubbed a known gang member, other door staff or a personal friend.

The queuing order exhibits various status designations and privileges as to who queues, pays and gets searched. Namely, 'who counts' in the door world. The door space, in effect, becomes the distinct ghetto of the door team and not management in a classic 'them and us' relationship. Thus, greater loyalty was shown to the door team and not to the management of the venue. In such work, memory and recall for faces and incidents develops fast as you identify troublemakers from the past. If you were new to the particular door, you would typically mainly work inside the venue and only temporarily front the door, mentored by a door person with more experience.

The entrance game could be artful, with the door staff using persuasion, tact, diplomacy and negotiation skills. This could involve a range of scripted refusals or 'knock backs'. Commonly, the customer appeals to other door staff to over-rule the previous decision, which is rarely done as a united front is vital. The door staff can use distancing strategies by shifting blame onto management as being responsible for a specific door policy. In a more technical sense, the authority of the door staff is legitimated by their employment by the licensee to keep order by 'reasonable force' if necessary. This involves boundary work as to what can be legally and morally sanctioned in the control of aggressive clientele by means of self-defence and/or protection of person and property. In interactional terms, it is based on the local, ongoing achievement of the situated door order.

The management of what the doormen often termed 'respect' is integral to the maintenance of a situated door order. What this amounts to is a type of pseudo honour borne out of a combination of fear and admiration, but it is a resource that is traded on in practically doing the doors. The interactional management of respect is a type of lay knowledge involving strategies and tactics of avoidance, humiliation, submission, reputation, deference, confrontation and structured escalation.

Door work, then, was a type of discretionary satisficing between what they formally can do and informally what they have to do. It is also a game of damage limitation in that the cardinal rule was getting the conflict outside the premises as swiftly and safely as possible. It then becomes the responsibility of the police as regards public disorder. The door order is classically a negotiated one (Strauss et al., 1963) between doormen, customers and management. It is one that is displayed symbolically for relevant co-present audiences, be it other door staff, gang members, management or customers. Part of door work, then, involves reading and giving off signs that are self-explicating in that setting. You have to know when and how to both back down and stay your ground on the door when dealing with people. Staying calm, managing physical distance, eye contact and controlling the conversation are all part of the common-sense resources employed in that work. In this sense, it is integrally a matter of performance (Goffman, 1967).

Hobbs et al. (2002) list local knowledge, verbal skills, bodily capital and fighting ability as part of the 'door trade'. For them, the working practices and occupational culture of door staff constitute a 'door lore' that centres on 'the art and economics of intimidation' (Hobbs et al., 2002: 352). What Hobbs et al. describe as 'their own informal and pragmatic techniques of containment' (2002: 352).

Despite being a fragmented and rather nomadic occupation (B. Sanders, 2005), there was a strong sense of community among bouncers, displayed in part by interaction rituals including dress code, socializing habits, and argot and gestures, including appropriate hand-shakes. Such a community, although not formally or collectively unionized, was deeply 'symbolically constituted' (Delanty, 2003). What Fincham (2008), in his study of the blurring between work and leisure of bicycle messengers, usefully refers to as 'subcultural affiliation'. He argues that the strict binary divide between work and leisure cannot be easily applied to some occupations, with bouncers being clearly one of them.

It is commonly acknowledged that bouncers are doing a type of private policing and are the primary agents of social control in the night-time economy (Hadfield, 2002; Hobbs et al., 2000, 2002, 2003a; Lister, 2002; Lister et al., 2000, 2001a, 2001b, 2001c; Winlow, 2001; Winlow et al., 2001). What Rigakos (2002) would refer to as a 'new para police'. Although bouncers are clear gate-keepers and regulators in the night-time economy spaces (Monaghan, 2006), they typically trade on an autonomous distinction and distance from the police and, for some, a pronounced cynical distrust of them.

Drawing on the famous work of the Chicago school sociologist E. C. Hughes, bouncing was centrally about the 'dirty work' of the night-time economy (Hughes, 1951, 1962, 1971). Dealing with intoxicated customers and all that that brings were routinely part of such work. E. C. Hughes wrote of the need to study: 'arrangements and devices by which men make their work tolerable, or even glorious to themselves and others' (1971: 342). Part of this was, for me, about the authority of the door staff in both admitting and refusing entry to the venue.

Ashforth and Kreiner (1999) suggest that 'dirty workers' use a variety of taint techniques to protect their identities from the threats posed by the stigma of their work, in particular, arguing that work-group cultures function as effective buffers, providing ideologies which enable group members to make sense of their work in esteem-enhancing ways. This was very evident with bouncers. Hansen Lofstrand et al. (2016), in their comparative ethnographic study of private security officers in Sweden and the UK, explore how the workers manage and repair self-esteem and manage 'dirty work' designations in a very stigmatized industry around their sense of self-worth and occupational purpose.

Part of the private policing, and for some dirty work, was also dealing with the drug economies in the night-time economy as a rather saturated and expected part of door work, certainly in city centre nightclubs and some pubs, although not all venues. Viewing the bouncers as the dealers is far too crude and erroneous, but the question of collusion is a complex and important one. Part of the door code was also orienting to what some door staff called 'the score on the door', if working in a high-profile nightclub in the city. A significant feature of this was the extent of any gang affiliation to a particular door. This was not all the door team, but usually some particular members of the door staff. Senior gang figures, or what they call 'heads', become icons and mythical figures in bouncing folklore. You heard more about them than you actually saw of them in doing routine door work. Related to this was orienting to drug dealing in an appropriate way. That is, recognizing and not stopping designated dealers endorsed by a certain gang affiliation, including bluffs by various customers who claimed to be 'connected'.

Ultimately, the drug economy and drug culture at the large London nightclub Sanders investigated was 'self-contained, self-policed and self-sufficient' (B. Sanders, 2005: 253), with a relatively small number of bouncers involved and not all. Similarly, my experience was that drug dealing in some venues that I worked in was tolerated when discreetly operated, and only became significant if violent incidents escalated because of it. People were searched on entry to some high-profile nightclubs, but this was often a basic search and certainly not one of police standard. Generally, most of the clubs were seen to operate a 'no drugs policy' but not in any strict way. A very strict policy would have been swimming against the recreational tide of the times.

There is a practitioner literature from working bouncers, including their emotional and gritty 'warts and all' memoirs, guides and manuals about door work (Barratt, 2004; Carson, 2005; Currie and Davies, 2003; Emburgh, 2010; Gadsden, 2006; Hammer, 2014; Holiday, 2011; Knapp, 2007; Lee, 2013; Marlow 2011; O'Keefe, 1997; Quinn, 1990; Stylianou, 2012; Thompson, 1994, 1999, 2001/2009; Trifari, 2008; Twemlow, 1980; Watts, 2005). Despite obvious problems with sensationalism and sentimentality, this is a rich source of insider lay accounts of doing door work and the biographical and experiential realities of being a bouncer.

This diverse range of door stories from current or former bouncers is a useful source of alternative data on door work. This literature is not fully engaged by the various researchers on door work, yet it is a practical literature that is consumed by bouncers for different reasons. There is a close and clear parallel here to football hooligan memoirs and self-confessionals. Redhead argues that such accounts can be partial and distorted but can and should act as a useful supplement and 'rough popular memory' (2009: 29) and certainly not be ignored or glossed over. Pearson, in his review of this genre, sensibly states: 'the "hit and tell" memoirs reveal a world of identity, local pride, camaraderie and humour' (2011: 14).

Door narratives, or the telling of bouncers' stories, are therefore an important and rich constitutive part of the subculture of door work and the identity of the bouncer self. Much of the time spent on the door was dedicated to both telling and listening to war stories, which were often highly humorous. It is a normalized part of the setting. In this sense, narratives are 'intrinsically collective acts' (Maines, 1993: 32). As Gergen and Gergen acutely observe: 'we live by stories – both in the telling and the doing of self' (1988: 18). 'War stories' also function as 'morality plays' (Toch, 1993), wherein the demanding emotional work of bouncing is valued by its participants. The question here is not about the detailed factual accuracy of the story but what it demonstrates about their world.

Heroic accounts in door stories, often told humorously, would typically glamorize the bouncer's involvement with gang members and exaggerate their valiant role in violent encounters. Door stories were a shifting mixture of reality, rumour, gossip and fabrications. What Monaghan (2002d) usefully described as 'in-group banter', which could be highly sexualized. I did not want to alert any suspicion by being too timid to tell or share 'door stories' and jokes, so I would laugh along initially and then tell my own later down the line. I often had to fabricate that I knew characters from the door world in the early days so as to fit in.

Bouncing credibility is often embellished with war stories, particularly where they have interacted with gang leaders or 'heads' – a sort of heroic 'lived to tell the tale' logic. Clearly, they are linked with typical views of bouncers as displaying forms of hyper-masculinity. War stories, as in other occupations, are part and parcel of the work they explicate rather than being separate from it. They constitute the classic 'shop talk' of the occupation, and humour played a large part in recounting incidents. Much of this talk, importantly, values the occupational worth of being a door person. Door stories serve various functions then, including explicating a door career, being instructive about the actual work and developing occupational camaraderie. In such stories, being a competent member of the door team requires that you speak the language or argot. It is not to suggest that this was a private language of the door staff, but it was an entitlement display, along with other aspects, of competent membership as a bouncer.

6.4 Managing situated 'ethical moments' on the door

The question of ethical parameters and limits plagued my mind throughout the fieldwork in a convoluted series of 'what if scenarios'. What if I witnessed serious injury or a serious crime, what would I do? What if restraint blurred into assault with a customer? What is reasonable force, if I came under attack with adrenaline flowing? Throughout the fieldwork, I was concerned with the tension between what I was occupationally expected to do as a bouncer, being paid for that duty, and my personal ethical and moral perception of harm and violence. I am convinced that I would have fully informed the police and hence blown my cover if there had been a serious incident, but fortunately this did not happen. In the latter parts of the fieldwork, as I had developed rapport with my fellow doormen, my 'what if scenarios' centred on What if I was found out?

I tried to abstain from making any value judgements throughout my analysis and my participation in the setting became part of my ongoing and varied 'guilty knowledge' (Adler, 1985; Becker, 1963; Carey, 1972; Polsky, 1967). The main problem around my duality was the problem of participation in any deviant activities. I attempted to be a 'credible witness' (Atkinson, 1990) and a 'marginal native' (Armstong, 1998) in my embedded ethnography, but I was obligated to do what was normal, accepted and expected in most situations.

I was 'native among the natives' (Zaman, 2008). Effectively, I was conducting a sort of 'fingers crossed ethnography' where I was concerned about my luck abruptly running out. In particular, I had a broad moral compass on the amount of controlled restraint I would use, if it was necessary. However, if violent situations emerged, I could not easily adopt a proxy role. My fellow bouncers had expectations of my conduct, and when adrenaline flows, such bracketing becomes blurred and difficult to maintain. This was a continual source of anxiety throughout the fieldwork.

Kate O'Brien (2009), in her semi-covert role as a female bouncer, reflects cogently on the ethical dilemmas of being a feminist researcher and squaring this with dealing with complex issues regarding the protection of vulnerable young women, in her fieldwork period. Role differentiation becomes quite blurred and challenging in practice. This is what O'Brien (2009) refers to as 'gendering the security gaze', which is a neglected and under-researched topic as most accounts trade on ideas of forms of hyper-masculinity. More inside accounts from feminist researchers is certainly called for in this area.

The brief vignettes that follow involve situational decisions and scenarios which display 'ethically important moments' (Guillemin and Gillam, 2004) for me. This is not to paint a romantic or heroic picture of the research, but rather a realistic one, warts and all. This is a world where you are presented with various ethical dilemmas that are worked out and managed, not solved, in the setting (Calvey, 2008). Ethical dilemmas, then, become a series of situated 'doings' and not only theoretical and idealized concepts.

Being recognized and managing denial

When a former student recognized me on the door, I had to assertively deny all knowledge of her. Because of her sustained insistence on knowing me, she was then refused entry to the premises and left with some friends feeling very bewildered. I felt guilty about this, but there seemed to be no other option at the time, particularly as it was very early on in the study.

Witnessing violence

I had witnessed a gang leader smash a bottle on a young customer's head. I had stopped him doing further damage by restraining him. I was on my own at this busy city-centre pub and managed to verbally calm them down without being attacked. After threatening me, they left the pub and violently wreaked havoc across the road at our sister venue, hospitalized a doorman, and randomly assaulted several customers. The riot police were eventually called to the premises and the gang, later identified as 'the Salford', fled, without any arrests being made. I had established my credibility in 'standing up to them' and 'showing my balls', but I severely doubted carrying on with the ethnography.

I became a witness to violence on several occasions. I did not intervene when a door was breached by a local gang from Cheetham Hill and a doorman was assaulted inside the club in front of me. I was warned it was personal and accordingly stood back. Another incident was when I witnessed a doorman physically assault a customer, followed by a group of doormen assaulting the same doorman by throwing him into a canal from a significant height. I helped fish the doorman out of the canal and told the police, who had been called by customers, that I had 'seen nothing'. This was at the request of the doorman, who did not want to be seen as 'a grass' and did not press any charges, despite several customer witness statements to the contrary and his self-evident broken nose. Thankfully, the doorman suffered superficial damage and no police action followed. These are clear complex moral compass issues where my personal version of morals can be at odds with what I am witnessing. In this way, covert participation is not endorsement of a value or belied system that is being researched.

Forcing entry to another door

When socializing with a group of doormen after a shift, and after excessive drinking and free entry into different nightclubs in the city centre, we tried to force entry into an expensive, ticketed dance event at the Manchester Evening News Arena late in the evening. I was caught up in the concerted push on the door and was in the crossfire of aggressive arguments between door staff and Arena staff. The police attended and issued a final warning that we would all be arrested and put in the 'fucking van'. We then wandered off laughing and shouting insults at both the police and venue staff.

Police surveillance and stab vests

One night, we were locked in the cellar of a nightclub after two young men approached the door after it had just closed, supposedly carrying guns. After watching CCTV footage it turned out they were carrying umbrellas because of the rainy weather. The nightclub had been the object of take-over bids by rival gangs having turf wars over selling recreational drugs in the venue. It was under police surveillance, hence we wore stab vests. Panic erupted, the staff were locked in the cellar and the police were called. Being under brief police surveillance whilst I had the bouncers under my surveillance was ironic. I nervously walked home and again doubted whether I should be doing this fieldwork.

Mistaken identity

I suffered from mistaken identity when, on entering a nightclub off duty for research purposes, I was stopped at the door by a well-known and very intimidating doorman from an infamous Manchester criminal family, who was eventually murdered. My heart stopped as I thought he had discovered my true research purposes and was going to get some retribution for this deception. But I was mistaken for somebody else and let in. Paranoia had got the better of me. I didn't spend long in the venue that evening and could not fully concentrate on observational matters.

Faking gang knowledge

On several occasions, customers would demand free entry and claim to be 'connected' to notorious gangs or leading criminal figures. If refused, threats were commonplace. Working out the real and bogus claims comes with the territory and was a stressful part of the job, particularly in the early days when I had little such local knowledge and regularly faked that I had much more. When I fronted the dance nightclub that was under police scrutiny due to gang problems, I falsely assured the head doorman that I could recognize all the 'heads' or local gang leaders on an important re-opening night at a club. The fact that the police gave us staff jackets to wear and were involved in undercover surveillance work themselves at the club that night made me very nervous. A local gang member threatened the door team later that night, causing the head doorman to resign on the spot and not return to that door. I followed his lead and, after the night's shift had ended, did not return either, much to my relief.

Turning the tape recorder off syndrome

A very different ethical moment is what I call 'turning the tape recorder off syndrome'. This occurred when a young doorman opened up to me about his longer term future, what you might call the brutalization of this type of work and the potential effects on his new-born son. I was drinking alone with him, at his invitation, and when I got the next round in, I quickly went to the toilet and turned the tape off. For me, this was a way of managing what I perceived as a type of ethical dilemma. I perceived continuing to tape record our conversation where he confided in me intimately about this 'shit work as a bouncer' as an invasion of his personal privacy and went beyond the remit of the study. Others might feel this is utterly hypocritical and a contradictory abandonment of realism.

This incident clearly points to the emotionally demanding nature of covert work. What I have loosely characterized as being part of a covert condition. Ethical decision-making then becomes a situated matter of judgement and not a prescriptive research manual right or wrong. Obviously, I continued to take mental notes and reflect on the situation, rather than decide not to publish the material in any way. Hence, there is contradiction and blurring here with situated ethical-decision making which is fascinating to further expose, dissect and unpack. There were other instances of this syndrome throughout the fieldwork that I had to manage. It is a type of situational ethical decision-making when a range of personal and private information was revealed to me about doormen and their lives outside their occupation, which is inevitable.

Dealing with the dealers

Whilst working on a busy nightclub in Manchester city centre at the weekend, I was informed by an experienced doormen to let two young rather trendy looking females into the venue without queuing or being searched. What he described as 'no questions asked' policy. On quizzing him further, he said that they worked for a well-known criminal drug dealer in the area and they were 'his girls'. Clearly the consequences of stopping them in their work was not on the agenda as they were very protected. Apparently, we were one club amongst several that they visited regularly. He joked about the girls going under the police radar for years. This was a type of guilty and potentially incriminating knowledge that I had to repress and go along with in the setting for obvious reasons.

This is not a definitive or exhaustive taxonomy of my experiences but a diverse range of fieldwork scenarios. There are no methodological strictly right or wrong answers here, but rather it is a demonstration of my covert condition. Tunnell reflects on the liberation of confessing and 'coming clean' in his research on property offenders and violent criminals: 'The methodologies of "muddy boots" and "grubby hands" implicitly mean taking sides, recognizing the politics of one's research, engaging in impression management and hedging the truth' (1998: 208).

I have attempted here to 'resurrect the ethical off-cuts' that are often sanitized out of published accounts and left on the 'cutting-room floor' (Smart, 2010). It has been a temporary immersion into the everyday life-world of some bouncers. What I hope to have presented is some dynamic 'ethically important moments' (Guilleman and Gillam, 2004) rather than a simplistic treatise on ethics or a step-by-step guide on ethical decision-making. It has been a reflexive exploration of a set of scenarios, from which to exercise your own moral and ethical imagination.

6.5 An optic on violence

In my case, by doing this covert type of fieldwork I clearly opened myself up to the problem of being a witness to activities that I might not personally agree with and might want to morally distance myself from. My logic was generally not to intervene, which would alter the course of what was naturally occurring. Moreover, essentially, I am not making moral judgements on the setting or the actions of the participants. In this sense, it was important for me to try to suspend my feelings, although sustaining this was difficult and challenging. I want to resist painting an exotic picture of doorman, which builds on their demonization. Part of this is getting a proportionate picture of violence in their world and not crudely falling into the trap of building an overly violent depiction of it. Dealing with violence or, in some cases, the fear of violence, was part of the occupational territory but not to the extent that it was 'all day, everyday'. Much of the conflict and potential episodes of violence were between intoxicated customers, with the bouncers typically defusing the situation, rather than violence between bouncers and customers, although this was also part of the game. To use visceral terms, I witnessed more vomit than blood during my six-month fieldwork period.

Monaghan (2003, 2004, 2006) in his study of bouncers also reflects on the 'personal turmoil' and sources of 'personal anxiety' in his ethnography, including his accounting of the use of force to the police. Indeed, for Monaghan, the territory of door work is saturated in legal risks, which doormen on the whole manage to skilfully navigate in ambiguous and difficult contexts.

Researchers can and do decide to conceal data, as not everything is revealed. Thus, research gets sanitized. This is particularly compounded by a covert role in terms of what is witnessed and revealed. Some incidents in my bouncer study I have deliberately decided to exclude from my account due to certain sensitivities.

When there were critical incidents of violence, not saturated, or more realistically episodes of anticipating violence, when doing the doors, it was very difficult to manage adrenaline in such situations. Effectively, the fear of violence was often the driver rather than the actuality of it. Gary Armstrong (1998), in his study of the Sheffield United football supporters, although his research was overt, was not as fortunate and on two occasions he was involved in minor physical confrontations. Ayres and Treadwell comment, on their overt ethnographic study of alcohol, cocaine use and violence in the night-time economy among English football firms, that many incidents are effectively normalized in the setting and hence are 'frequently unreported to the police' (2011: 88).

My investigative logic, not the situation, here is partly reminiscent of Steven Taylor's problems of observing abuse in a mental health institution. Part of his gate-keeping arrangements for gaining access for his participant observation study was that he had 'promised to maintain confidentiality and refrain from interfering in institutional activities' (Taylor, 1987: 289). Do the means justify the ends? It certainly does if routine abuse is uncovered and then investigated.

Taylor spent most of his time on a ward for what he termed the 'mentally retarded', where he witnessed the routine control of the vulnerable patients by abusive tactics by the guards. This practically translated into standing by as a witness while some patients were physically and emotionally abused. It presented an uncomfortable ethical dilemma for him throughout his fieldwork as these were, for him, 'immoral acts observed in the field' (Taylor, 1987: 380). These immoral acts included slapping patients, making them perform sexual acts and, with one, making a patient eat burning cigarettes. Taylor argues that abstract moral codes are difficult to apply in the field, particularly where the moral parameters are utterly alien to you. On his personal trauma, he states 'people who cannot deal with moral ambiguity probably should not do fieldwork' (Taylor, 1987: 294). For Taylor, researching abuse was ultimately more useful than direct intervention in a setting.

Bill Sanders (2005), in his study of bouncing culture in a large London nightclub, builds a proportionate and sensible picture of violence and door work, which I would endorse. Sanders accurately claims: 'However, given the thousands of punters who attended each weekend, violent incidents in the club involving bouncers were relatively infrequent. Furthermore, in the main, punters on the receiving end of bouncers' violence were not "innocent"' (2005: 252).

Silverstone, who investigated the rave culture in a London nightclub by working initially as a member of the bar staff and then as part of the security team, sensibly states on this: 'In terms of policing these spaces, violence was a rarity, as a working drug market did not want the police attention that might come with routine violence' (2006: 148). Silverstone is keen to distinguish between different types of night-time economies – pub space and urban spaces – which have different types of policing and incidences of violence in them. He refers to doormen as being 'part of the genealogy of working class muscle' (2006: 148) and accurately stresses that 'for the British government, bouncers have been the folk devil of choice' (2006: 149).

Violence and masculinity, particularly machismo and hyper forms of bravado on the door, provide both the cause and condition of the bouncer self. What I loosely describe as a 'choreography of bravado' that plays out in the doing of door work. Ultimately, some of the participants live up to the traditional label, while others resist it, which can serve to trap some of them in self-defeating cycles. Thus, everyday clichés and stereotypes residually group and classify what 'everybody knows about them' and in turn demonizes, vilifies and maligns them. Thus, the topic has a sort of intriguing 'armchair value'. If these men are typically 'the lads' of the counter-school culture (Willis, 1977), then they have grown up and are now doing doors.

The majority of the door teams were masculine. I worked with only one female door member, who, as pointed out by Hobbs et al. (2007) and O'Brien et al. (2008) in their two-year ethnographic study of female door work, seemed to perform a more gender specialist role in defusing aggressive females, as well as some gender transgression and mimicry, which ultimately results in 'reinforcing gendered codes that underpin violence work' (O'Brien et al., 2008: 170).

We must continually question and challenge the typical stereotypes about bouncers, which tend to crudely lump them together homogeneously as ultimately all about hyper-masculinity, which is a dangerous and crude generalization to make. Understanding the versions of masculinity that bouncers perform in complex ways is tied up with their ideas of credible bodily self-images and their enacted types of physicality and violence (Monaghan and Atkinson, 2014).

My witnessing of violence, and more generally being a participant observer in this context, has some parallels to Westmarland's innovative overt study of gender and policing. She usefully describes her feelings of angst about whistleblowing as 'encounters with ambiguity' (2001: 531), particularly on the blurring between violence, excessive and reasonable force. She did not view herself as any sort of 'ethnographic referee' as she tried to understand the 'world view' of a particular occupational group. She does acknowledge that her 'thoughts were not of how to stop the violence or to report it, but to concentrate on watching it develop in order to record the reactions of those involved' (2001: 532). Similar to my own research, she 'raises a number of difficult ethical scenarios which do not have a coherent or uniform solution for ethnographers' (2001: 533), which become discretionary and situated personal judgements.

6.6 Emotionality, embodiment and risk-taking in ethnography

This ethnography was of a sensual and embodied kind. It was the voluntary and deliberate experience of risk-taking and edgework (Lyng, 1990, 2005). At times, I felt I was at the limits of my deception and doubted how long I could sustain this role. Within edgework, risk becomes intimately part of the phenomenological experience. For me, this was 'the buzz' of doing doors, which was an intoxicating mixture of pleasure, thrill and adrenaline alongside stress, fear, anxiety and apprehension.

Lee Monaghan (2003, 2004, 2006) conducted an 'embodied ethnography' in his study of the occupational subculture of nightclub and pub security staff or doormen in Southwest Britain from 1997 to 2001. Monaghan describes his role as adopting 'an active membership role' (2004: 455) as a doorman in seven city-centre licensed premises over fourteen months. Part of his contact was also socializing with them in both nightclubs after work, as I did. Monaghan had contact with around sixty doormen, some of whom he interviewed in the latter stages of his fieldwork.

An interesting point is that Monaghan's methodological approach was not covert but his normalization in the setting was vital. For Monaghan, his fieldwork role was intimately linked to his bodily capital and bodily co-presence, which in his case was a history of boxing and weight-lifting. Although the customers would not have known about his study, Monaghan is clear about his overt stance to his door colleagues: 'I divulged information about my academic interests and affiliation to most door staff with whom I regularly worked' (2004: 455–456).

For Monaghan, in doing such fieldwork, 'the multidimensional body becomes a topic of, and resource in, ethnographic fieldwork' (2006: 238). For Monaghan, such risky fieldwork is clearly embodied and emotional edgework. As he reflects: 'using my body to research "other bodies" in a risk environment was sociologically valuable but also personally troublesome' (2006: 226).

My research also has some parallels with Diphoorn (2013), in her overt ethnography of private policing in Durban, South Africa. For her the 'emotionality of participation' is imperative for the analysis of the research setting, which involved the management of violence with armed response units. For her, participation in such a research setting is not a fixed state but involves active, reluctant and passive modes. For Diphoorn, one needs to 'further understand the dialectic between emotion and method' (2013: 222).

I genuinely felt that I had gained an understanding of being a bouncer as a 'lived experience' by covert means that I could not have achieved overtly. In the latter stages, I strongly wanted to reveal my true identity to the door community I worked with but due to a combination of guilt and risk management I left by not turning up for my shift, binning my mobile phone and avoiding the venues where I had worked. This sort of 'disappearing act' was my fieldwork exit strategy, but I felt that I had empathetically got 'under their skin' and 'walked in their shoes' for a brief time. I felt that I had earned some entitlement to talk about the bouncer's world in an authentic way, which was not a belligerent hit-and-run proxy version of it.

My fieldwork was partly a type of embodied activity, in a disguised format, which was performatively intense. As Coffey puts it: 'Fieldwork is necessarily an embodied activity. Our body and the bodies of others are central to the practical accomplishment of fieldwork' (1999: 59). My covert presentation involved an engineering of my physical self, similar to Daniels (1983), as she deliberately lost weight and cultivated certain aspects of femininity in her investigation of military psychiatry. Part of what Daniels (1980) elegantly titled her book chapter as 'Getting In and Getting On: The Sociology of Infiltration and Ingratiation'.

I am partly inspired by Wacquant's famous study of boxing (1992, 1995, 2000, 2005), particularly his seminal book *Body and Soul: Notebooks of an Apprentice Boxer* (2000), which shifted from covert to overt over his three-year fieldwork period. His embodied approach has clear parallels to bouncing, with his passionate drive to inhabit their craft and habitus. Body image and bodily capital are the keys to a more intimate and nuanced understanding of bouncer work as a craft to a certain extent.

For Wacquant, boxing, which is widely demonized and vilified, is a visceral pursuit and in order to understand it, put basically, the researcher had to try the 'sensuous pizzazz' (Waquant, 2005: 464) for themselves. The central argument of his book is about entering the boxers' bodies as they collectively learn their trade in order to understand meaning-making. For Wacquant, his apprentice membership was an 'invaluable methodological springboard' (2005: 462). Like Wacquant, I similarly felt that I had entered a distinctive subculture and habitus, with its own rules, rituals and social logic, in which I could only stay for a temporary period. What I previously describe as a form of 'sub-aqua ethnography' (Calvey, 2000).

As Palmer similarly reflected on the risk and dilemmas of her overt fieldwork on alcohol-based sporting subcultures: 'the nature of my fieldwork required a particular kind of image management. … This meant letting dangerous behaviour such as heavy drinking, physical horseplay and banter unfold unbridled by researcher intervention' (2010: 435).

The covert research role I deliberately chose clearly was a type of high-risk methodology (Wolf, 1991). Jacob-Pandian states that the ethnographer: 'does not become a native but is forever in the process of becoming a native' (1975: 170). I was deliberately attempting to become a type of intimate insider but on a faked basis. Ironically, genuine friendships did also develop from this faked position. Doing covert work is thus not devoid of ethicality but displays different, subtle forms of it in a situated manner (Calvey, 2008).

Similar to Pearson (2009), in his covert study of football hooliganism, I was walking a legal tightrope in doing such a study. My participant observation, like his, meant breaking the law in certain situations, not in a cavalier, belligerent or romantic sense, but in a situational one. Hence, my ethnography at the edge, which involved certain aspects of illegality and criminality, was a 'lived intensity' (Ferrell and Hamm, 1998) and 'experiential immersion' (Ferrell, 1998).

6.7 Conclusions: the post-fieldwork self in a study that never quite finishes

The idea of the post-field self was a significant one for me. The nature of the covert fieldwork was psychologically intense and emotionally demanding. What I previously referred to as a form of nomadic 'sub-aqua ethnography' (Calvey, 2000). Despite my previous wording of a book chapter entitled 'Getting on the Door and Staying There' (2000), I also faced similar exit problems to Ditton (1977), in his study of fiddling and pilferage in a bakery. Hence, Ditton states: 'In fact (and this, I suggest, is perhaps the mark of the truly accepted observer) I had far greater problems in getting out' (1977: 5). Managing my exit process became more delicate and complicated than I anticipated. I had finished the study when a senior doorman at the Hacienda nightclub confirmed that I was 'in the firm', and I did not want that association to negatively follow me around in my private life. Being in their 'firm' might have consequences, which I wanted to avoid at all costs. It was time to leave the field.

Ward (2008), in her experiential study of drug sellers in London, experienced problems of distancing with her study and felt a sense of betrayal of the friendships she had used to do her study. I can fully empathize with her ambivalent position. I had 'surrendered' (Wolff, 1964) to the setting culturally and psychologically, accepting certain rules, mores and activities, which had to be emotionally managed, both during and after the fieldwork period.

So on several occasions after I had left the field, when I was recognized by various bouncers, I felt that I had to sustain my door identity and, what I loosely call, 'go back into character', making fabricated jokes about early retirement, low wages and personality clashes with pushy managers. Most of the door staff assumed I was still working on the doors and had just moved around a few of them. On some occasions, I would purposively let them think this if it was more expedient in the situation. Sometimes, this resulted in free entry to the club and not queuing, as I did not want to offend them. While inside the club, I felt like and partly acted like I was still on duty as a doorman having some leisure time, classically like the policeman who is never off duty. It was like being stuck in an incessant research project that never quite finished.

I hope to have presented door work not as exotica or crude subjugation but as a particular type of emotional labour (Hochschild, 1979, 1983). I have attempted to present a brief glimpse of the reality which engages bouncers in their own terms. The bouncers in the research are, if unwittingly, genuine collaborators in the project to whom I am indebted in many ways. The field experience of getting on, staying on and leaving the door has been a powerful one that is not wiped away by another project, and nor should it be. It has reminded me of the need to record people's lives, in all their richness, more creatively, honestly and modestly. I enjoyed what one doorman called the 'buzz' from working on doors from 'the inside'. Indeed, it is an addictive one. However, I was simultaneously relieved to have eventually melted back into the anonymous crowd.

My ethnography attempts to be a realistic 'warts and all' navigation of this peculiar covert journey. This is a strong and sustained push for understanding bouncing and their everyday world as a lived experience. It has parallels with Ferrell and Hamm's description of criminological Verstehen, based on Weber. Ferrell and Hamm argue: 'to explore the lived politics of pleasure and pain, fear and excitement; to think with the body as well as the mind' (1998: 14).

The irony of some of these 'faked friendships' was that they formed the basis of some genuine, if temporary, affections, bonds and trust I developed with the door team. I look back fondly on some of those memories. I managed my dual identity as best I could. It is cogently summed up by the seminal anthropologist Evans-Pritchard: 'One becomes, at least temporarily, a sort of double marginal man, alienated from both worlds' (1976: 24).

My research generated some press interest, which included an interview titled 'Drugs, guns and fights: all in a night's work' for the *Times Higher Education* by Adam James in February 2001, a short piece in *The Guardian* by David Ward in December 2000 provocatively titled 'I don't want to get no bullet over no bullshit', and a televised interview with Nick Higham as part of the Festival of Science, broadcast on *BBC News 24* in October 2006. The local press were far more sensationalist in their coverage, including 'Bouncers in world of guns and drugs' on the front page of *Manchester Evening News*, followed by 'The danger on the doors' in the *Manchester Metro* and, finally, 'Bouncer revelation man leaves the country',

Manchester Evening News, all in early December 2000 by journalist Ed Swinden. Clearly, such public coverage is beneficial in terms of public dissemination, but it glamorizes and stereotypes the topic, which was the opposite of my intentions in doing the research project.

6.8 Learning exercise

Examine the different 'ethical moments' discussed in section 6.4 above and reflect on them in the following ways:

1. If you witnessed violence in a covert fieldwork setting, would you feel the need to whistleblow to the police?

2. Would you prefer to have a key informant or gate-keeper in doing dangerous covert fieldwork? Explain your decision.

3. If your moral compass and sensibilities are different from those you study, could you still undertake your research?

4. Would you feel guilty in doing covert fieldwork? If so, how would you manage it?

7

A REVIVAL IN COVERT RESEARCH

It is my contention that both the contemporary appetite and popularity for covert research is growing in various academic communities, for a number of different reasons. This is additionally interesting and somewhat ironic in the current context of increasing ethical regimentation. What I hope to do in this chapter is to explore the reasons and contexts for this renaissance or revival, which are not coherently interrelated, but come from multiple sources. I have categorized and made sense of these sources, respectively, as autoethnography, covert social networks, cyber ethnography, investigative journalism and visual ethnography. Clearly, each area is a field in itself, but what I hope to do is to display how these disparate developments have collectively resulted in a contemporary revival of covert research.

7.1 Autoethnography

The rise of autoethnography, or what some would endorse as a 'new narrative turn', is linked to complex issues in the human and social sciences about otherness, biography and self in fieldwork. Autoethnography has now become a popular catch-all phrase, of various styles and modes, including self-ethnography (Alvesson, 2003; Reed-Danahay, 1997), personal ethnography (Crawford, 1996), self-stories (Denzin, 1989), first-person accounts (Ellis, 1998), personal narrative (Ellis and Bochner, 2000), autoethnographic vignette (Humphreys, 2005), narratives of the self (Gergen and Gergen, 1988) and ethnographic memoir (Tedlock, 1991). This genre is clearly deeply underpinned by the primacy of autobiography in different shapes and forms.

The autoethnographic genre, although relatively new, has been well documented (Atkinson, 2006; Bochner and Ellis, 2002; Ellis, 1995, 1999, 2000, 2007, 2009; Ellis and Bochner, 1990, 2000, 2006; Ellis et al., 2011; Ellis and Rawicki, 2013; Goldschmidt, 1977; Hayano, 1979; Holman Jones et al., 2013; Humphreys, 2005; Reed-Danahay, 1997; Sikes, 2013; Whitinui, 2014). Autoethnography is clearly a diverse style and genre and not a unified paradigm. In such a genre, emotion becomes a resource to evoke and explore and not avoid (Denshire, 2014).

Autoethnography has some parallels to insider research. Brannick and Coghlan (2007) usefully define insider research as: 'research by complete members of organizational systems and communities in and on their own organizations' (2007: 59). This autoethnographic turn opens up, for many, innovative ways of writing, inscribing and expressing the ethnographic self, which can include covert forms. Some autoethnographies have retrospective and biographical characteristics at their core, where informed consent can obviously be difficult to obtain. Typically, the researcher draws on their situated experiences, which is familiar and intimate to them. For me, autoethnography presents a rich set of occasions for both 'varieties of opportunistic research' (Riemer, 1977) and 'accidental ethnography' (Fujii, 2015). It appears as if the standard ethical dilemmas about informed consent, which have plagued covert research, are obviated or side-stepped in some autoethnographies, particularly if they are retrospective accounts.

Some early examples of biographical ethnographies would not describe their style as autoethnographic as this is a relatively new label. Bruno Bettelheim, an Austrian scholar working within analytic psychology, explored his year-long personal experiences of extreme psychological brutalization while in a Nazi concentration camp in 1938–1939 by covertly observing the behaviour of both guards and inmates. This now classic account was published, after several rejections, in 1943 as a journal paper and latterly more extensively in his popular book *The Informed Heart* (1960). Melville Dalton's classic *Men Who Manage: Fusions of Feeling and Theory in Administration* (1959), which is one of the case studies in Chapter 2, would be comfortably classified now as autoethnography.

Fred Davis, from a sociological Chicago school tradition, conducted covert research on the cabdriver over a six-month period in 1948 in Chicago by being employed as one. His study was later published in 1959. Davis was interested in what he characterized as 'facets of fleeting relationships' (1959: 158). The study, of what he later described as 'a fantastic potpourri of scribblings' (Davis, 1974: 313), explored the cabdrivers' typology of fares, with tipping being 'the central moral focus of his work' (Davis, 1974: 313).

Ned Polsky's famous study of poolroom hustling, *Hustlers, Beats, and Others* (1967), carried out over eight months during 1962 and 1963, was clearly embedded in his own auto-biographical experience in pool rooms for over twenty years, mainly around New York. John Irwin entered graduate school as an ex-convict. Having been imprisoned for five years for the armed robbery of a gas station, his influential book *The Felon* (1970), which became a classic in criminology and prison studies, clearly draws on his lived experiences as a criminal as well as interview data with a variety of other career criminals, such as hustlers, junkies and thieves. Holdaway's (1983) *Inside the British Police Force* and Young's (1991) *An Inside Job* are clear examples within the field of police studies, which are discussed more fully in Chapter 5.

Joanna Ryan with Frank Thomas, in *The Politics of Mental Handicap* (1987), offer a moving account of life on the wards dealing with people, children and adults with a range of disabilities and mental health problems. It is based on the six-month diary of Frank Thomas, who worked as a nursing assistant and volunteer in what was then called a 'sub-normality hospital'. Importantly, the diary was not written for publication, unlike many recent autoethnographies, but was a personal record of a man trying to make sense in his life and work experiences on the ward. It became a means of preserving his sanity. Ryan adds the academic commentary and perspectives from psychology and mental health fields.

Thomas kept a secret diary which was concealed from staff and patients but he was not involved in any role pretence while working on the ward. This account is an important way to expose the realities of bitter dehumanization, disposal and exclusion. When first published, it was widely regarded as methodologically novel in getting much closer to the lived experiences of being what was then termed 'mentally handicapped'. The book was to have an important impact on social policy in the field. Ryan describes the aim of the dairy as:

> A daily record, but interspersed with hind sights, opinions, conclusions. A great deal is not very tasteful. But then it is not a very tasteful situation. It is written as I felt it at the time – crude, vulgar, sometimes obscene. It may offend your sensibilities. It should do. (1987: 30)

The rich first-hand experiences of Richard Jones (1995) about prison life, encouraged by Irwin (1970), is drawn from his diaries after his year-long sentence in a maximum-security prison, where he collaborated, with permission, with his academic teacher on various publications. In such a unique and surreptitious collaboration not everyone knew of his dual role. More recently, there has been a call to value the distinct tradition of convict autoethnography from former prisoners. Newbold et al. elegantly argue: 'the passion engendered by the experience of incarceration can add color, context, and contour to data collection, findings, and analysis and may therefore be regarded as an essential thread in the tapestry of criminological inquiry' (2014: 439).

A somewhat controversial and provocative figure in autoethnography is Carol Rambo, formerly Rambo-Ronai. Some of her work includes life history narratives of adult survivors of childhood sexual abuse and trauma, a sensitive and taboo topic, where informed consent is problematic and retrospective debriefing is naïve. Her 'layered account' of her own childhood sexual abuse is remarkable and pioneering and is offered as a 'new writing format' (Ronai, 1995: 395). Ronai bravely and provocatively states at the outset of her award-winning 1995 paper: 'I am a survivor of child sex abuse. I am also a sociologist, a wife, a friend, and many other identities one might imagine for an adult, white female. The boundaries of these identities converge, blur, and separate as I write' (1995: 395–396).

Ronai's 'layered account' has also involved her introspective and retrospective reflections on her ambiguous role identities as a past striptease dancer:

> The trickster/researcher must 'tease out' the ambiguity of existing structures by putting them into play. Hanging suspended in the dance or play of ambiguity is the potential for new impressions to be added to the mystic sketch pad of consciousness. (Ronai and Ellis, 1989: 419)

Another controversial figure is Lauren Slater, a social psychologist who famously repeated the Rosenhan experiment individually. Her controversial book, *Lying: A Metaphorical Memoir* (2001), also offers, to me, some interesting covert food for thought. In this autobiographical book about her childhood memories and feigned mental health problems, the lines between truth and deceit are deliberately blurred in her provocative accounts of her 'narrative truth'. The book is full of vivid lived experiences, including her attendance at Alcoholics Anonymous, where she deliberately deceived the group about her drink problem. My interest here is in the artfulness of her deception. I am not advocating the widespread adoption of her 'narrative truth' style but her emotional exposition of deception 'laid bare' is worth further exposition.

A range of interesting autoethnographies have explored total institutions of various sorts over the years. There are few covert studies of the military due to obvious access and sensitivity issues. Cromer (1988) conducted a covert participant observation study of a basic training course in the Israeli Defence Forces.

This was effectively an autoethnographic account in that Cromer was doing his compulsory national service at the time. There was no gate-keeping and the other draftees were not aware of the study. Cromer uses Goffman in his analysis of the 'mortification of self' in the army as a 'total institution'. In particular, Cromer examines how new draftees deal with their initiation into army life by trying to pass the time more quickly. He writes under the broad themes of seeking information, passing time and killing time.

Kivett and Warren (2002) look at social control and the micro-politics of 'trouble' in a group home for delinquent boys, a residential behaviour-modification treatment centre or quasi-total institution in a Midwestern town in the United States. In particular, Kivett and Warren explored the escalation and de-escalation processes in managing the behaviour of young people in the setting. Kivett worked as a member of the support staff for around two years and his autoethnographic account provides the data for the study. Kivett opportunistically took 'mental notes in the field, full notes as soon as possible afterwards' (Kivett and Warren, 2002: 8).

Kirke (2010) offers an autoethnography of the British Army, which explores rule bending and breaking, including cases of informal revenge and disobedience. Data were extensively longitudinal in covering thirty years when he was a commissioned offer in the Royal Artillery. The research started life in 1974 as a 'self-motivated personal study' (Kirke, 2010: 364) that included personal memories in retrospect and a private observational journal. The study became formalized while Kirke was at the Department of Social Anthropology at Cambridge University in 1993/1994. Various interviews were conducted and consent given, when practicable at the later stages of the study. Kirke stresses that 'the driving ethical principle was to do no harm' (2010: 364).

Taber (2010), when faced with similar access problems in researching the Western National Defence Force, used autoethnography, because access would have required a type of bounded censorship. Indeed, for her as a feminist, it was a fortuitous development as she did not want to limit her critical analysis. Taber was familiar with the military, having grown up in a military family, attended military college and did thirteen years of military service. Her autoethnography became a 'reflexivity of discomfort' (Taber, 2010: 19) as she began to question and challenge the military culture in which she was embedded.

In terms of critique, the autoethnographic genre has been accused of narcissism or self-obsession and self-indulgence. Ings usefully argues that there are 'cautions and opportunities inherent in the methodology' (2014: 675). Atkinson (1997a) poses the very interesting early question of 'narrative turn or blind alley?' Another interesting question is posed by Sparkes (2002), who asks whether autoethnography is self-indulgence or something more?

Medford (2006) raises the issue of mindful slippage in autoethnography, as authors typically strive to present truthful experiential accounts. For her, despite the commitment to critical self-reflexivity, slippage is implicated in decisions on what to include and exclude in accounts. Medford argues that 'sometimes it seems appropriate – even necessary – to abbreviate, edit or otherwise modify our life stories in our writing' (2006: 853). Her concern is how we justify 'what gets purposely lost in the retelling' (2006: 854), which leads her to call for an 'ethic of accountability'.

Delamont takes a stronger line in her critique. She recognizes the 'rising acceptance' (2009: 51) of autoethnography in methodological communities but ultimately argues that there has been a 'narcissistic substitution of autoethnography for research' (2009: 51). For her, a 'retreat into autoethnography is an abrogation of the honourable trade of the scholar' (2009: 61). Tolich (2010) usefully raises the problems of gaining retrospective informed consent, with many autoethnographers effectively blurring and fudging the issue of how they account for implicating people without their permission in their narratives.

Ellis, Adams and Bochner (2011), in a comprehensive overview of autoethnography, claim that autoethnography challenges canonical ways of doing research and representing others. For them, autoethnography heightens and complicates 'relational ethics' as, by using personal experience, other people, often friends, are implicated. A complexity here is that informed consent cannot, in some cases, be realistically gained but it is realistically obviated or side-stepped.

Ellis rather evangelically states in an edited handbook of autoethnography: 'autoethnography is not simply a way of knowing about the world, it has become a way of being in the world, one that requires living consciously, emotionally and reflexively' (2013: 10). I do not subscribe to such a dogmatic blind faith in autoethnography, but the genre is useful, on the rise and has a part to play in the revival of covert methodology.

The point of exploring this turn is to show how it contributes in some ways to a covert revival in that many of these experiential accounts are retrospective and have obviated the need for informed consent. I have some scepticism over the rather self-indulgent and self-obsessed nature of this autoethnographic turn, which can prioritize experience over analysis, but my purpose here is to demonstrate its place in the renaissance of covert research. Clearly, autoethnography is not a unified methodological style and is a very diverse and fragmented grouping. What is important to remember is that it would be erroneous to equate all autoethnography with covert research, as this is not the case.

Autoethnography is an innovative way, among several others, of challenging conventional and canonical ways of doing ethnography and representing others. Because it is an increasingly populist genre, autoethnography, for me, can run the risk of becoming a fashionable and empty 'catch-all' phrase and slogan that loses analytic precision and clarity. Having said that, the creative gains are substantial. Although, for some, the philosophical push of autoethnography is a fusion of art and science, for me, the push is a more literary one.

With the lack of any strict and purist criteria, several hybrid versions of autoethnography can be housed under this umbrella, which can be highly productive. It is not a tradition in need of rescuing (Atkinson, 2006), but an emergent, expanding and provocative one. Covert research, although it clearly takes a very different stance on 'relational ethics' and 'collaborative witnessing', has productive links to the autoethnographic turn.

Various interesting issues immediately spring to mind here. First, the sensitive, even taboo, and stigmatized areas. Second, the exploration of the blurring between biography, identity and self. Third, the creative writing styles adopted, which attempts to break out from conventional 'ways of knowing' and expressing. Could this be both a sentiment and format for future covert research? Despite the various critiques of autoethnography, it has much to contribute to ethnography. Ultimately, for me, autoethnography is a methodological 'work in progress', that has some productive links to covert research.

7.2 Covert social networks

A covert network is a social network that has elements of secrecy about it, and that leads the actors involved, in many cases, to try to keep their identities hidden. Some of the very early work in this area can be traced to George Simmel's influential research on secret societies (1906). Some of the work done in this relatively new field has historical aspects, as in studies of the suffragette social movement (Crossley et al., 2012) or the Provisional Irish Republican Army (Stevenson and Crossley, 2014). Although much of the work in this area focuses on terrorist and criminal networks, a wide variety of protest and social movements, deviant subcultures, dark, underground, illegal and clandestine networks are also explored (Asal and Rethemeyer, 2006; Baker and Faulkner, 1993; Crossley, 2007; Enders and Su, 2007; Klerks, 2001; Krebs, 2001; Raab and Milward, 2003; Sageman, 2004).

The interest in covert social networks has increased in recent years as such networks are objects of study for policymakers as well as academics. With the former, various agencies need to minimize the risk to the public from criminal and terrorist by disrupting their activities. The analysis of such covert social networks is primarily relational and is typically based on quantitative data, which can be spatially and graphically organized (Broccatelli et al., 2016), such as kinship ties, communication structures and co-participation in events. The analysis of covert social networks, then, relies heavily on forms of social network analysis (Crossley, 2002; Diani and McAdam, 2003; Scott, 2000, 2002).

The increasing interest in covert social networks could lead to more interest in covert fieldwork more generally, and possibly from different sections of the more quantitative social science community.

7.3 Cyber ethnography

In the cyber or virtual world, which is very different from the traditional fieldwork locations, online locales, communities, populations and spaces are fair research game. The questions of privacy, harm, ownership, censorship, legality, illegality, informed consent have not gone away and, if anything, are more difficult to regulate in this diffuse and fragmented environment. Consequently, various researchers from different fields have become concerned with internet methodology and in particular the ethical dilemmas, moves and tactics involved in researching this new locale in a more dedicated manner. Namely, the issue of lurking.

Cyberspace has, in many ways, become what I describe as a 'covert playground'. Informed consent takes on a new shape in such an arena, which has become a serious concern for some researchers in their ongoing attempt to develop specific internet ethics and protocols for various online ethical dilemmas (Buchanan, 2004; Denscombe, 2005; Flicker et al., 2004; Hine, 2005; Madge, 2007). Carusi and Jirotka (2009) describe the field of internet and online ethics as an 'ethical labyrinth'. The Association of Internet Researchers produced some ethical guidelines in 2002 (modified in 2012).

It is not to say that virtual research is ethically belligerent or cavalier by design, as various researchers use online informed consent forms and are explicit about their research role. Cyber ethnography is diverse but the particular nature of this field opens up, wittingly and unwittingly, many more spaces and opportunities for covert research. The computer has not only become a second self (Turkle, 1984) but a cyber-self (Robinson, 2007) where people can and do conceal and fake identities in a multiplicity of ways. What Robinson describes as 'the creation of cyber personas' (2007: 98) and 'identity play' (Turkle, 1995, 1999), which can be blurred narratives, that are partly true and false. Cyberspace, then, becomes a space to act out various real and imagined scenarios, which can be liberating and playful as well as more sinister. Is the person the age, gender or ethnicity they proclaim to be? A case of a virtual 'dance of identity' (Vrooman, 2002: 52) and game of 'transformed digital self-representation' (Yee et al., 2009: 30).

Clearly, locating the field in cyberspace has altered, and accordingly some researchers have argued for an alternate configuration of the field site. Virtual ethnographers have successfully shifted the notion of on- and off-line space and new mobile and multi-sited methodologies to investigate it (Hine, 2000, 2005). The typical researcher fudge here, which legitimates types of lurking, takes several forms. First, the research domain is a public one, hence the researcher lurking is not invasive or intrusive. Namely, as long as anonymity is used, which is standard research practice, cyber life becomes fair research game. Second, it is regularly stated that little or no harm was done to the participants due to the distance, remoteness and absence of intrusion between the researcher and the researched. Third, the public nature of the materials tends to suggest that the data are effectively fair game. The end result of this is that a range of sensitive topics can be explored, with the standard ethical protocol of informed consent being typically obviated.

Let us look at some examples of online covert lurking across different topics. Slater's (1999) work on Internet Relay Chat studies the exchange of explicit 'sex pics' among a number of users in a covert study over the course of a year in a type of bartering subculture. Sharp and Earle (2003) covertly study commercial internet sex by looking at over 5,000 personal reviews by male clients of sex workers on a 'punters' website.

Blevins and Holt (2009) explore the sensitive topic of the virtual subculture of Johns, male heterosexual clients of sex workers, in ten cities in the United States, who had the highest arrest rates for prostitution, via a sample of posts from specific public web forums run by and for male customers who visit female prostitutes. They legitimate their lurking as: 'the research team did not interact with any of the subjects who post in these forums. Instead, we acted as strict observers within these forums' (Blevins and Holt, 2009: 624). Blevins and Holt stress: 'These types of studies will improve our knowledge of the ways the Internet facilitates deviant communication and crime in the new millennium' (2009: 639).

Ashford (2009) argues that research on virtual online sex environments 'readily displays the fluid self' (2009: 310), which includes false and masked virtual identities. For Ashford, such research 'should pose new questions for the academy and its organs of ethical control' (2009: 310). Renninger (2015) explores the stigmatized topic of asexuality in the era of social media and the networked poly-media environment. For him, asexuality is a minority group, which is very distinct from other sexualities. His analysis is based on time spent lurking on asexual websites during 2012 and 2013.

Langer and Beckman (2005) examined two Danish public access websites which discussed the use of cosmetic surgery. It was used mainly by women, with a smaller number of men, and typically discussed choice of surgery, body image, common fears, horror stories and practical tips. The study was conducted over a sixteen-month period where postings were followed and extracted for content analysis. They argue that netnography (Kozinets, 2010) is a valuable method for investigating cosmetic surgery and that, more generally, 'the covert study of public online communication about sensitive research topics is both legitimate and ethical' (Langer and Beckman, 2005: 200).

Hammersley and Treseder (2007) investigated pro-anorexia or extreme dieting websites. They view internet identity as an important methodological and analytic problem of trust. Indeed, the subtitle of their paper asks 'who's who in "pro-ana" websites?' The pro-anorexia websites encourage self-starvation and severe dieting to gain a certain media-driven body image and are mainly populated by young vulnerable women who suffer from eating disorders and body dysmorphia.

Day and Keys (2008) examine starving in cyberspace by exploring pro-eating disorder websites and doing feminist-inspired discourse analysis on the content, after collecting it from public search engines. Day and Keys legitimate their lurking as: 'no attempts were made to deceive those visiting the sites by, for example, TK "posing" as a self-starver or someone seeking advice on weight loss. Rather the method of "lurking" was adopted (reading the messages without taking part)' (2008: 6).

Coleman (2010) explores online dieting by lurking on the Weight Watchers UK website, which is a very popular website for such activities. She looks at how the dieting website creates new kinds of dieting temporalities in order to manage expectations about weight loss, given the typical recidivism rates of dieting. The success stories that she draws from the website are part of an evangelical push for new subscribers. Clarke (2015) similarly explores the 'dieting self' by becoming a paying member of an online weight loss group for three months, although disguised his actual body type, which was a tall and athletic male.

Smith and Stewart (2012) examine the body perceptions and health behaviours in an online bodybuilding community. For Smith and Stewart, the online community revealed a dedication to extremes and risk taking and a mind-set of hyper-masculinity, including steroid use. Various forum postings, which had a global network, were followed during a one-year period. Smith and Stewart argue: 'we therefore maintained a purely observational status wherein we played the role of specialized "lurkers"' (2012: 974).

Lurking is an obvious strategy than can be used to investigate extreme cyber hate (Back et al., 1996; Daniels, 2009; Mock, 2000; Whine, 1999; Zickmund, 1997). Vrooman (2002) explores flaming and abusive rants conducted for status and prestige by covertly observing the interactions of a cyber-community dedicated to this activity, during four months of lurking. Daniels (2009) covertly surveyed cloaked websites, which actively conceal authorship and have temporary sites, as cyberspaces for propaganda, extreme values and cyber-racism in the digital era. Daniels argues: 'Cloaked websites can disguise a variety of political agendas' (2009: 676). Shachaf and Hara (2010), explore internet trolls through multiple methods, which included email interviews, content analysis and online covert observations. Shachaf and Hara argue for more general analysis that attempts to: 'understand motivations and behaviours of various types of vandals, hackers and trolls' (2010: 368).

It is clear that a diverse range of sensitive topics have been explored by covert lurking and it is reasonable to assume that this is likely to increase. Murthy argues that 'the rise of digital ethnographies has the potential to open new directions in ethnography' (2008: 837). According to Murthy, the four new technologies of online questionnaires, digital video, social networking websites and blogs present a range of methodological possibilities and problems that will impact on the research relationship. Murthy argues that: 'social researchers cannot afford to continue the overall trend of side-stepping digital methods in the future' (2008: 838). Moreover, Murthy describes digital ethnography as a 'covert affair', stressing: 'my survey of digital ethnographies reveals a disproportionate number of covert versus overt projects' (2008: 839).

Hallett and Barber (2014) state that traditional ethnographic research in a cyber-era needs to change and adapt:

Many people have a different frame of reference than ten or twenty years ago; they text, Facebook, blog, and use Second Life. Studying people and organizations without considering the digital spaces where they define, express, and develop communities, images, and relationship would be inadequate. The time has come for ethnography to respond. (2014: 326)

It is clear that cyber lurking has been used extensively to explore a range of topics, with some of these being classified as covering sensitive topics and vulnerable groups, in ways that traditional ethnographies would have been stifled by ethical regimes. Clearly, as more researchers use multiple methods, the spaces and opportunities for doing covert work at some stage of the research are likely to expand. The ease and convenience of collecting digital data, in contrast to more time-consuming traditional face-to-face methods also promotes the use of cyber ethnography.

7.4 Investigative journalism

Clearly, not all investigative journalism is covert, although it has become rather synonymous with covert tactics. Obviously, investigative journalism is a dedicated field in itself, which cannot be covered in detail here. I aim to reflect on some leading contemporary examples in the field across different topics. Early examples from this field are discussed in Chapter 2 on the origins of covert research, including the pioneering work of Nellie Bly on mental health and institutionalization (see the case study in the learning exercises of the end of that chapter).

Investigative journalism is, in many ways, the intellectual poor cousin of the social sciences, with some academics wishing to distance themselves from types of 'quick and dirty' journalistic reporting. For me, investigative journalism represents a bold and disruptive field, which is not as fettered by the more formalistic ethical hang-ups and fetishes of the social sciences, although it is often more tightly bound by legal restrictions. Although driven by obviously different criteria and expectations, social science has some lessons to learn from this field. In some ways, investigative journalism has hijacked undercover research from the social sciences as it typically produces covert accounts across a range of topics at a much faster pace, although some investigations may be carried out in the long term.

Investigative journalism has a rich and distinctive history and its own particular problems, ideologies and debates. I don't wish to treat investigate journalism as an extension or species of an academic covert tradition. However, I do want to articulate and flag up the parallels and potential opportunities for positive cross-fertilization between the two disciplines. Investigative journalism has various descriptions and forms, including adversarial journalism, advocacy reporting, public service journalism, citizen journalism and exposé reporting. Like autoethnography, not all investigative journalism is covert, but some of those working in the field regularly use covert tactics and methods.

Feldstein (2006) argues that many forms of investigative reporting are associated with 'muckraking', a term used by American president Theodore Roosevelt in 1906 to describe journalists negatively as trouble-making dirt diggers. For some, the label and the popular image remains. Goddard (2006) reflects on the historical regulation of undercover journalism in the UK from 1960 to 1980. Goddard stresses that undercover journalism has risen in profile and popularity due to the personality-led investigations, which can become celebrity-driven rather than debunking strictly in the 'public interest'. Goddard also stresses that the increasing exploitation of surveillance-style technology and miniaturized technology has led to such techniques becoming more widely visible on television. Goddard argues that undercover journalism is about compromises between the principles of social responsibility, public interest, privacy and justifiable invasion. Ettema and Glasser cogently state: 'Investigative reporting can be journalism at its most politically vigorous and methodologically rigorous. Sometimes, however, it is also journalism at its most vulnerable' (2007: 491).

The Irish investigative journalist Donal MacIntyre cogently sums up their covert condition as he reflects on his early work in his autobiographical book *MacIntyre*:

In the course of a day I have assumed four different personalities, worn four different wardrobes and spoken four different street dialects, and left a little bit of me behind in each of those worlds. … There is no blueprint, no Scotland Yard course or City University module to prepare you for this kind of work. … The job goes beyond normal health and safety regulations and is outside every EU working directive. (1999: 7–8)

Let us turn to some examples of covert investigative journalism. Journalist Robin Page provided an early covert account of homelessness in *Down among the Dossers* (1973). Page's work with the vulnerably housed when he was a civil servant had fuelled his interest in this social group. As a civil servant, he saw the homeless frequently from the 'official' perspective, but decided to become a down and out himself to understand street poverty first-hand in Brighton, the south coast and London.

Gunter Wallraff is a famous, award-winning German investigative journalist, now exiled in Holland. *13 Undesired Reports* (1969), published in *Stern* magazine is an early piece of his work where he described his undercover experiences of being an alcoholic, a homeless street person and a worker in a chemicals factory. In researching his book *Lead Story* (1977), Wallraff joined the staff of *Bild*, Germany's biggest tabloid newspaper, under a pseudonym and exposed their muckraking practices. This story was the basis of his film *The Man Inside*, released in 1990. Walraff also worked undercover as a Turkish migrant temporary worker in a steel factory, at a Burger King fast food takeaway and in a chemical factory, and published his experiences in *Lowest of the Low* (1985). This became a best-selling book and was translated into several languages. His motivations are often politicized ones to demonstrate social injustices and expose institutional corruption. He has faced several lawsuits over the years for his allegations.

His most recent work is a documentary film called *Black on White: A Journey through Germany* (2009) and his recent book *Reports From the Brave New World* (Wallraff, 2009), highlight instances of shocking racial discrimination and violent racism. In the film, Wallraff spent a year mocked up in the disguise of a Somali immigrant with the help of a theatre make-up artist. It seems extreme, but, for Walraff, it was necessary to display how racism operates in modern Germany. Some of the black community advocacy groups in Germany have been offended by Wallraff's account, labelling it cavalier and belligerent.

Donal MacIntyre has become a household name for undercover reporting and exposé journalism in the UK, mainly on the subject of criminality. He began his television career at the BBC in the early 1990s and became famous for his BBC series *MacIntyre Investigates* in 1999. In this series, over eighteen months, and using hidden micro cameras and bugging devices, he covertly investigates a range of different settings, including Chelsea football hooligans, a fashion model agency, a care home for adults with learning difficulties and confidence tricksters. Some of his cases have resulted in prosecutions. Since this series, he has done various overt investigations of high-profile gangsters, including the Noonan family in Manchester, resulting in his award-winning film *A Very British Gangster*. Paul Connolly, another Irish investigative journalist, and his team have more recently explored the underground economy, secret sex lives including swingers, outdoor sex, street begging, sham marriages and welfare fraud.

A number of investigative journalists have explored the breadline by covert means. Barbara Ehrenreich, in her bestselling book *Nickel and Dimed: Undercover in Low-wage USA* (2002), which later became a play, worked undercover as a low-wage worker over a two-year period, accepting various breadline jobs and living in cheap, transient lodgings. These jobs included cleaning, waitressing, being a nursing home aide and a retail clerk for a large supermarket. For Ehrenreich, a PhD-educated journalist: 'the only way to find out was to get out there and get my hands dirty' (2002: 4). The book became a *New York Times* bestseller.

In light of her lack of relevant job experience, she presented herself as a 'divorced homemaker re-entering the workforce after many years' (Ehrenreich, 2002: 5). Ehrenreich wishes to strongly dispel a heroic picture of investigative journalism and to paint a more mundane one: 'So this is not a story of some death-defying "undercover" adventure. Almost anyone could do what I did – look for jobs, work those jobs, try to make ends meet. In fact, millions of Americans do it every day, and with a lot less fanfare and dithering' (Ehrenreich, 2002: 6). In her concluding chapter, Ehrenreich reflects on the flexible and fluid artfulness of the covert role: 'It's not just the work that has to be learned in each situation. Each job presents a self-contained social world, with its own personalities, hierarchy, customs and standard' (2002: 194). Ehrenreich shows in an updated second book, *Nickel and Dimed: On Not Getting By in America* (2008), that underpaid work has deteriorated further.

Fran Abrams was commissioned by *The Guardian* newspaper to survive on the breadline by earning the minimum wage in a series of casual temporary jobs in the UK. These jobs included a night cleaner at the Savoy hotel in London, a pickle factory worker in South Yorkshire and a care assistant in Scotland. Her journey of making ends meet was collected in *Below the Breadline: Living on the Minimum Wage* (Abrams, 2002).

Journalist Polly Toynbee went on a similar journey, captured in *Hard Work: Life in Low-pay Britain* (2003). Toynbee analyses poverty and the low-wage economy in British society by living on a run-down London council estate herself and taking on a variety of minimum-wage jobs. She worked as a hospital porter, a dinner lady, a cake packer, telemarketer, and a nursing home care assistant. In some of these jobs she only did one shift. Her self-imposed 'social exclusion' included no connection with her support network of family and friends. She shopped on a very tight budget with no luxuries and spent hours searching for work with dismissive agencies. She feels that cheap labour is a highly exploited and devalued work-force, and that attitudes need to change. This book repeated her previous work experiment, captured in *A Working Life* (1971), where she worked undercover on a maternity ward and in soap, cake and car factories.

Award-winning Australian journalist Elisabeth Wynhausen took leave from *The Australian* newspaper and went undercover, as an older job seeker, for ten months. She explored the downside of Australia's growing underclass and working poor in *Dirt Cheap: Life at the Wrong End of the Job Market* (2005). She acknowledges the inspiration of Ehrenreich's (2002) book. Her casual, unskilled jobs included packing eggs in a poultry factory, a cafeteria worker, an office cleaner, a retail checkout worker, a sales assistant in a chain store and a hotel kitchen hand in a nursing home, as she moved from state to state, including the cities of Sydney and Melbourne. She had an emergency fund, a car and her own apartment. She had to break into the credit card when the wages could not cover her costs of living, as low-cost accommodation was impossible to find. Her account reveals work-place harassment and bullying to this marginalized workforce, which she wants to oppose.

Celebrated French journalist Florence Aubenas searched for casual work during a time of recession in Caen, France, where she rented a furnished room. She had no special skills or qualifications and became an anonymous job seeker at employment centres. She joined the unemployment queue as an undercover journalist, eventually getting some causal hours working as a night cleaner on minimum wage in offices, holiday villas and on an English Channel ferry service. Her account of her journey in *The Night Cleaner* (2011), published in French in 2010, became an international bestseller. She finished the journalistic experiment when she got employed on a permanent contract, which took six months. On her fabricated covert role, Aubenas states in the preface: 'I preserved my identity, my name, and my ID, but I signed on as out-of-work, with just a baccalaureate in my pocket' (2011: viii).

This covert role involved her in a series of denials and risky negotiations, as Aubenas states in the preface: 'Just once, a young woman in a temping agency rumbled me. She was following the rule book. I asked her to keep my secret, and she did so. The vast majority of the men and women I encountered didn't ask me any questions' (2011: viii).

Following the success of her earlier undercover book, Ehrenreich shifted focus to the corporate world of business executives in *Bait and Switch: The Futile Pursuit of the Corporate Dream* (2006). For this book, she was inspired by reports of increasing deskilling and degradation in the middle classes rather than in the working classes. Her covert infiltration initially involved using her maiden name to construct a fake career history.

This investigation of the corporate world lasted a year and involved internet job searches, networking events and expansive career coaching. This covert project also meant Ehrenreich became more involved in the impression management of her body image and personality, which took an emotional toll. She states: 'I underwent a physical makeover and, although perhaps less successfully, attempted to soften my normally blunt persona into something more "likeable" and "team player"-like' (2006: 215). Ehrenreich is concerned with the psychological brutalization of the rising number of unemployed executives who are competing with each other for a shrinking number of career opportunities. Ehrenreich poignantly reflects: 'The tragedy is that they could be doing so much more' (2006: 236).

An extreme and very brave form of disguise was a gender experiment by American journalist Norah Vincent in *Self-Made Man*: *My Year Disguised as a Man* (2006). She is a gay woman who disguised herself as an effeminate man, including false beard and frontal appendage, to explore male culture over eighteen months. She used the name Ned, her tomboy name from childhood. She pushed her comfort zone by joining a bowling team, going to a strip bar, visiting a men's retreat, working in door-to-door sales and staying in a monastery. She suffered guilt syndromes about her deception and did eventually reveal her true self. This was followed by *Voluntary Madness: My Year Lost and Found in the Loony Bin* (2010), where she went undercover in three very different mental institutions, a public clinic, a private clinic and an alternative healing space.

Turning to some high-profile European examples, since writing his remarkable novel *Gomorrah: Italy's Other Mafia* (2007), about the Neapolitan Mafia, Roberto Saviano has been in hiding and is still currently under police protection. He has received several assassination threats from the Mafia. His novel was also made into a cinema film in 2008, which was awarded the Grand Prix of the Jury at the Cannes Film Festival.

He began his journalistic work on the book in 2001, consulting police records and court transcripts as well as taking jobs that allowed first-hand contact with the mob. He worked undercover in Camorra-controlled factories, construction sites and even as a waiter and photographer at a Camorra mob wedding. In the book, Saviano gained access to what he calls the 'baby soldiers' of the Di Lauro clan, who averaged thirteen to sixteen years old, and who, astonishingly, wore bullet proof vests in their line of criminal work. The Comorra is a normalized part of the social and cultural fabric of Italian life. Saviano recounts how he saw his first murder, of a local anti-Mafia priest, at fourteen, and how it radicalized him.

A bestseller in Italy and available in fifty-three languages, *Gomorrah* was a literary sensation and has currently sold 10 million copies. Saviano uses a mosaic of human stories to highlight the extent of Camorra global power, not just in the Naples area but throughout Italy and beyond. Silvio Berlusconi, the former controversial Italian Prime Minister, has accused Saviano of exaggerating mafia potency. Saviano does provide a partisan yet passionate account. He emotively claims: 'I was born in the land of the Gomorrah, in the territory with the most homicides in Europe, where savagery is interwoven with commerce, where nothing has value except what generates power' (2007: 300).

His fight against organized crime continues and he remains under police protection. In a recent candid interview, Saviano poetically reflects: 'I've turned into a monster myself by analysing and studying the world of organised crime from every angle. ... You even end up learning to think like they do' (2014: 33). In a critical book review, Collins asks 'How deep inside did he get? Not that far, as we shall see' (2009: 516), feeling that Saviano presented a rather sensationalist and glamorized account.

Mark Daly, a Scottish investigative journalist, worked undercover for Greater Manchester Police (GMP) in 2003 examining racism within the force. He was discovered and arrested by the police on 'suspicion of obtaining a pecuniary advantage by deception' and then bailed. The backdrop to his study was the publication in February 1999 of the high-profile Stephen Lawrence Inquiry conducted by Sir William Macpherson, which branded London's Metropolitan Police institutionally racist. After months of intensive training as a probationary officer, he then worked the beat as a standard police constable for two months, based in Stockport, Greater Manchester. Daly wishes to stress that most of the racist attitudes and language came from a minority of probationary recruits rather than beat constables.

The Secret Policeman was screened on television in 2003 and caused controversy and outcry. The then Home Secretary and several senior police officers condemned the racism it had exposed. The Campaign for Racial Equality launched a formal inquiry. Ten of the police officers involved resigned from three forces and twelve more were disciplined following a Police Complaints Authority (PCA) investigation, in agreement with the Independent Police Complaints Commission (IPCC). A follow-up documentary, *The Secret Policeman Returns* (2008), which was not undercover, examined if the promises to root out institutional racism had been kept, and explored the reality of being a Black Minority Ethnic (BME) police officer. For Daly, although police culture was changing, it was not progressive enough.

Undercover Mosque (2007) was part of Channel 4's *Dispatches* series, which is its flagship current affairs programme. It used an undercover reporter, who secretly recorded footage for a year in various British mosques, to expose extremist rants from Muslim preachers. The programme team were accused of faking evidence by West Midlands Police, who launched an inquiry after a public outcry. Ofcom, the broadcasting regulator, investigated the programme and eventually exonerated the team of journalists involved.

A follow-up programme, *Undercover Mosque: The Return* (2008), again used undercover film footage as well as some interviews with Muslim academics and prominent Islamic preachers. This programme focused on three Islamic institutions in London that were controlled by fundamentalist Saudi Arabian groups. The female reporter attended prayer meetings at a moderate British mosque and secretly filmed sermons given to the women-only congregation in which female preachers recite extremist and intolerant beliefs towards homosexuality and other religions. The follow-up documentary was not reacted to in the same emotive way.

For six months, Russell Sharp went undercover as a soldier undergoing basic training at the Infantry Training Centre at the Gatterick Garrison in Yorkshire to investigate bullying in the British Army. The backdrop to this was the Deepcut inquiry (2006), which was a government review of the circumstances surrounding the deaths – suspected suicides – of four soldiers at Princess Royal Barracks, Deepcut, between 1995 and 2002. *The Undercover Soldier* (2008) was screened by the BBC and did not show any filmed evidence of ill treatment, although Sharp personally claimed to have witnessed several incidents of bullying himself and heard of numerous accounts from other trainees. Sharp was discharged from the army and was not found out, despite coming close to his cover being blown. The documentary led to the suspension of five instructors, although the BBC was widely criticized by serving soldiers for the bias and sensationalist nature of the investigation.

Gina Welch, in her book *In the Land of Believers: An Outsider's Extraordinary Journey into the Heart of the Evangelical Church* (2010), went undercover for two years, attending an evangelical Baptist church in Virginia, United States, for Christian conservatives. Welch, an atheist and also raised as a secular Jew, joins in with the worship rituals of the congregation devoutly, despite their homophobia and dogmatic pro-life politics. Welch discovers, to her surprise, that she appreciates their sense of community and generosity, but is uneasy with their prejudices. When she accompanies the church on a mission to Alaska to 'save' one hundred souls, she is overcome with guilt for deceiving people in what she describes as feeling 'toxic'. She begins to call friends anxiously for support and eventually quits the experiment, calling for more comprehension rather than vilification of extremist religious groups which have become important social movements in American society.

In *God in a Brothel: An Undercover Journey into Sex Trafficking and Rescue* (2011), a former New Zealand policeman Daniel Walker presents his four-year undercover investigation of the highly profitable global sex trafficking trade, from a mainly Christian interventionist stance. Various victims of sex slavery, mainly female children and young people, were rescued and various pimps were prosecuted. Walker posed as a sex tourist and predator himself and suffered emotional risk, physical danger and risked his marriage in such work, which he recounts in the book. Walker has since founded an organization to try to combat global sex trafficking.

Investigative journalism as a field is clearly highly fragmented and contested. For me, some forms of intimate journalism (Harrington, 1997, 2003) and ethnographic journalism (Cramer and McDevitt, 2004; Hermann, 2014) can offer social scientific covert research some robust lessons about ethical scenarios, deception and moral transgression. It is important to remember that much investigative journalism, unlike much social science, is subject to continuous review by legal teams, who are empowered to prevent publication, as well as the press having an expedient 'public interest' defence available to them, unlike most academic social scientists.

Debates around the social context of deception within journalism have been centred on notions of adequate justification (Elliott and Culver, 1992) and acceptable deception (Lee, 2004). Lee elegantly characterizes their dilemma as: 'lying to tell the truth' (2004: 97). The code of conduct from the National Union of Journalists (NUJ), covering UK and Irish members, which was established in 1936 and updated in 2011, makes relevant reading. Point five, from twelve principles, states: 'Obtains material by honest, straightforward and open means, with the exception of investigations that are both overwhelmingly in the public interest and which involve evidence that cannot be obtained by straightforward means' (https://www.nuj.org.uk/about/nuj-code/). Not all journalists are members of this organization and clearly it does not have a global remit but the sentiment of 'public interest' appears to be a common driving force in the journalistic community.

7.5 Visual ethnography

Visual methods in social research have been routinely used. Visual anthropology, visual sociology and the field of visual studies are distinctive fields that I will not attempt to review here. Various anthropological and sociological discussions over the years (Banks, 2001; Chaplin, 1994; Emmison and Smith, 2000; Harper, 1998; Prosser, 1998; Prosser et al., 2008; Rose, 2001; Ruby, 2000) have drawn attention to the importance of studying people's visual sense of space and place. Lee and Ingold elegantly note that: 'walking around is fundamental to the everyday practice of social life and too much anthropological fieldwork' (2006: 67). My specific interest and gaze here, as with the other sources of revival, is with the covert aspects of this field.

Various visual researchers (Feld and Basso, 1996; Ingold, 2000; Low and Lawrence-Zuniga, 2003; Pink, 2006, 2007b, 2008b) have drawn particular critical attention to how a visual ethnography of movement, routes and mobilities can reveal important insights into how urban places and spaces are constituted and contested in complex ways. Many of these contexts are public so covert methodology can become an intrinsic part of such a multi-layered gaze. Like the modern *flâneur*, who, drawing on the classical philosopher Walter Benjamin, 'seeks refuge in the crowd' (Benjamin, 1999: 21) and whose mobile gaze is drawn to 'the luster of the crowd' (Benjamin 1968: 193), it is a mobile methodology that is suited to various contemporary urban public environments.

The recent and very innovative developments in sensory ethnography (Pink, 2015) have some covert implications. What Pink (2010) has broadly referred to as an 'anthropology of the senses'. When Pink discusses 'walking with video' (2007b) as a creative anthropologic way to document memory, feelings, senses, visuals and emotional geography with participants in various public locations, it would be safe to assume that passers-by are not routinely asked for their consent to be recorded. More generally, the attempt to explore alternative data, including bodily movements, kinaesthetic understanding, audio-visual realms, memories, haptic and spatial environments, clearly opens up more spaces, moves and tactics, both witting and unwitting, for creative and imaginative covert research.

Also linked to this 'visual turn', and what Henny termed a 'more visual sociology' (1986: 1), is the democratization of documentation and information-sharing through social networking and new media. This is a complex field, which requires dedicated examination, but suffice it to say that covert practices are implicated in this.

The use of photographs in field research has long been used as a way of enhancing the research context and bringing an intimacy to the participants and their real-time settings (Becker, 1974). Thus, photo-documentation is not only data recording but a part of the reflexive imagination of the researcher. Clearly, much photo-documentation is done with consent, but certainly not all. With the saturated use of mobile phone technology, ubiquitous photography (Hand, 2012) is likely to become much more widespread, which is often expediently and quickly done without consent.

A good example of this is the increasing use of mobile phones to film and document prison life in the UK by prisoners without the consent of prison authorities. Ironically, such uploaded amateur selfies and short films have highlighted the problems of violence, drug abuse and congestion in modern prison culture and, following widespread media attention, the need for urgent reform. The Channel 4 documentary *The Secret Life of Prisons*, broadcast in November 2016, used such footage illegally taken by inmates inside jails across the country.

There has been an increase in the amount of researching using visual methodology and hence increasing ethical concerns about this being done in rather random and maybe even reckless ways in some cases. Prosser et al. (2008) argue that researchers need to be vigilant regarding their visual ethics. They state: 'At present applications to conduct empirical visual research are given a label "handle with care" by IRBs and ethics committees' (2008: 28–29). There are increasing opportunities in this field, in the internet age and with the YouTube generation, for a lot more covert games, moves and tactics.

7.6 Conclusions

There are adequate grounds to claim that there is a revival in covert research. The evidence comes from a variety of different sources, which are not incremental or integrated. With the increasing popularity of mixed methods research, it is conceivable that covert research could play a more complementary role in such an approach, rather than a purist one. However, such a revival does not constitute a paradigm shift and covert research should still remain a relatively niche position in the social sciences and a very fragmented field or diaspora.

7.7 Learning exercise

1. Do you agree that covert research is becoming more popular?

2. List the different fields in which this revival has emerged in order of what you consider to be the most important?

3. Will covert research become a more mainstream discipline in the social sciences or remain a niche field in the future?

8

CONCLUSIONS

8.1 Reflections, musings and troubles

These conclusions are more accurately a series of ongoing intellectual reflections, musings and further troubles that will not go away around the complex issues of deception. One of the key messages here is that important lessons can be learnt from covert research, which, in some cases, can echo and relate to the wider social research community. Covert research should, for me, be part of a routine methodological imagination and toolkit in the social sciences, not absent from it or difficult to locate. Moreover, for me, the craft of covert research is an artful business. Getting close to participants and not letting them get close to you in a sustained manner is an emotional and challenging endeavour.

From my archival dig and recovery of a submerged and very dispersed tradition, it appears to be that covert research is far more extensive and diverse than first anticipated. This is compounded by some rather sanitized research accounts, which underplay, gloss over and can deny any use of covert tactics and moves. Hilbert (1980) referred to covert participant observation as an 'unstudied phenomenon'. Although it has been studied more since then, it is still, for me, profoundly under-theorized. So, on closer inspection, what we have are 'varieties of covert research' using a 'continuum of deception'. What I have tried to resist is constructing an exotic, heroic and exaggerated view of covert research, which is crude and simplistic.

My intention was never to develop a prescriptive research guide or recipe manual of good and best practices on how to do covert research. Rather, my intention has been to compare and contrast different covert scenarios and covert conditions, to see what can be reflectively learnt as part of the development of a wider critical methodological imagination.

It is my contention that the history and direction of the social sciences would definitely not have been the same without covert research. The social science community has a typically ambivalent relationship to these, if you will, covert transgressors. Namely, a sort of love/hate one. There is a hesitation to celebrate them, yet a recognition of a need for them, even if only to play the expedient 'ethical sitting duck' and 'moral straw person'. Thus, these covert studies have for too long a period provided convenient case studies for ethicists and methodologists as examples of bad ethics, poor social research design and flawed fieldwork decision-making rather than being more instructively recognized and appreciated.

Moreover, because covert research, on closer inspection, is realistically a diverse continuum and rarely purist, it could become more common in mixed or multiple methods strategies of researchers. Some of the conventional methodological literatures crudely typify covert research as exclusively purist and hence ignore the large number of diverse semi-covert studies that exist. This, in turn, diminishes the complementary contribution that covert methodology has made to social research.

A more sensible way then to analyse covert research, as stated previously, is to view it as a complex continuum rather than as a fixed decision comprising a strictly polarized dichotomy between overt and covert. On close inspection, much of the inflated reactions to and controversies around covert research are often centred on a few extreme purist examples as belligerent transgressors. Indeed, much covert research role has been emergent and unwitting rather than deliberately planned. Namely, it has been conducted by drift rather than design. Moreover, much covert research typically involves gate-keeping arrangements with key informants in the field. Also, many ethnographers, within standard overt roles, have used what can broadly be referred to as concealment practices, such as eavesdropping, both wittingly and unwittingly, throughout their research.

Social scientists clearly do not operate in a vacuum. Their fieldwork actions are constrained and restrained by a set of ethical obligations and commitments which sensibly safeguard researchers, the public and the universities from hostile intrusive research. This book is not about crudely blaming or pointing the finger at ethical regimentation, but understanding the important and mediated role it plays in shaping research activity and in particular covert research.

Covert research, for me, can be a highly opportunistic strategy and tactic that makes sense when researching a range of public crowds, mobs and social movements. This is not the remit of this book, but what I am appealing to here is that such an arena, as well as others, is open to types of opportunistic bystander research where one can easily collect eavesdropped data and make public observations. Clearly, this is not without risks and must be sensibly executed, although obviously researchers cannot control all aspects of the research setting or the unintended consequences arising from it.

Why do covert research then? What is the motivation behind such a move? My choice to do covert research, as outlined previously, is neither a sensationalist nor romantic one. For me, doing covert research is an innovative and creative research strategy and choice. It is one way, and certainly not the only way, of getting closer to an intimate and nuanced understanding of the actors' perspective in various settings, free of the status restrictions and expectations of the overt academic research role. Undercover work can be a curious type of 'stranger' role, a distinct and different type of insider role.

A key question here is: Can this method gain the researcher something different? Where is the extra benefit? For me, it definitely can add value and provide a different layer. In terms of ethnographic intimacy or empathetic understanding, you can get closer to your subject. It is not to say that covert research is a panacea. It is not always appropriate or practical. Undertaking covert research is not a decision to be taken lightly or frivolously as it comes with ethical costs. However, to regard these ethical dilemmas as a set of methodological horrors to be hidden away or cast under the intellectual carpet is botched and erroneous. Rather, we should embrace the complexities of doing covert research as incitements not barriers.

Despite the assumption that covert research is utterly inappropriate and hence redundant when researching sensitive topics and vulnerable groups, such an approach can be appropriate in some settings. We need only look at Buckingham et al.'s *Living with the Dying* (1976) and Scheper-Hughes' *Parts Unknown: Undercover ethnography of the organs-trafficking underworld* (2004) as controversial but highly instructive covert examples. There are a range of other examples to draw on as regards sensitive topics. This is not to say that covert research becomes a *carte blanche* blanket application as it is not always appropriate or, in a very small amount of cases, legally allowed. Nevertheless, the envelope for covert research could be pushed further in appropriate ways in many more settings instead of being hurriedly closed.

Hopefully, the diverse cases considered in the covert diaspora display the importance of covert research as part of a standard methodological toolkit and normal repertoire, rather than necessarily being associated with exotica, extremity or transgression. On closer inspection, covert research has rarely caused significant harm to the participants. This is not to say that it is harm- and risk-free, but to say that the harm can be exaggerated. It is my contention that the method typically offends social scientific sensitivities rather than public norms. This is not an excuse to do antagonistic heroic or crude exposé and crusader research under the banner of covert research, but to open up imaginative and innovative ways of doing social research in a wider range of mundane settings.

Covert research has been and is still commonly accused of suffering from forms of partisanship, bias and 'going native'. To trade on Howard S. Becker's famous paper (1967), covert research has on the simple face of it 'taken a side', but this does not mean to say that covert researchers necessarily endorse the values and views of whatever side you have taken and has lost any critical commentary and reflective ability in doing so.

Erving Goffman's presidential address, 'The Interaction Order' (1982), at the American Sociological Association (ASA) was delivered months before he passed away. In the conclusions to his address, Goffman urges: 'There's nothing in the world we should trade for what we do have: the bent to sustain in regard to all elements of social life a spirit of unfettered, unsponsored inquiry' (1982: 17). I would like to feel that covert research is firmly part of that spirt of inquiry.

Linstead et al. (2014) stress that in researching what they call 'the dark side of organization', a range of methodologies must be considered. They argue that: 'Hidden, concealed, clandestine or sensitive work poses a range of challenges to researchers who need to avail themselves of various direct, indirect and even covert methods in order to pursue their inquiries effectively' (2014: 177).

For me, much covert research is a particular form of emotion work both in carrying out a demanding role and in writing up, and sometimes not disclosing, sensitive data and guilty knowledge. Van Maanen argues that 'convincing ethnography will always be something of a mess, a mystery, and a miracle' (2010: 251). For me, covert ethnography has a role to play in a 'convincing ethnography'.

For me, in my covert case study of bouncers, I genuinely felt that I had gained an enhanced and more intimate understanding of being a bouncer as a lived and a sensory experience by covert means that I could not have achieved overtly. That is not to say that you cannot study bouncers overtly, which has been successfully done in the field. Obviously, I was still a temporary tourist in that world and my entitlement had parameters. I have tried to display the emotional and demanding nature of doing such covert work, under what I described as 'sub aqua ethnography' (Calvey, 2000), and the identity imprint that it had on me for a lengthy period of time after the study had finished. I still sanitized out some details from my experience of 'being there' (Geertz, 1988) and briefly 'walking in their shoes'.

I hope to have avoided presenting bouncers, to trade on the famous Alvin Gouldner (1968) phrase, as part of a 'zoo keeping' study. I hope my temporary yet lived experience as one has not turned them into 'exotic subcultural others' as academic narrative can so often do. Managing my 'secret self' was a key part of my study but hopefully that did not descend into a narcissistic self-obsession.

What I have attempted to do in my covert ethnography of bouncing was to present my version of an 'autoethnographic portrait' (Rambo, 2005), which has partly been about managing guilt syndromes, emotional discomfort, witnessing violence and sustaining deliberate deception. Covert research is clearly not to everyone's taste, but the commitment is to fairly explore different, not better, ways of constructing narratives. I share some sensibilities with Ronai as she accurately reflects:

> In my attempt at artful sociology, emotional sociology, and sociological introspection, my goal was to help the reader connect my experience with their own. By discussing lived emotional experience, readers are confronted with the things they have in common with the author and they are less likely to dismiss the situations of others as freakish and not their concern. (1997: 427–428)

Rich social research is deeply artful in general terms but the covert role is particularly demanding. Passing in some settings seems far closer to method acting, which most students are not ordinarily versed in. Covert research seems an extreme and skilled version of passing; it is not mysterious. Some researchers have an appetite and taste for it and others do not. I hope that this book has exposed and examined the covert craft and condition in a variety of settings and contexts. What we often have with covert research are complex 'ethical algorithms' that are difficult to work out, plan for and plot in any exact way.

As no study can be exhaustive or definitive and has to be abandoned at some point, regrettably, some significant covert studies will have been inevitably overlooked or, worse still, omitted. As stated previously, my demanding archival search has involved both closer readings of familiar studies and tropes and completely new discoveries of unknown studies. As there appears to be little cross-fertilization of covert work across the social science family of disciplines, this book goes some small way to recognizing, appreciating and sharing that covert corpus. Obviously, my readings of these covert studies are not privileged, but merely particular.

For me, covert work forms a central and robust part of the future of ethnography, in various guises. It should not be resigned to the intellectual dustbin of lost footnotes and cursory comments. Moreover, it should be given a more central and standard position in the introductory social research textbooks rather than trivialized as exotic or extreme. This serves to over-simplify and truncate its history and breadth.

The various ethical dilemmas that I managed in doing covert research on bouncers displays a robust type of moral imagination (Johnson, 1985; Kiragu and

Warrington, 2013; Moberg and Seabright, 2000) rather than necessarily testifying to the absence of one. This moral imagination is a way of both reflecting and acting on the ethical complexities of risk, harm, consequence and implication in the field in real time as it occurs. After all, managing ethics is a situated doing and not just a textbook exercise. The crude view of covert research would be that covert researchers are somewhat ethically immune and lack sensitivity when the exact opposite can be the case. What I hope to have shown, when using deception, is the complexity of ethical and moral dilemmas and the artfulness of their situated management. It is a sort of ethical algorithm, a calculus of balances between harm, risk and consequence in fieldwork choices and tactics. Naturally, there are legalities and sensitivities within which covert research should operate sensibly, as any methodology should. Hopefully, I have dispelled the overly heroic and romanticized picture of the covert researcher who feels that 'anything goes'.

The comments of Harold Garfinkel, the originator of ethnomethodology, resonate when he reflects on the complexity of social life and the clumsy tendencies of analysis:

> The attempt to approximate some sort of precision in the study of human conduct is not unlike the task of swatting flies with a hammer. Apart from the fact that one must make the tenuous assumption that the fly will remain still, one must be willing to settle for a low batting average while facing the prospect of leaving the room in a shambles when the game is done. (2005: 99)

Clearly, covert research does not hold all the answers but we need a broad range of methodological strategies in our arsenal to cope sensibly with the complexity of real-world research.

I do not offer covert research as a form of methodological panacea, which would be naïve and erroneous. The covert researcher is not removed from bias, partisanship and fetish. It is a rich method of investigation but has obvious ethical problems as well suffering from instigation tactics. Problems of interpretation and understanding are not removed by taking a covert position. It is one method among many, which attempts to make sense of complex phenomena. As Van Dongen and Fainzang sensibly caution, 'just as distance is not a guarantee of objectivity, familiarity is not knowledge' (1998: 247).

For me, the parameters of covert research need to be further explored and, when appropriate, pushed. If I want to explore a range of sensitive topics then covert research should not be quickly dismissed. The list of topics is endless when you think about the application of covert research seriously. Put rather bluntly, the social science community is missing a trick. Your own biographical, occupational and cultural backyards can become sites of and resources for covert study.

Interesting opportunities can and do quickly evolve, without the need for formal ethical approval to stifle it. I would like to stress here that this is not to say that 'anything goes' as we need to develop sensible and appropriate strategies to research vulnerable groups and sensitive topics, but this should not inevitably and necessarily exclude and outcast covert research as a 'methodological pariah'.

Tillman-Healy (2001, 2003) argues for friendship as a method of qualitative inquiry and a kind of fieldwork site, where the data are naturally occurring. She views this method as being framed within an 'ethic of friendship', with clear informed consent. I agree with this innovative move as friendship can be a rich source of topics and data and many covert accounts depend on forms of fake and passing friendship. However, vitally, for me, friendship research would not always strictly require informed consent and could become more blurred in practice.

For me, covert research clearly carries on Weber's classical spirit of *Verstehen* but in a different way. It disrupts our traditional ways of 'telling about society' (Becker, 2007) and should become a more standard 'trick of the trade' (Becker, 1998). Research governance needs to be relaxed, not removed, for in-depth covert research into a range of topics. What I call the 'textbook mentality' needs to recognize and appreciate the messy reality of situated research and the imaginative role that covert research can play in that messy research world. Put more basically, covert research is not a horror to be hidden away and swept under the methodological carpet.

I genuinely feel that we need to be more creative and imaginative in how we think about storytelling and storytellers. Covert research can be part of that creative stimulus. Gordon reminds us that sociology has a privileged mandate for conjuring up social life but: 'we have more to learn about how to conjure in an evocative and compelling way' (2008: 22). Neither do I present covert research as a species of newness, creativity or innovation, the latest narrative fad for you to be dazzled by. I hope that I have demonstrated that covert research has historical roots and is concerned with significant methodological and analytical troubles that will not easily go away.

Van Den Hoonaard concludes his useful book on ethics with some cautionary sentiments. He states:

> Ethnographic fieldwork is fleeing into the hands of journalists who have largely remained free of the ethics-review constraints that researchers commonly face. Undercover police and security personnel now engage in the kinds of research previously reserved for social researchers. (2011: 288)

The use of covert research has different and dispersed purposes for journalists and practitioners. For me, covert research, in part, still needs to be rehabilitated within the social sciences and, if you will, recovered for the next generation of researchers. Covert research has been hijacked by investigative journalism, which, with less ethical angst and playing a different narrative game, typically covers the interesting covert ground much quicker than social science could ever do. Namely, it is quick and dirty ethnography. Despite the differences, much more cross-fertilization should take place between the two. The spirit of investigative journalists should be applauded.

Covert research needs to come out of its stigmatized methodological closet and become a much more routine and normalized part of the creative imagination of the social scientist. It is not to say that the marginal status of covert research is a unified matter with all criticisms and critics sharing the same universalistic type of rejection in the social sciences. More realistically, as with most debates, it is a complex continuum with some being sympathetic and others being repulsed. This book is not intended to be definitive or exhaustive. However, I do hope this study is reasonably authoritative and provides a useful resource for further investigations of covert research.

I hope that I have provided a thoughtful account of covert research that incites further recoveries of covert gems and voices in the social sciences that I have omitted, or indeed add new dimensions and complexities to the familiar ones I have discussed. Although I do not expect covert research to become the sociological mainstream, I hope that the intellectual pariah label has become more difficult to quickly and crudely attach. Hopefully covert research has been demystified, and it becomes part of the more standard methodological repertoire of the social scientist, if appropriate. My goal is not to crudely popularize covert research but to give it a fairer reading.

This book is not a new qualitative manifesto or, worse still, a covert call to arms, but more a taking stock and rehabilitation of a submerged and vibrant covert tradition. I do not wish to reify covert research in any way as it is not always appropriate and has clear ethical costs and consequences. Having said that, covert research should be clearly recognized and appreciated as a type of inventive method (Lury and Wakeford, 2012), along with others. It has the capacity to be an 'irritant', to borrow Lury and Wakeford's useful critical term. Moreover, it has the capacity to disrupt the somewhat stifling mentality on ethicality and challenge the pervasive moralism (Hammersley and Traianou, 2012) in research ethics. Part of this disruption, for me, would be in giving covert research a fairer reading. I am calling here for types of passionate covert immersion and warts-and-all confessionals that are not led by romanticism or sensationalism, but a sustained desire to engage with social actors and their stories in different but authentic ways.

Atkinson characterizes his recent book, *For Ethnography*, as 'something of a manifesto, a personal statement of commitment and of enthusiasm' (2015: 189).

I have a similar 'for covert research' sentiment. This is not on any sentimentality grounds but on the basis that some, not all, covert work genuinely stands out. For Atkinson 'well-crafted' ethnographies will endure and stand the test of time. Clearly, ethnographic quality varies, as Atkinson stresses, but for me, some covert research has a secure place in the sociological craft.

Of course, fully embracing a covert position, for some, is a step too far and will be resisted as a methodological taboo and offence. Such transgression and trespassing has no part in their intellectual landscape. My intention is not to convert people but give covert research a fairer reading. What I hopefully have presented in the book is the richness of the covert corpus. In doing this, I hope I have also revealed a diverse collection of complex ethical scenarios resulting from a covert stance rather than a simple set of methodological recipes and crude step-by-step guides. My aim was to expose and explore the covert condition and its particular sensibility. Covert research will probably still remain a niche position in social research, but hopefully not a maverick, exotic and demonized one.

I want this book, in some small way, to recover some key covert research from its submerged and index/footnote status. It has been somewhat of an archival monster, a demanding yet worthwhile task in historically charting and mapping the covert diaspora. Various studies have emerged, beyond the usual suspects conventionally referred to in the literatures. These studies deserve both recovery and recognition. Indeed, I have been personally surprised by the amount and diversity of the covert corpus and its legacy in the social science community, and this has been a rewarding intellectual re-education for me.

Hopefully, this book acts as a disruptive incitement for scholars and students to take covert research more seriously. I hope that the recovery and, to a certain extent, revival of covert research will lead to a greater recognition and appreciation of its historical role in shaping social scientific disciplines. For me, covert research deserves both a clearer and stronger voice in the future.

Above all, undertaking this project has reawakened my sense of curiosity and wonderment in the wealth and richness of the social world. It has been a rich and at times demanding covert sociological odyssey for me. I hope the book, in some modest ways, has the same effect on you, the reader.

8.2 Learning exercise

Below are some key questions that you might want to reflect on and explore. When you began reading this book, you might have held some strong and possibly emotive 'gut reactions' and 'armchair views' to covert research. That is valid. Now you have finished reading the book and digested its arguments, this exercise is effectively a sort of reflective 'before and after' quiz.

1. Why do covert research?

2. Can and should it be justified?

3. Are covert researchers unethical? Do they self-regulate their ethical conduct?

4. Would you use eavesdropping as a technique to gain data in a study?

5. Would you whistleblow in an organization you worked in, if you felt it was necessary?

6. Should covert researchers be more ethically regulated?

7. What are the limits and parameters of covert research?

8. Do the ends justify the means in social research?

9. Why has covert research been so maligned and demonized?

10. What range of interesting topics has covert research covered?

11. Has covert research been influential?

12. Is there a robust place for covert research in the contemporary social science community?

BIBLIOGRAPHY

Abrams, F. (2002) *Below the Breadline: Living on the Minimum Wage*. London: Profile Books.

Addington, J. (2012) 'Introduction to early intervention in first episode psychosis', in K. M. Boydell and H. Bruce Ferguson (eds), *Hearing Voices: Qualitative Inquiry in Early Psychosis*. Waterloo, Ontario: Wilfred Laurier Press. pp. 1–9.

Adler, P. A. (1985) *Wheeling and Dealing: An Ethnography of an Upper-level Drug Dealing and Smuggling Community*. New York: Columbia University Press.

Adler, P. and Adler, P. A. (1987) *Membership Roles in Field Research*. Thousand Oaks, CA: Sage.

Adler, P. and Adler, P. A (1998) 'Foreword: moving backward', in F. Ferrell and M. S. Hamm (eds), *Ethnography at the Edge: Crime, Deviance and Field Research*. Boston, MA: Northeastern University Press. pp. xii–xvi.

Adler, P. and Adler, P. A. (1999) 'Book review of Chapkis, Wendy (1997) *Live Sex Acts: Women Performing Erotic Labor.* New York: Routledge.

Adriaenssens, S. and Hendrickx, J. (2011) 'Street-level informal economic activities: estimating the yield of begging in Brussels', *Urban Studies*, 48(1): 23–40.

Agar, Michael H. (1980) *The Professional Stranger: An Informal Introduction to Ethnography*. New York: Academic Press.

Albert, S. (2011) 'Spontaneous pleasure: sex between women in public places', *Sexualities*, 14(6): 669–680.

Allan, S., Sonwalkar, P. and Carter, C. (2007) 'Bearing witness: Citizen journalism and human rights issues', *Globalisation, Societies and Education*, 5(3): 373–389.

Allan, S. and Thorsen, E. (eds) (2009) *Citizen Journalism: Global Perspectives*. New York: Peter Lang.

Alpert, G. P. and Noble, J. J. (2009) 'Lies, true lies, and conscious deception: police officers and the truth', *Police Quarterly*, 12(2): 237–254.

Alvesson, M. (2003) 'Methodology for close-up studies: struggling with closeness and closure', *Higher Education*, 46(2): 167–193.

Analoui, F. (1995) 'Workplace sabotage: its styles, motives and management', *Journal of Management Development*, 14(7): 48–65.

Anderson, L. (2006) 'Analytic autoethnography', *Journal of Contemporary Ethnography*, 35(4): 373–395.

Anderson, N. (1923/1961) *The Hobo: The Sociology of the Homeless Man*. Chicago, IL: University of Chicago Press (reprint, originally published in 1923).

Andriotis, K. (2010) 'Heterotopic erotic oases: the public nude beach experience', *Annals of Tourism Research*, 37(4): 1076–1096.

Anteby, M. (2010) 'Markets, morals, and practices of trade: jurisdictional disputes in the US commerce in cadavers', *Administrative Science Quarterly*, 55(4): 606–638.

Arendt, H. (1963) *Eichmann in Jerusalem: A Report on the Banality of Evil.* New York: Penguin.

Armstrong, G. (1998) *Football Hooligans: Knowing the Score.* Oxford: Berg.

Arquilla, J. and Ronfeldt, D. (eds) (2001) *Networks and Netwars.* Santa Monica, CA: Rand.

ASA (1999) *Ethical Guidelines for Good Research Practice.* London: Association of Social Anthropologists of the UK and the Commonwealth. www.theasa.org/

Asal, V. and Rethemeyer, R. (2006) 'Researching terrorist networks', *Journal of Security Education*, 1(4): 65–74.

Asch, S. E. (1955) 'Opinions and social pressure', *Scientific American*, 193(5): 31–35.

Ashford, C. (2009) 'Queer theory, cyber-ethnographies and researching online sex environments', *Information & Communications Technology Law*, 18(3): 297–314.

Ashforth, B. E. and Kreiner, G. E. (1999) '"How can you do it?": Dirty work and the challenge of constructing a positive identity', *Academy of Management Review*, 24(3): 413–434.

Ashton, P. (2013) *Undercover.* MondayBooks.Com.

Association of Internet Researchers (http://aoir.org/ethics/)

Atkinson, P. A. (1981) *The Clinical Experience:The Construction and Reconstruction of Medical Reality.* Farnborough: Gower.

Atkinson, P. A. (1990) *The Ethnographic Imagination: Textual Constructions of Reality.* London: Routledge.

Atkinson, P. A. (1997a) 'Narrative turn or blind alley?', *Qualitative Health Research*, 7(3): 325–344.

Atkinson, P. A. (1997b) *The Clinical Experience: The Construction and Reconstruction of Medical Reality.* Aldershot: Ashgate. 1st edition 1981.

Atkinson, P. A. (2006) 'Rescuing autoethnography', *Journal of Contemporary Ethnography*, 35(4): 400–404.

Atkinson, P. A. (2015) *For Ethnography.* London: Sage.

Atluri, T. (2009) 'Lighten up?! Humour, race and Da off colour joke of Ali G', *Media, Culture and Society*, 31(2): 197–214.

Aubenas, F. (2011) *The Night Cleaner.* Cambridge: Polity Press.

Ayres, T. C. and Treadwell, J. (2011) 'Bars, drugs and football thugs: alcohol, cocaine use and violence in the night-time economy among English football firms', *Criminology & Criminal Justice*, 12(1): 83–100.

Babbage, C. (1830) *Reflections on the Decline of Science in England, and on Some of its Causes.* London: Fellowes.

Babbie, E. (2004) 'Laud Humphreys and research ethics', *International Journal of Sociology and Social Policy*, 24(3/4/5): 12–19.

Back, L., Keith, M. and Solomos, J. (1996) 'The new modalities of racist culture: technology, race, and neo-fascism in the digital age', *Patterns of Prejudice*, 30(2): 3–28.

Bader, C. (1999) 'When prophecy passes unnoticed: new perspectives on failed prophecy', *Journal for the Scientific Study of Religion*, 38(1): 119–131.

Bailey, J. R. and Ford, C. M. (1994) 'Of methods and metaphors: theater and self-exploration in the laboratory', *Journal of Applied Behavioral Science*, 30(4): 381–396.

Bain, R. (1925) 'The Impersonal Confession and social research', *Journal of Applied Sociology*, 9: 356–361.

Bainbridge, W. S. (1997) *The Sociology of Religious Movements*. New York: Routledge.

Baker, W. and Faulkner, R. (1993) 'The social organisation of conspiracy: illegal networks in the heavy electric equipment industry', *American Sociological Review*, 58(6): 837–860.

Balch, R.W., Farnsworth, G. and Wilkins, S. (1983) 'When the bombs drop: reactions to disconfirmed prophecy in a millennial sect', *Sociological Perspective*, 26(2): 137–158.

Balch, R. W. and Taylor, D. (1977) 'Seekers and saucers: the role of the cultic milieu in joining a UFO cult', *American Behavioral Scientist*, 20(6): 839–860.

Banks, M. (2001) *Visual Methods in Social Research*.1st edn. London: Sage.

Banks, M. (2007) *Using Visual Data in Qualitative Research*. London: Sage.

Bannon, J. (2013) *Running with the Firm: My Double Life as an Undercover Hooligan*. London: Ebury Press.

Barnes, J. A. (1963) 'Some ethical problems in modern fieldwork', *British Journal of Sociology*, 14(2): 118–134.

Barnes, J. A. (1983) 'Lying: a sociological view', *Australian Journal of Forensic Sciences*, 15(4): 152–158.

Barnes, J. A. (1994) *A Pack of Lies: Towards a Sociology of Lying*. Cambridge: Cambridge University Press.

Barratt, M. J. and Lenton, S. (2010) 'Beyond recruitment? Participatory research with people who use drugs', *International Journal of Internet Research Ethics*, 3(1): 69–86.

Barratt, R. (2004) *Doing the Doors: A Life on the Door*. London: Milo Books.

Barrera, D. and Simpson, B. (2012) 'Much ado about deception: consequences of deceiving research participants in the social sciences', *Sociological Methods & Research*, 41(3): 383–413.

Barton, B. (2007) 'Managing the toll of stripping: boundary setting among exotic dancers', *Journal of Contemporary Ethnography*, 36(5): 571–596.

Batchelor, S. (2009) 'Girls, gangs and violence: assessing the evidence', *Probation Journal*, 56(4): 399–414.

Batson, C. D., Cochran, P. J., Biederman, M. F., Blosser, J. L., Ryan, M. J. and Vogt, B. (1978) 'Failure to help when in a hurry: callousness or conflict', *Personality and Social Psychology Bulletin*, 40(1): 97–101.

Batson, D. and Ventis, L. (1982) *The Religious Experience: A Social Psychological Perspective*. New York: Oxford University Press.

Baumrind, D. (1964) 'Some thoughts on ethics of research: after reading Milgram's Behavioral Study of Obedience', *American Psychologist*, 19(6): 421–423.

Beah, I. (2007) *A Long Way Gone: Memoirs of a Boy Soldier*. New York: Farrar, Straus and Giroux.

Bearman, P. (2005) *Doormen*. Chicago, IL: University of Chicago Press.

Becker, H. S. (1951) 'The professional dance musician and his audience', *American Journal of Sociology*, 57(2): 136–144.

Becker, H. S. (1953) 'Becoming a marijuana user', *American Journal of Sociology*, 59(3): 235–242.

Becker, H. S. (1963) *Outsiders: Studies in the Sociology of Deviance*. New York: Free Press.

Becker, H. S. (1967) 'Whose side are we on?', *Social Problems*, 14(3): 239–247.

Becker, H. S. (1974) 'Photography and sociology', *Studies in the Anthropology of Visual Communication*, 1(1): 3–26.

Becker, H. S. (1998) *Tricks of the Trade: How to Think about Your Research While You're Doing it*. Chicago, IL: University of Chicago Press.

Becker, H. S. (2003) 'The politics of presentation: Goffman and total institutions', *Symbolic Interaction*, 26(4): 659–669.

Becker, H. S. (2007) *Telling about Society*. Chicago, IL: University of Chicago Press.

Beecher, H. K. (1955) 'The powerful placebo', *Journal of the American Medical Association*, 159(17): 1602–1606

Bell, D. (2001) 'Book review of *Public Sex/Gay Place* by W. L. Leap', *Progress in Human Geography*, 25(1): 132–133.

Belshaw, C. (2010) 'Response', *Nursing Ethics*, 17(1): 133–134.

Benjamin, W. (1968) *Illuminations: Essays and Reflections*. Edited by Hannah Arendt and translated by Harry Zohn. New York: Schocken.

Benjamin, W. (1999) *The Arcades Project*. Translated by H. Eiland and K. McLaughlin. Cambridge, MA: Harvard University Press.

Berkowitz, D. (2006) 'Consuming eroticism: gender performances and presentations in pornographic establishments', *Journal of Contemporary Ethnography*, 35(5): 583–606.

Berkun, M. M., Bialek, H. M., Kern, R. P. and Yagi, K. (1962) 'Experimental studies of stress in men', *Psychological Monographs*, 76, No.15.

Bettelheim, B. (1943) 'Individual and mass behaviour in extreme situations', *Journal of Abnormal and Social Psychology*, 38(4): 417–452.

Bettelheim, B. (1960) *The Informed Heart*. New York: Free Press.

Bhardwa, B. (2013) 'Alone, Asian and female: the unspoken challenges of conducting fieldwork in dance settings', *Dancecult: Journal of Electronic Dance Music*, 5(1): 39–60.

Bittner, E. (1973) 'Objectivity and realism in sociology', in G. Psathas (ed.), *Phenomenological Sociology*. New York: Wiley. pp. 109–125.

Blackman, S. (2007) 'Hidden ethnography: crossing emotional borders in qualitative accounts of young people's lives', *Sociology*, 41(4): 699–716.

Blass, T. (2002) 'The man who shocked the world', *Psychology Today*, 35(2): 68–74.

Blass, T. (2004) *The Man Who Shocked the World: The Life and Legacy of Stanley Milgram*. London: Basic Books.

Blevins, K. R. and Holt, T. J. (2009) 'Examining the virtual subculture of Johns', *Journal of Contemporary Ethnography*, 38(5): 619–648.

Bloome, D., Sheridan, D. and Street, B. (1993) *Reading Mass-Observation Writing: Theoretical and Methodological Issues in Researching the Mass-Observation Archive*. Brighton: University of Sussex.

Bloor, M. and Ward, F. (2006) *Keywords in Qualitative Methods: A Vocabulary of Research Concepts*. London: Sage.

Bly, N. (1888) *Six Months in Mexico*. New York: American Publishers.

Bly, N. (1887) *Ten Days in a Mad-House*, Published with *'Trying to Be as Servant' and 'Nellie Bly as a White Slave'*. New York: Ian L. Munro Publishers.

Boas, F. (1919) 'Scientists as Spies', *The Nation*, 20 December, New York: Joseph H. Richards Publishers.

Bochner, P. and Ellis, C. (eds) (2002) *Ethnographically Speaking: Autoethnography, Literature and Aesthetics*. Walnut Creek: Alta Mira Press.

Bok, S. (1978) *Lying: Moral Choice in Public and Private Life*. New York: Pantheon Books.

Bok, S. (1982) *Secrets: On the Ethics of Concealment and Revelation*. New York: Pantheon Books.

Bok, S. (1982) 'Freedom and risk', in M. Bulmer (ed.), *Social Research Ethics: An Examination of the Merits of Covert Participant Observation*. London: Macmillan. pp. 166–184.

Bone, J. (2006) 'The longest day: flexible contracts, performance-related pay and risk shifting in the UK direct selling sector', *Work, Employment & Society*, 20(1): 109–127.

Bosk, C. L. and De Vries, R. G. (2004) 'Bureaucracies of mass deception: Institutional Review Boards and the ethics of ethnographic research', *ANNALS of the American Academy of Political and Social Science*, 595: 249–263.

Bourdieu, P. (1977) *Outline of a Theory of Practice*. Cambridge: Cambridge University Press.

Bourdieu, P. (1983) 'Erving Goffman: discoverer of the infinitely small', *Theory, Culture & Society*, 2(1): 112–113.

Bourdieu, P. (1984) *Distinction: A Social Critique of the Judgement of Taste*. London: Routledge.

Bourdieu, P. (1990) *The Logic of Practice*. Stanford, CA: Stanford University Press.

Bowie, D. and Chang, J. C. (2005) 'Tourist satisfaction: a view from a mixed international guided package tour', *Journal of Vacation Marketing*, 11(4): 303–322.

Brandt, A. (1978) 'Racism and research: the case of the Tuskagee syphilis study', *Hastings Centre Report*, 8(6): 21–29.

Brannan, M. (2016) 'Power, corruption and lies: Mis-selling and the production of culture in financial services', *Human Relations* (Online First 2 November 2016), pp 1–27.

Brannick, T. and Coghlan, D. (2007) 'In defense of being "native": the case for insider academic research', *Organizational Research Methods*, 10(1): 59–74.

Brannigan, A. (2004) *The Rise and Fall of Social Psychology: The Use and Misuse of the Experimental Method*. New York: Aldine de Gruyter.

Brannigan, A. (2009) 'The defense of situationalism in the age of Abu Ghraib', *Theory and Psychology*, 19(5): 698–704.

Brannigan, A., Nicholson, I. and Cherry, F. (2015) 'Introduction to the special issue: Unplugging the Milgram machine', *Theory & Psychology*, 25(5): 551–563.

Brewer, J. D. (1993) 'Sensitivity as a problem in field research: a study of routine policing in Northern Ireland', in C. M. Renzetti and R. M. Lee (eds), *Researching Sensitive Topics*. Newbury Park, CA: Sage. pp. 125–145.

Brewster, Z. (2003) 'Behavioural and interactional patrons: tipping techniques and club attendance', *Deviant Behaviour: An Interdisciplinary Journal*, 24(3): 221–243.

Briggs, D. (2013) *Deviance and Risk on Holidays: An Ethnography of British Tourists in Ibiza*. London: Palgrave Macmillan.

Briggs, D. and Ellis, A. (2016) 'The Last Night of Freedom: Consumerism, Deviance and the "Stag Party"', *Deviant Behavior*, Published Online 1 November 2016.

British Psychological Society (2013) *Ethics Guidelines for Internet-mediated Research*. Leicester: BPS. INF206/1.2013.

Broccatelli, C., Everett, M. and Koshinen, J. (2016) 'Temporal dynamics in covert networks', *Methodological Innovations*, 9: 1–14.

Brock, T. C. and Guidice, G. D. (1963) 'Stealing and temporal orientation', *Journal of Abnormal and Social Psychology*, 66(1): 91–94.

Brotsky, S. and Giles, D. (2007) 'Inside the "Pro-ana" community: a covert online participant observation', *Eating Disorders: The Journal of Treatment and Prevention*, 15(2): 93–109.

Brown, K. M. (1986) 'Establishing difference: culture, 'race', ethnicity and the production of ideology', *Journal of Sociology*, 22(2): 175–186.

Bryman, A. (2008) *Social Research Methods* (3rd edn). Oxford: Oxford University Press (1st edn, 2001).

BSA (2002) *Statement of Ethical Practice for the British Sociological Association*. Durham: British Sociological Association, www.britsoc.co.uk/the-bsa/equality/statement-of-ethical-practice.aspx.

Buchanan, E. A. (ed.) (2004) *Readings in Virtual Research Ethics*. Hershey, PA: Information Science Publishing.

Buckingham, R. W., Lack, S. A., Mount, B. M. and MacLean, L. D. (1976) 'Living with the dying: use of the technique of participant observation', *Canadian Medical Association Journal*, 115 (18 December): 1211–1215.

Buckle, A. and Farrington, D. P. (1984) 'An observational study of shoplifting', *British Journal of Criminology*, 24(1): 63–73.

Buckle, A. and Farrington, D. P. (1994) 'Measuring shoplifting by systematic observation: a replication study', *Psychology, Crime & Law*, 1(2): 133–141.

Budiani, D. (2007) 'Facilitating organ transplants in Egypt: an analysis of doctor's discourse', *Body & Society*, 13(3): 125–149.

Buford, B. (1991) *Among the Thugs*. London: Secker and Warburg.

Bulmer, M. (1982a) 'When is disguise justified? Alternatives to covert participation observation', *Qualitative Sociology*, 5(4): 251–264.

Bulmer, M. (1982b) 'Are pseudo-patient studies justified?', *Journal of Medical Ethics*, 8(2): 65–71.

Bulmer, M. (1982c) 'Ethical problems in social research: the case of covert participant observation', in M. Bulmer (ed.), *Social Research Ethics: An Examination of the Merits of Covert Participant Observation*. London: Macmillan. pp. 3–14.

Bulmer, M. (1982d) 'The merits and demands of covert participant observation', in M. Bulmer (ed.), *Social Research Ethics: An Examination of the Merits of Covert Participant Observation*. London: Macmillan. pp. 217–251.

Bulmer, M. (1983) 'The methodology of the taxi-dance hall: an early account of Chicago ethnography from the 1920s', *Journal of Contemporary Ethnography*, 12(1): 95–120.

Bulmer, M. (1984) *The Chicago School of Sociology*. Chicago, IL: University of Chicago Press.

Burger, J. M. (2009) 'Replicating Milgram: would people still obey today?', *American Psychologist*, 64(1): 1–11.

Burgess, R. G. (1983) *Experiencing Comprehensive Education: A Study of Bishop McGregor School*. London: Methuen.

Buroway, M. (1979) *Manufacturing Consent*. Chicago, IL: Chicago University Press.

Buzard, J. (2003) 'On AutoEthnographic Authority', *The Yale Journal of Criticism*, 16(1): 61–91.

Cahn, W. (1973) 'Report on the Nassau County Jail', *Crime & Delinquency*, 19(1): 1–14.

Calder, A. (1995) 'Mass-Observation 1937–49', in M. Bulmer (ed.), *Essays on the History of British Sociological Research*. Cambridge: Cambridge University Press. pp. 121–136.

Calder, J. D. (1999) *Intelligence, Espionage and Related Topics: An Annotated Bibliography of Serial, Journal, and Magazine Scholarship, 1844–1998*. Westport, CT: Greenwood Press.

Calvert, C. (2000) *Voyeur Nation: Media, Privacy and Peering in Modern Culture*. Boulder, Colorado: Westview Press.

Calvey, D. (2000) 'Getting on the door and staying there: a covert participant observational study of bouncers', in G. Lee-Treweek and S. Linkogle (eds), *Danger in the Field: Risk and Ethics in Social Research*. London: Routledge. pp 43–60.

Calvey, D. (2008) 'The art and politics of covert research: doing "situated ethics" in the field', *Sociology*, 42(5): 905–918.

Calvey, D. (2013) 'Covert ethnography in criminology: a submerged yet creative tradition in criminology', *Current Issues in Criminal Justice*, 25(1): 541–550.

Campbell, H. (1980) 'Rastafari: culture of resistance', *Race and Class*, 22(1): 1–22.

Carnahan, T. and McFarland, S. (2007) 'Revisiting the Stanford Prison Experiment: could participant self-selection have led to the cruelty?', *Personality and Social Psychology Bulletin*, 33(5): 603–614.

Carey, J. T. (1972) 'Problems of access and risk in observing drug scenes', in J. D. Douglas (ed.), *Research on Deviance*. New York: Random House. pp. 71–92.

Carley, K. (2006) 'Destabilization of covert networks', *Computational and Mathematical Organization Theory*, 12(1): 51–66.

Carson, B. (2005) *Show No Fear: A Bouncer's Diary*. London: Athena Press.

Carusi, A. and Jirotka, M. (2009) 'From data archive to ethical labyrinth', *Qualitative Research*, 9(3): 285–298.

Caudhill, W., Redlich, F. C., Gilmore, H. R. and Brody, E. B. (1952) 'Social structure and interaction processes on a psychiatric ward', *American Journal of Orthopsychiatry*, 22(2): 314–334.

Caudhill, W. (1958) *The Psychiatric Hospital as a Small Society*. Cambridge, MA: Harvard University Press.

Cavan, S. (1966) *Liquor Licence: An Ethnography of Bar Behaviour.* Chicago, IL: Aldine.

Chambliss, W. J. (1975) 'On the paucity of original research on organized crime', *American Sociologist*, 10(1): 36–39.

Chang, J. C. (2009) 'Taiwanese tourists' perceptions of service quality on outbound guided package tours: a qualitative examination of the SERVQUAL dimensions', *Journal of Vacation Marketing*, 15(2): 165–178.

Chapkis, W. (1997) *Live Sex Acts: Women Performing Erotic Labor.* New York: Routledge.

Chapkis, W. (2010) 'Productive tensions: ethnographic engagement, complexity, and contradiction', *Journal of Contemporary Ethnography*, 39(5): 483–497.

Chaplin, E. (1994) *Sociology and Visual Representation*. London: Routledge.

Charmaz, K. (2004) 'Premises, principles, and practices in qualitative research: revisiting the foundations', *Qualitative Health Research*, 14(7): 976–993.

Charmaz, K. and Olesen, V. (1997) 'Ethnographic research in medical sociology: its foci and distinctive contributions', *Sociological Methods & Research*, 25(4): 452–494.

Charters, S., Fountain, J. and Fish, N. (2009) 'You felt like lingering: experiencing "real" service at the winery tasting rooms', *Journal of Travel Research*, 48(1): 122–134.

Christensen, L. (1988) 'Deception in psychological research: when is its use justified?', *Personality and Social Psychology Bulletin*, 14(4): 664–675.

Clare, A. (1976) *Psychiatry in Dissent: Controversial Issues in Thought and Practice*. London: Tavistock.

Clarke, A. (2015) 'Governing the dieting self: conducting weight-loss via the internet', *Journal of Sociology*, 51(3): 657–673.

Clarke, L. (1996) 'Participant observation in a secure unit: care, conflict and control', *Nursing Times Research*, 1(6): 431–440.

Clarke, L. (2004) 'Real-world ethics and nursing research: a response to Martin Johnson', *Nursing Times Research*, 9(5): 389–391.

Clawson, M. A. (1989) *Constructing Brotherhood: Class, Gender and Fraternalism*. Princeton, NJ: Princeton University Press.

Coffey, A. (1999) *The Ethnographic Self: Fieldwork and the Representation of Identity.* London: Sage.

Cohen, L. (2011) 'Migrant supplementarity: remaking biological relatedness in Chinese military and Indian five-star hospitals', *Body & Society*, 17(2–3): 31–54.

Cohen-Almagor, R. (2014) 'After Leveson: recommendations for instituting the public and Press Council', *The International Journal of Press/Politics*, 19(2): 202–225.

Coleman, R. (2010) 'Dieting temporalities: interaction, agency and the measure of online weight watching', *Time & Society*, 19(2): 265–285.

Collins, R. (2009) 'How organized is international crime?' *Contemporary Sociology*, 38(6): 516–521.

Colosi, R. (2010a) 'A return to the Chicago school? From the "subculture" of taxi dancers to the contemporary lap dancer', *Journal of Youth Studies*, 13(1): 1–16.

Colosi, R. (2010b) *Dirty Dancing? An Ethnography of Lap-Dancing*. Abingdon: Willan Publishing.

Corbett, D. (2003) *Both Sides of the Fence: A Life Undercover*. Edinburgh: Mainstream Publishing.

Corrigan, O. (2003) 'Empty ethics: the problem with informed consent', *Sociology of Health and Illness*, 25(3): 769–792.

Corzine, J. and Kirby, R. (1977) 'Cruising the truckers: sexual encounters in a highway rest area', *Urban Life*, 6(2): 171–192.

Coy, P. G. (2001) 'Shared risks and research dilemmas on a Peace Brigades International team in Sri Lanka', *Journal of Contemporary Ethnography*, 30(5): 576–606.

Cramer, J. and McDevitt, M. (2004) 'Ethnographic journalism', in S. H. Iorio (ed.), *Qualitative Research in Journalism: Taking it to the Streets*. London: Routledge. pp.127–143.

Crawford, L. (1996) 'Personal ethnography', *Communications Monographs*, 63(2): 158–170.

Cressey, P. G. (1983) 'A comparison of the roles of the "sociological stranger" and the "anonymous stranger" in field research', *Urban Life*, 12(1): 102–120.

Cressey, P. G. (1932) *The Taxi-Dance Hall: A Sociological Study in Commercialized Recreation and City Life*. Chicago, IL: University of Chicago Press.

Cromer, G. (1988) 'Time perspectives and time usage in a basic training course in the Israeli Defence Forces', *Small Group Behaviour*, 19(1): 67–78.

Crossley, N. (2002) *Making Sense of Social Movements*. Maidenhead, UK: Open University Press.

Crossley, N. (2007) 'Social networks and extra-parliamentary politics', *Sociology Compass*, 1(1): 222–236.

Crossley, N., Edwards, G., Harries, E. and Stevenson, R. (2012) 'Covert social movement networks and the secrecy-efficiency trade off: the case of the UK suffragettes (1906–1914)', *Social Networks*, 34(4): 633–644.

Crow, G., Wiles, R., Heath, S. and Charles, V. (2006) 'Research ethics and data quality: the implications of informed consent', *International Journal of Social Research Methodology*, 9(2): 83–95.

Crown, S. (1975) '"On being sane in insane places": a comment from England', *Journal of Abnormal Psychology*, 84(5): 453–455.

Currie, T. and Davies, J. (2003) *Bouncers: Their Lives in Their Own Words*. London: Milo Books.

Dabney, D. A., Hollinger, R. C. and Dugan, L. (2004) 'Who actually steals? A study of covertly observed shoplifters', *Justice Quarterly*, 21(4): 693–728.

Dalton, M. (1959) *Men Who Manage: Fusions of Feeling and Theory in Administration*. New York: John Wiley and Sons.

Daniels, A. K. (1980) 'Getting in and Getting on: the sociology of infiltration and ingratiation', in M. Mackie (ed.), *Sociology's Relations with the Community*. Calgary, Canada: University of Calgary Press. pp. 85–97.

Daniels, A. K. (1983) 'Self-deception and self-discovery in fieldwork', *Qualitative Sociology*, 6(3): 195–214.

Daniels, J. (2009) 'Cloaked websites: propaganda, cyber-racism and epistemology in the digital era', *New Media & Society*, 11(5): 659–683.

Darley, J. M. and Latané, B. (1968) 'Bystander intervention in emergencies: diffusion of responsibility', *Journal of Personality and Social Psychology*, 8(4): 377–383.

Darley, J. M. and Latané, B. (1970) *The Unresponsive Bystander: Why Doesn't He Help?* New York: Appleton Century Crofts.

Darmon, M. (2012) 'A people thinning institution: changing bodies and souls in a commercial weight-loss group', *Ethnography*, 13(3): 375–398.

Davidson, J. (2006) 'Covert research', in V. Jupp (ed.), *The SAGE Dictionary of Social Research Methods*. London; Sage, pp. 48–50.

Davis, D. A. (1976) 'On being detectably sane in insane places: base rates and psychodiagnosis', *Journal of Abnormal Psychology*, 85(4): 416–422.

Davis, F. (1959) 'The cabdriver and his fare: facets of a fleeting relationship', *American Journal of Sociology*, 65(2): 158–165.

Davis, F. (1974) 'Stories and sociology', *Urban Life and Culture*, 3(3): 310–316.

Dawson, L. (1999) 'When prophecy fails and faith persists: a theoretical overview', *Nova Religio: The Journal of Alternative and Emergent Religions*, 3(1): 60–82.

Day, K. and Keys, T. (2008) 'Starving in cyberspace: a discourse analysis of pro-eating disorder websites', *Journal of Gender Studies*, 17(1): 1–15.

De Maria, W. (2008) 'Whistleblowers and organizational protesters: crossing imaginary borders', *Current Sociology*, 56(6): 865–883.

Dein, S. (1997) 'Lubavitch: a contemporary messianic movement', *Journal of Contemporary Religion*, 12(2): 191–204.

Delamont, S. (2009) 'The only honest thing: autoethnography, reflexivity and small crises in fieldwork', *Ethnography and Education*, 4(1): 51–63.

Delanty, G. (2003) *Community*. New York: Routledge.

Delph, E. W. (1978) *The Silent Community: Public Homosexual Encounters*. Beverly Hills, CA: Sage.

Denscombe, M. (2005) 'Research ethics and the governance of research projects: the potential of internet home pages', *Sociological Research Online*, 10(3).

Denshire, S. (2014) 'On auto-ethnography', *Current Sociology Review*, 62(6): 831–850.

Denzin, N. K. (1968) 'On the ethics of disguised observation', *Social Problems*, 15(4): 502–504.

Denzin, N. K. (1989) *Interpretive Interactionism*. London: Sage.

Denzin, N. K. (2010) *The Qualitative Manifesto: A Call to Arms*. Walnut Creek, CA: Left Coast Press.

Denzin, N. K. and Erikson, K. (1982) 'On the ethics of disguised observation', in M. Bulmer (ed.), *Social Research Ethics: An Examination of the Merits of Covert Participant Observation*. London: Macmillan. pp. 142–151.

Desroches, F. (1990) 'Tearoom trade: a research update', *Qualitative Sociology*, 13(1): 39–61.

Deuchar, R. and Holligan, C. (2010) 'Gangs, sectarianism and social capital: a qualitative study of young people in Scotland', *Sociology*, 44(1): 13–30.

Diamond, S. S. and Morton, D. R. (1978) 'Empirical landmarks in social psychology', *Personality and Social Psychology Bulletin*, 4(2): 217–221.

Diamond, T. (1992) *Making Gray Gold: Narratives of Nursing Home Care*. Chicago, IL: University of Chicago Press.

Diamond, T. (2006) '"Where did you get the fur coat, Fern?" Participant observation in institutional ethnography', in D. Smith (ed.), *Institutional Ethnography as Practice*. Lanham, MD: Rowman & Littlefield. pp. 45–63.

Diani, M. and McAdam, D. (2003) *Social Movements and Networks*. Oxford: Oxford University Press.

Dicks, B., Flewitt, R., Lancaster, L. and Pahl, K. (2011) 'Multimodality and ethnography: working at the intersection', *Qualitative Research*, 11(3): 227–237.

Dingwall, R. (2006) 'Confronting the anti-democrats: the unethical nature of ethical regulation in social science', *Medical Sociology Online*, 1(1): 51–58.

Dingwall, R. (2008) 'The ethical case against ethical regulation in humanities and social science research', *Twenty-First Century Society*, 3(1): 1–12.

Diphoorn, T. (2013) 'The emotionality of participation: various modes of participation in ethnographic fieldwork of private policing in Durban, South Africa', *Journal of Contemporary Ethnography*, 42(2): 201–225.

Ditton, J. (1977) *Part-time Crime: An Ethnography of Fiddling and Pilferage*. London: Macmillan.

Dodge, M., Starr-Gimeno, D. and Williams, T. (2005) 'Puttin' on the sting: Women police officers' perspectives on reverse prostitution assignments', *International Journal of Police Science & Management*, 7(2): 71–85.

Dodson, L. and Zincavage, R. M. (2007) '"It's like a family": caring labor, exploitation, and race in nursing homes', *Gender & Society*, 21(6): 905–928.

Domingo, D., Quandt, T., Heinonen, A., Paulussen, S., Singer J. B. and Vujnovic, M. (2008) 'Participatory journalism practices in the media and beyond', *Journalism Practice*, 2(3): 326–342.

Donath, J. (1998) 'Identity and deception in the virtual community', in M. Smith and P. Kollock (eds), *Communities in Cyberspace*. London: Routledge. pp. 29–59.

Donnelly, C. M. and Wright, B. R. E. (2013) 'Goffman goes to church: face saving and the maintenance of collective order in religious services', *Sociological Research Online*, 18(1).

Donovan, F.(1919) *The Woman Who Waits*. Boston, MA: Richard G. Badger.

Donovan, F. (1929) *The Saleslady*. Chicago, IL: University of Chicago Press.

Donovan, F. (1938) *The Schoolma'am*. New York: Frederick A. Stokes.

Douglas, B. and Tewksbury, R. (2008) 'Theaters and sex: an examination of anonymous sexual encounters in an erotic oasis', *Deviant Behaviour*, 29(1): 1–17.

Douglas, J. (1976) *Investigative Social Research: Individual and Team Field Research*. Beverly Hills, CA: Sage.

Doyle, P. (2004) *Hot Shots Heavy Hits: Tales from an Undercover Drug Agent*, Boston, MA: Northeastern University Press.

Egan, D. R. (2006) 'Resistance under the black light: exploring the use of music in two exotic dance clubs', *Journal of Contemporary Ethnography*, 35(2): 201–219.

Ehrenreich, B. (2002) *Nickel and Dimed: Undercover in Low-wage USA*. London: Granta Books.

Ehrenreich, B. (2006) *Bait and Switch: The Futile Pursuit of the Corporate Dream.* London: Granta Books.

Ehrenreich, B. (2008) *Nickel and Dimed: On Not Getting By in America.* London: Holt Paperbacks.

Eilstrup-Sangiovanni, M. and Jones, C. (2008) 'Assessing the dangers of illicit networks: why Al-Qaida may be less threatening than we think', *International Security*, 33(2): 7–44.

Elliott, D. and Culver, C. (1992) 'Defining and analyzing journalistic deception', *Journal of Mass Media Ethics*, 7(2): 69–84.

Ellis, C. (1995) *Final Negotiations: A Story of Love, Loss and Chronic Illness.* Philadelphia, PA: Temple Press.

Ellis, C. (1998) 'Exploring loss through autoethnographic inquiry: autoethnographic stories, co-constructed narratives, and interpretive interviews', in J. H. Harvey (ed.), *Perspectives on Loss: A Sourcebook.* Philadelphia, PA: Taylor and Francis. pp. 49–62.

Ellis, C. (1999) 'Heartfelt autoethnography', *Qualitative Health Research*, 9(5): 669–683.

Ellis, C. (2000) 'Creating criteria: an autoethnographic story', *Qualitative Inquiry*, 6(2): 273–277.

Ellis, C. (2004) *The Ethnographic I: A Methodological Novel about Autoethnography.* Walnut Creek, CA: AltaMira Press.

Ellis, C. (2007) 'Telling secrets, revealing lives: relational ethics in research with intimate others', *Qualitative Inquiry*, 13(1): 3–29.

Ellis, C. (2009) *Revision: Autoethnographic Reflections on Life and Work.* Walnut Creek, CA: Left Coast Press.

Ellis C. (2013) 'Carrying the torch for autoethnography', in S. Holman Jones., T. Adams and C. Ellis (eds), *Handbook of Autoethnography.* Walnut Creek, CA: Left Coast Press. pp. 9–12.

Ellis, C., Adams, T. E. and Bochner, A. P. (2011) 'Autoethnography: an overview', *Forum: Qualitative Social Research*, 12(1), Article 10.

Ellis, C. and Bochner, A. P. (eds) (1990) *Composing Ethnography.* Walnut Creek, CA: AltaMira Press.

Ellis, C. and Bochner, A. P. (2000) 'Autoethnography, personal narrative, reflexivity', in N. K. Denzin and Y. S. Lincoln (eds), *Handbook of Qualitative Research* (3rd edn). Thousand Oaks, CA: Sage. pp. 733–768 (1st edn, 1994).

Ellis, C. and Bochner, A. P. (2006) 'Analyzing analytic autoethnography: an autopsy', *Journal of Contemporary Ethnography*, 35(4): 429–449.

Ellis, C. and Rawicki, J. (2013) 'Collaborative witnessing of survival during the Holocaust: an exemplar of relational autoethnography', *Qualitative Inquiry*, 19(5): 366–380.

Emburgh, B. (2010) *The Bouncer.* London: Universe.

Emmerich, N. (2013) 'Between the accountable and the auditable: ethics and ethical governance in the social sciences', *Research Ethics*, 9(4): 175–86.

Emmerich, N. (2016) 'Reframing research ethics: towards a professional ethics for the social sciences', *Sociological Research Online,* 21(40): 7.

Emmison, M. and Smith, P. (2000) *Researching the Visual: Images, Objects, Contexts and Interactions in Social and Cultural Inquiry.* London: Sage.

Enders, W. and Su, X. (2007) 'Rational terrorists and optimal network structure', *The Journal of Conflict Resolution*, 51(1): 33–57.

Erikson, K. T. (1967) 'A comment on disguised observation in sociology', *Social Problems*, 14(4): 366–373.

Economic and Social Research Council framework for research ethics (2015) January, Swindon: ESRC.

Ettema, J. S. and Glasser, T. L. (2007) 'An international symposium on investigate journalism: introduction', *Journalism*, 8(5): 491–494.

Evans-Pritchard, E. E. (1976) *Witchcraft, Oracles and Magic among the Azande.* Oxford: Clarendon Press.

Faden, R. and Beauchamp, T. L. (1986) *A History and Theory of Informed Consent.* Oxford: Oxford University Press.

Farber, I. E. (1975) 'Sane and insane: constructions and misconstructions', *Journal of Abnormal Psychology*, 84(6): 589–620.

Farquhar, L. (2013) 'Performing and interpreting identity through Facebook imagery', *Convergence: The International Journal of Research into New Media Technologies*, 19(4): 446–471.

Farrington, D. P. and Kidd, R. F. (1977) 'Is financial dishonesty a rational decision?', *British Journal of Social and Clinical Psychology*, 16(2): 139–146.

Farrington, D. P. and Knight, B. J. (1979) 'Two non-reactive field experiments on stealing from a "lost" letter', *British Journal of Social and Clinical Psychology*, 18(3): 277–284.

Farrington, D. P. and Knight, B. J. (1980) 'Stealing from a "lost" letter: effects of victim characteristics', *Criminal Justice and Behaviour*, 7(4): 423–436.

Feld, S. and Basso, K. (eds) (1996) *Senses of Place.* Santa Fe, NM: School of American Research Press.

Feldstein, M. (2006) 'A muckraking model: investigative reporting cycles in American history', *The Harvard International Journal of Press/Politics*, 11(2): 105–120.

Ferdinand, J., Pearson, G., Rowe, M. and Worthington, F. (2007) 'A different kind of ethics', *Ethnography*, 8(4): 519–544.

Ferrell, J. (1998) 'Criminological *Verstehen*: inside the immediacy of crime', in J. Ferrell, and M. S. Hamm (eds), *Ethnography at the Edge: Crime, Deviance, and Field Research.* Boston, MA: Northeastern University Press. pp. 20–43.

Ferrell, J. and Hamm, M. S. (1998) 'True confessions: crime, deviance, and field research', in J. Ferrell, and Mark S. Hamm (eds), *Ethnography at the Edge: Crime, Deviance, and Field Research.* Boston, MA: Northeastern University Press. pp. 2–20.

Festinger, L., Riecken, H. W. and Schachter, S. (1956) *When Prophecy Fails: A Social and Psychological Study of a Modern Group that Predicted the Destruction of the World.* Minneapolis, MN: University of Minnesota Press.

Fielding, N. (1981) *The National Front.* London: Routledge and Kegan Paul.

Fielding, N. (1982) 'Observational research on the National Front', in M. Bulmer (ed.), *Social Research Ethics: An Examination of the Merits of Covert Participant Observation.* London: Macmillan. pp. 80–104.

Fijnaut, C. (1995) *Undercover: Police Surveillance in Contemporary Perspective.* The Hague: Kluwer Law International.

Fincham, B. (2008) 'Balance is everything: bicycle messengers, work and leisure', *Sociology*, 42(4): 618–634.

Fine, G. A. (1993) 'Ten lies of ethnography: moral dilemmas of field research', *Journal of Contemporary Ethnography*, 22(3): 267–294.

Fine, G. A. (2003) 'Towards a people ethnography: developing a theory from group life', *Ethnography*, 4(1): 41–60.

Fine, G. A. and Manning, P. (2003) 'Erving Goffman', in G. Ritzer (ed.), *The Blackwell Companion to Major Contemporary Theorists*. Oxford: Blackwell. pp. 34–63.

Fine, G. A. and Martin, D. D. (1990) 'Partisan view: sarcasm, satire, and irony as voices in Erving Goffman's asylums', *Journal of Contemporary Ethnography*, 19(1): 89–115.

Fistein, E. and Quilligan, M. (2011) 'In the lion's den? Experiences of interaction with research ethics committees', *Journal of Medical Ethics*, 38(4): 224–227.

Fleisher, M. (1989) *Warehousing Violence*. Thousand Oaks, CA: Sage.

Fletcher, J. (1966) *Situation Ethics: The New Morality*. Westminster: John Knox Press.

Flick, C. (2016) 'Informed consent and the Facebook emotional manipulation study', *Research Ethics*, 12(1): 14–28.

Flicker, S., Haans, D. and Skinner, H. (2004) 'Ethical dilemmas in research on Internet communities', *Qualitative Health Research*, 14(1): 124–134.

Flowers, A. (1998) *The Fantasy Factory: An Insider's View of the Phone Sex Industry*. Philadelphia, PA: University of Pennsylvania Press.

Foot-Whyte, W. (1943) *Street Corner Society: The Social Structure of an Italian Slum*. Chicago, IL: University of Chicago Press.

Forrest, B. (1986) 'Apprentice-participation: methodology and the study of subjective reality', *Journal of Contemporary Ethnography*, 14(4): 431–453.

Fox, N., Ward, K. and O'Rourke, A. (2005) 'Pro-anorexia, weight-loss drugs and the internet: an "anti-recovery" explanatory model of anorexia', *Sociology of Health and Illness*, 27(7): 944–971.

Frank, A. W. (2004) 'After methods, the story: from incongruity to truth in qualitative research', *Qualitative Health Research*, 14(3): 430–440.

Frank, K. (1998) 'The production of identity and the negotiation of intimacy in a "gentle-man's club"', *Sexualities*, 1: 175–202.

Frank, K. (2002) *G-Strings and Sympathy: Strip Club Regulars and Male Desire*. Durham, NC: Duke University Press.

Frank, K. (2003) '"Just trying to relax": masculinity, masculinizing practices, and strip club regulars', *The Journal of Sex Research*, 40(1): 61–75.

Frank, K. (2007) 'Thinking critically about strip club research', *Sexualities*, 10(4): 501–517.

Fujii, L. E. (2015) 'Five stories of accidental ethnography: turning unplanned moments in the field into data', *Qualitative Research*, 15(4): 525–540.

Gadsden, M. J. (2006) *Memoirs of a Bouncer: The Real Men in Black*. London: AuthorHouse.

Galliher, J. F. (1982) 'The protection of human subjects: a re-examination of the profes-sional code of ethics', in M. Bulmer (ed.), *Social Research Ethics: An Examination of the Merits of Covert Participant Observation*. London: Macmillan. pp. 152–165.

Galliher, J. F., Brekhus, W. H. and Keys, D. P. (2004) *Laud Humphreys: Prophet of Homosexuality and Sociology*. Madison, WI: University of Wisconsin Press.

Game, A. and Metcalfe, A. W. (1996) *Passionate Sociology*. London: Sage.

Gans, H., J. (1968) 'The participant-observer as a human being: observations on the personal aspects of field work', in H. S. Becker et al. (eds), *Institutions and the Person: Papers presented to Everett C. Hughes*. Chicago, IL: Aldine. pp. 300–317.

Gans, H. J. (1999) 'Participant observation: in the era of ethnography', *Journal of Contemporary Ethnography*, 28(5): 540–548.

Garfinkel, H. (1963) 'A conception of, and experiments with, "trust" as a condition of stable concerted actions', in O. J. Harvey (ed.), *Motivation and Social Interaction*. New York: Ronald Press. pp. 187–238.

Garfinkel, H. (1967) *Studies in Ethnomethdoology.* Englewood Cliffs, NJ: Prentice-Hall.

Garfinkel, H. (2005) *Seeing Sociologically: The Routine Grounds of Social Action*. London: Routledge.

Garland, J. and Treadwell, J. (2010) 'No surrender to the Taliban: football hooliganism, Islamophobia and the rise of the English Defence League', *Papers from the British Criminology Conference*, 10: 19–35.

Gavin, J., Rodham, K. and Poyer, H. (2008) 'The presentation of "Pro-Anorexia" in online group interactions', *Qualitative Health Research*, 18(3): 325–333.

Gawande, A. (2010) *The Checklist Manifesto: How To Get Things Right*. London: Profile Books.

Gay, E. (1888) 'The toiling women', 'Song of the shirt', 'Working in the wet', *St Pauls Globe*, April.

Geertz, C. (1973) *The Interpretation of Cultures: Selected Essays*. New York: Basic Books.

Geertz, C. (1988) *Works and Lives: The Anthropologist as Author*. Cambridge: Polity Press.

Geertz, C. (1995) *After the Fact.* Cambridge, MA: Harvard University Press.

Gergen, K. J. and Gergen, M. M. (1988) 'Narrative and the self as relationship', in L. Berkowitz (ed.), *Advances in Experimental Social Psychology*. San Diego, CA: Academic Press. pp. 17–56.

German, M. (2007) *Thinking Like a Terrorist: Insights of a Former Undercover Agent*. Dulles, VA: Potomac Books.

Gershon, I. (2014) 'Publish and be damned: new media publics and neoliberal risk', *Ethnography*, 15(1): 70–87.

Giddens, A. (2009) *Sociology* (6th edn). Cambridge: Polity Press (1st edn, 1989).

Gillespie, A. A. (2008) 'Cyber-stings: policing sex offences on the internet', *The Police Journal*, 81(3): 196–208.

Gilligan, C. (1993) *In a Different Voice: Psychological Theory and Women's Development*. Cambridge, MA and London: Harvard University Press.

Goddard, P. (2006) 'Improper liberties: regulating undercover journalism on ITV, 1967–1980', *Journalism*, 7(1): 45–63.

Goffman, A. (2009) 'On the run: wanted men in a Philadelphia ghetto', *American Sociological Review*, 74(3): 339–357.

Goffman, A. (2014) *On the Run: Fugitive Life in an American City.* Chicago, IL: University of Chicago Press.

Goffman, E. (1952) 'On cooling the mark out: some aspects of adaption to failure', *Psychiatry*, 15(4): 451–463.

Goffman, E. (1959) *The Presentation of Self in Everyday Life*. New York: Doubleday Anchor Books.

Goffman, E. (1961) *Asylums: Essays on the Social Situation of Mental Patients and Other Inmates*. New York: Doubleday.

Goffman, E. (1967) *Interaction Ritual: Essays on Face-to-Face Behaviour*. New York: Doubleday.

Goffman, E. (1968) *Stigma: Notes on the Management of Spoiled Identity*. Harmondsworth: Penguin.

Goffman, E. (1974) *Frame Analysis*. Boston, MA: Northeastern University Press.

Goffman, E. (1983) 'The interaction order: American Sociological Association Presidential Address 1982', *American Sociological Association*, 48(1): 1–17.

Goffman, E. (1989) 'On fieldwork' (transcribed by L. H. Lofland), *Journal of Contemporary Ethnography*, 18(2): 123–132.

Goggin, G. (2014) 'Facebook's mobile career', *New Media & Society*, 16(7): 1068–1086.

Gold, R. L. (1958) 'Roles in sociological field observations', *Social Forces*, 36(3): 217–223.

Goldman, J. (ed.) (2006) *Ethics of Spying: A Reader for the Intelligence Professional*. Lanham, MD: Scarecrow Press.

Goldsmid, H. J. (1886) *Dottings of a Dosser, Being Revelations of the Inner Life of Low London Lodging-Houses*. London: T. Fisher Unwin.

Goldschmidt, W. (1977) 'Anthropology and the coming crisis: an autoethnographic appraisal'. *American Anthropologist*, 79(2): 293–308.

Gonos, G. (1976) 'Go-Go dancing: a comparative frame analysis', *Urban Life*, 5(2): 189–220.

Goode, E. (1996) 'The ethics of deception in social research: a case study', *Qualitative Sociology*, 19(1): 11–33.

Gordon, A. (2008) *Ghostly Matters: Haunting and the Sociological Imagination*. Minneapolis and London: University of Minnesota Press.

Gouldner, A. (1968) 'The sociologist as partisan: sociology and the welfare state', *American Sociologist*, 3(2): 103–116.

Graham, L. (1995) *On the Line at Subaru-Isuzu: The Japanese Model and the American Worker*. Ithaca, NY: ILR Press.

Gregory, S. W. (1982) 'Accounts as assembled from breaching experiments', *Symbolic Interaction*, 5(1): 49–63.

Griffin, J. H. (1961) *Black Like Me*. New York: Souvenir Press.

Griffiths, M. and Whitty, M. (2010) 'Online behavioural tracking in internet gambling research: ethical and methodological issues', *International Journal of Internet Research Ethics*, 3(1): 104–117.

Griffiths, P. (2008) 'Ethical conduct and the nurse ethnographer: consideration of an ethic of care', *Journal of Research in Nursing*, 13(4): 350–361.

Grodzinsky, F. S. and Tavani, H. T. (2010) 'Applying the "contextual integrity" model of privacy to personal blogs in the blogosphere', *International Journal of Internet Research Ethics*, 3(1): 38–47.

Groombridge, N. (1999) 'Perverse criminologies: the closet of Doctor Lombroso', *Social and Legal Studies*, 8(4): 531–548.

Grove, S. J. and Fisk, R. (1992) 'Observational data collection methods for services marketing: an overview', *Journal of the Academy of Marketing Science*, 20(3): 217–224.

Guilleman, M. and Gillam, L. (2004) 'Ethics, reflexivity and "ethically important moments in research"', *Qualitative Inquiry*, 10(2): 261–280.

Gunter, A. (2008) 'Growing up bad: black youth, "road" culture and badness in an East London neighbourhood', *Crime, Media Culture*, 4(3): 349–366.

Gurney, P. (ed.) (1988) *Working Class Life in Bolton in the 1930s: A Mass Observation Anthology*. Brighton: University of Sussex Library, Mass Observation Archive.

Hackler, J. C. (1971) 'Book review of *Tea Room Trade*', *Journal of Research in Crime and Delinquency*, 8(1): 119–121.

Hadfield, P. (2002) 'Open all hours', *Police Review*, 16 August, 110/5686: 21.

Hadfield, P., Lister, S. and Traynor, P. (2009) 'This town's a different town today: policing and regulating the night-time economy', *Criminology and Criminal Justice*, 9(4): 465–485.

Haenfler, R. (2004) 'Rethinking subcultural resistance: core values of the straight edge movement', *Journal of Contemporary Ethnography*, 33(4): 406–436.

Haggerty, K. D. (2004) 'Ethics creep: governing social science research in the name of ethics', *Qualitative Sociology*, 27(4): 391–414.

Hall, T. (2003) *Better Times than This: Youth Homelessness in Britain*. London: Pluto Press.

Hallett, R. E. and Barber, K. (2014) 'Ethnographic research in a Cyber Era', *Journal of Contemporary Ethnography*, 43(3): 306–330.

Hallsworth, S. and Young, T. (2008) 'Gang talk and gang talkers: a critique', *Crime Media Culture*, 42(2): 175–195.

Hamer, B. (2008) *The Last Undercover: The True Story of an FBI Agent's Dangerous Dance with Evil*. New York: Hachette Book Group.

Hammer, H. (2014) *Bars, Bouncers, Bad Guys and Beyond: A Kick Ass Guide for Bouncers and Security Officers*. Amazon Digital Services LCC.

Hammersley, M. (2009) 'Against the ethicists: on the evils of ethical regulation', *International Journal of Social Research Methodology*, 12(3): 211–226.

Hammersley, M. (2010) 'Creeping ethical regulation and the strangling of research', *Sociological Research Online*, 15(4): 16.

Hammersley, M. and Traianou, A. (2011) 'Moralism and research ethics: a Machiavellian perspective', *International Journal of Social Research Methodology*, 14(5): 379–390.

Hammersley, M. and Traianou, A. (2012) *Ethics in Qualitative Research: Controversies and Contexts*. London: Sage.

Hammersley, M. and Treseder, P. (2007) 'Identity as an analytic problem: who's who in "Pro-ana" websites?', *Qualitative Research*, 7(3): 283–300.

Hamo, M., Kampf, Z. and Shifman, L. (2010) 'Surviving the "mock interview": challenges to political communicative competence in contemporary televised discourse', *Media, Culture & Society*, 32(2): 247–266.

Hand, M. (2012) *Ubiquitous Photography*. Cambridge: Polity Press.

Haney, C., Banks, C. and Zimbardo, P. (1973) 'Interpersonal dynamics in a simulated prison', *International Journal of Criminology and Penology*, 1: 69–97.

Hansen Lofstrand, C., Loftus, B. and Loader, I. (2016) 'Doing dirty work: stigma and esteem in the private security industry', *European Journal of Criminology*, 13(3): 297–314.

Hardyck, J. A. and Braden, M. (1962) 'Prophecy fails again: a report of a failure to replicate', *Journal of Abnormal and Social Psychology*, 65(2): 136–141.

Harper, D. (1998) 'An argument for visual sociology', in J. Prosser (ed.), *Image Based Research: A Sourcebook for Qualitative Researchers*. London: Routledge. pp. 24–41.

Harré, R. (1979) *Social Being: A Theory for Social Psychology.* Oxford: Basil Blackwell.

Harrington, W. (1997) *Intimate Journalism: The Art and Craft of Reporting Everyday Life*. London: Sage.

Harrington, W. (2003) 'What journalism can offer ethnography', *Qualitative Inquiry*, 9(1): 90–104.

Harris, A. (2008) 'The artist as surgical ethnographer: participant observers outside the social sciences', *Health*, 12(4): 501–514.

Harris, M. B. (1974) 'Mediators between frustration and aggression in a field experiment', *Journal of Experimental Social Psychology*, 10(6): 561–571.

Haslam, D. (1999) *Manchester England: The Story of the Pop Cult City*. London: Fourth Estate.

Hayano, D. M. (1979) 'Auto-ethnography: paradigms, problems and prospects', *Human Organization*, 38(1): 99–104.

Hayward, K. and Hobbs, D. (2007) 'Beyond the binge in "booze" Britain: market-led liminalization and the spectacle of binge drinking', *The British Journal of Sociology*, 58(3): 437–456.

Hebl, M. R., Foster, J. B., Mannix, L. M. and Dovidio, J. F. (2002) 'Formal and interpersonal discrimination: a fields of bias toward homosexual applications', *Personality and Social Psychology Bulletin*, 28(6): 815–825.

Hedgecoe, A. (2016) 'Reputational risk, academic freedom and research ethics review', *Sociology*, 50(3): 486–501.

Hefley, K. (2007) 'Stigma management of male and female customers to a non-urban adult novelty store', *Deviant Behaviour*, 28(1): 79–109.

Henle, M. and Hubble, M. B. (1938) 'Egocentricity in adult conversations', *Journal of Social Psychology*, 9: 227–234.

Henny, L. (1986) 'Theory and practice of visual sociology', *Current Sociology*, 34(3): 1–23.

Hermann, A. K. (2014) 'Ethnographic journalism', *Journalism*, 11 December, 1–19.

Herrera, C. D. (1997) 'A historical interpretation of deceptive experiments in American Psychology', *History of the Human Sciences*, 10(1): 23–36.

Herrera, C. D. (1999) 'Two arguments for "covert methods" in social research', *British Journal of Sociology*, 50(2): 331–343.

Herrera, C. D. (2003) 'A clash of methodology and ethics in "undercover" social science', *Philosophy of the Social Sciences*, 33(3): 351–362.

Herring, S. C., Job-Sluder, K., Scheckler, R. and Barab, S. (2002) 'Searching for safety online: managing "trolling" in a feminist forum', *The Information Society*, 18(5): 371–383.

Heslop, R. (2012) 'A sociological imagination: Simon Holdaway, police research pioneer', *Police Practice and Research: An International Journal*, 13(6): 525–538.

Higgs, M. (1906) *Glimpses into the Abyss*. London: P. S. King and Son.

Higham, N. (2006) Televised interview with Dave Calvey, BA Festival of Science, *BBC News 24*, broadcast 24 October.

Hilbert, R. A. (1980) 'Covert participant observation: on its nature and practice', *Urban Life*, 9(1): 51–78.

Hine, C. (2000) *Virtual Ethnography*. London: Sage.

Hine, C. (2005) *Virtual Methods: Issues in Social Research on the Internet*. Oxford. Berg.

Hinshaw, S. P. (2005) 'Objective assessment of covert antisocial behaviour: predictive validity and ethical considerations', *Ethics & Behaviour*, 15(3): 259–269.

Hobbs, D., Hadfield, P., Lister, S. and Winlow, S. (2002) 'Door lore: the art and economics of intimidation', *British Journal of Criminology*, 42(2): 352–370.

Hobbs, D., Hadfield, P., Lister, S. and Winlow, S. (2003a) *Bouncers: Violence and Governance in the Night-Time Economy*. Oxford: Oxford University Press.

Hobbs, D., Lister, S., Hadfield, P., Winlow, S. and Hall, S. (2000) 'Receiving shadows: governance and liminality in the night-time economy', *British Journal of Sociology*, 51(4): 701–717.

Hobbs, D., O'Brien, K. and Westmarland, L. (2007) 'Connecting the gendered door: women, violence and door work', *British Journal of Sociology*, 58(1): 21–38.

Hobbs, D., Winlow, S., Hadfield, P. and Lister, S. (2005) 'Violent hypocrisy', *European Journal of Criminology*, 2(2): 161–183.

Hobbs, D., Winlow, S., Lister, S. and Hadfield, P. (2003b) 'Bouncers and the social context of violence: masculinity, class and violence in the night-time economy', in E. Stanko (ed.), *The Meanings of Violence*. London: Routledge. pp. 165–184.

Hochschild, A. R. (1973) *The Unexpected Community: Portrait of an Old-Age Subculture*. Englewood Cliffs, NJ: Prentice-Hall.

Hochschild, A. R. (1979) 'Emotion work, feeling rules and social structure', *American Journal of Sociology*, 85(3): 551–575.

Hochschild, A. R. (1983) *The Managed Heart: Commercialization of Human Feeling*. Berkeley, CA: University of California Press.

Hoffman, M. (1971) 'Book review: *Tearoom Trade*', *Archives of Sexual Behaviors*, 1(1): 98–100.

Hofling, C. K., Brotzman, E., Dalrymple, S., Graves, N. and Bierce, C. (1966) 'An experimental study of nurse–physician relations', *Journal of Nervous and Mental Disease*, 143(2): 171–180.

Holdaway, S. (1982) '"An inside job": a case study of covert research on the police', in M. Bulmer (ed.), *Social Research Ethics: An Examination of the Merits of Covert Participant Observation*. London: Macmillan. pp. 59–79.

Holdaway, S. (1983) *Inside the British Police: A Force at Work*. Oxford: Basil Blackwell.

Holiday, I. (2011) *The Bouncer's Bible* (2nd edn). London: Outskirts Press.

Holloway, I. (1997) *Basic Concepts for Qualitative Research*. London: Wiley-Blackwell.

Holman Jones, S., Adams, T. E. and Ellis, C. (eds) (2013) *Handbook of Autoethnography*. Walnut Creek, CA: Left Coast Press.

Holmes, M. (2010) 'The emotionalization of reflexivity', *Sociology*, 44(1): 139–154.

Holt, T. J., Blevins, K. R. and Kuhns, J. K. (2014) 'Examining diffusion and arrest avoidance practices among Johns', *Crime & Delinquency*, 60(2): 261–283.

Homan, R. (1978) 'Interpersonal communication in Pentecostal meetings', *Sociological Review*, 26(3): 499–518.

Homan, R. (1980) 'The ethics of covert methods', *The British Journal of Sociology*, 33(1): 46–59.

Homan, R. (1991) *The Ethics of Social Research*. London: Macmillan.

Homan, R. (1992) 'The ethics of open methods', *British Journal of Sociology*, 43(3): 321–332.

Homan, R. (2001) 'The principle of assumed consent: the ethics of gatekeeping', *Journal of Philosophy of Education*, 35(3): 329–343.

Homan, R. and Bulmer, M. (1982) 'On the merits of covert methods: a dialogue', in M. Bulmer (ed.), *Social Research Ethics: An Examination of the Merits of Covert Participant Observation*. London: Macmillan. pp. 105–124.

Hong, L. K. and Duff, R. W. (1977) 'Becoming a taxi-dancer: the significance of neutralization in a semi-deviant occupation', *Sociology of Work and Occupations*, 4(3): 327–342.

Hong, L. K. and Duff, R. W. (1997) 'The center and the peripheral: functions and locations of dance clubs in Los Angeles', *Journal of Contemporary Ethnography*, 26(2): 182–201.

Horowitz, I. L. (1967) *The Rise and Fall of Project Camelot*. Cambridge, MA: MIT Press.

Hosmer, L. (1896) 'Factory girls in a big city', *St Louis Post-Dispatch*, 26 November.

Howard, R. with Fennell, T. (2008) *Ronnie's Looking for Trouble: The True Story of Britain's Most Brutal Undercover Cop*. London: Mainstream Publishing.

Howe, D. P. (2009) 'Reflexive ethnography, impairment and the pub', *Leisure Studies*, 28(4): 489–496.

Hubbard, J. A. (2005) 'Eliciting and measuring children's anger in the context of their peer interactions: ethical considerations and practical guidelines', *Ethics & Behaviour*, 15(3): 247–248.

Hubble, N. (2006) *Mass-Observation and Everyday Life: Culture, History, Theory*. London: Palgrave.

Hudson, S., Snaith, T., Miller, G. A. and Hudson, P. (2001) 'Distribution channels in the travel industry: using mystery shoppers to understand the influence of travel agency recommendations', *Journal of Travel Research*, 40(2): 148–154.

Hughes, E. C. (1951) 'Work and the self', in J. Rohrer and M. Sherif (eds), *Social Psychology at the Crossroads*. New York: Harper & Brothers. pp. 313–323.

Hughes, E. C. (1962) 'Good people and dirty work', *Social Problems*, 10(1): 3–11.

Hughes, E. C. (1971) 'Work and self', in E. C. Hughes, *The Sociological Eye: Selected Papers*. Chicago, IL: Aldine–Atherton. pp. 338–347.

Hughey, M. W. and Daniels, J. (2013) 'Racist comments at online news sites: a methodological dilemma for discourse analysis', *Media, Culture & Society*, 35(3): 332–347.

Humphreys, L. (1970) *Tearoom Trade: Impersonal Sex in Public Places*. Chicago, IL: Aldine.

Humphreys, L. (1975) *Tearoom Trade: Impersonal Sex in Public Places* (Enlarged edition). Chicago, IL: Aldine.

Humphreys, L. (1980) 'Social science: ethics of research', *Science*, 207(4432): 713–714.

Humphreys, M. (2005) 'Getting personal: reflexivity and autoethnographic vignettes', *Qualitative Inquiry*, 11(6): 840–860.

Hunt, S. (2002) 'Neither here nor there': the construction of identities and boundary maintenance of West African Pentecostals', *Sociology*, 36(1): 147–169.

Hunter, D. L. H. (2008) 'The ESRC research ethics framework and research ethics review at UK universities: rebuilding the Tower of Babel REC by REC', *Journal of Medical Ethics*, 34(11): 815–820.

Hutton, F. (2006) *Risky Pleasures? Club Cultures and Feminine Identities.* Aldershot: Ashgate.

Hylander, I. and Granstrom, K. (2010) 'Organizing for a peaceful crowd: an example of a football match', *Forum: Qualitative Social Research*, 11(2).

Ingold, T. (2000) *The Perception of the Environment*. London: Routledge.

Ings, W. J. (2014) 'Narcissus and the muse: supervisory implications of autobiographical, practice-led PhD design theses', *Qualitative Research*, 14(6): 675–693.

Iphofen, R. (2006) 'Ethical scrutiny', *Times Higher Education*, 8 September.

Iphofen, R. (2009) *Ethical Decision Making in Social Research: A Practical Guide.* Basingstoke: Palgrave Macmillan.

Iphofen, R. (2011) 'Ethical decision making in qualitative research', *Qualitative Sociology*, 11(4): 443–446.

Irwin, J. (1970) *The Felon*. Englewood Cliffs, NJ: Prentice-Hall.

Israel, M. (2004) 'Strictly confidential?', *British Journal of Criminology*, 44(5): 715–40.

Jackall, R. (1988) *Moral Mazes.* New York: Oxford University Press.

Jacob-Pandian, E. (1975) 'Participant observation, liminality and the science of man', *International Journal of Contemporary Sociology*, 12(3/4): 167–180.

Jacobs, B. A. (1992) 'Undercover deception: reconsidering presentations of self', *Journal of Contemporary Ethnography*, 21(2): 200–255.

James, A. (2001) 'Drugs, guns and fights: all in a night's work', *Times Higher Education*, 23 February.

Jane, E. A. (2014) 'Beyond antifandom: cheerleading, textual hate and new media ethics', *International Journal of Cultural Studies*, 17(2): 176–190.

Janetzko, D. (2008) 'Nonreactive data collection on the internet', in N. Fielding, R. M. Lee and G. Blank (eds), *The Sage Handbook of Online Research Methods*. Los Angeles, CA: Sage.

Jeffcut, P. (1996) 'Between management and the managed: the processes of organizational transition', in S. Linstead, R. Grafton-Small and P. Jeffcutt (eds), *Understanding Management*. London: Sage. pp. 174–194.

Jewkes, Y. (2011) 'Autoethnography and emotion as intellectual resources: doing prison research differently', *Qualitative Inquiry*, 18(1): 63–75.

Johnson, M. (1985) 'Imagination in moral judgment', *Philosophy and Phenomenological Research*, 46(2): 265–280.

Johnson, M. (2004) 'Real-world ethics and nursing research', *Nursing Times Research*, 9(4): 251–262.

Jones, J. H. (1981) *Bad Blood: The Tuskegee Syphilis Experiment*. New York: Free Press.

Jones, R. S. (1995) 'Uncovering the hidden social world: insider research in prison', *Journal of Contemporary Criminal Justice*, 11(2): 106–118.

Kamata, S. (1982) *Japan in the Passing Lane: An Insider's Account of Life in a Japanese Auto Factory*. New York: Pantheon Books.

Karp, D. A. (1973) 'Hiding in pornographic bookstores: a reconsideration of the nature of urban anonymity', *Urban Life and Culture*, 1(4): 427–451.

Katz, A. M. and Fox, K. (2004) *The Process of Informed Consent. What's at Stake?* Final Report, Department of Social Medicine, Harvard Medical School, Children's Hospital, Boston, MA.

Katz, J. (2004) 'On the rhetoric and politics of ethnographic methodology', *The ANNALS of the American Academy of Political and Social Science*, 595(1): 280–308.

Katz, J. (2006) 'Ethical escape routes for underground ethnographers', *American Ethnologist*, 33(4): 499–506.

Kaufman-Scarborough, C. (2001) 'Sharing the experience of mobility-disabled consumers: building understanding through the use of ethnographic research methods', *Journal of Contemporary Ethnography*, 30(4): 430–464.

Kennedy, S. (1954) *The Klan Unmasked*. Gainesville, FL: University Press of Florida (formerly *I Rode with the Ku Klux Klan*) (1st edn, 1942).

Kienle, G. S. and Kiene, H (1997) 'The powerful placebo: fact or fiction', *Journal of Clinical Epidemiology*, 50(12): 1311–1318.

Kimmel, A. (1988) *Ethics and Values in Social Research*. London: Sage.

Kiragu, S. and Warrington, M. (2013) 'How we used moral imagination to address ethical and methodological complexities whilst conducting research with girls in school against the odds in Kenya', *Qualitative Research*, 13(2): 173–189.

Kirke, C. (2010) 'Orders is orders ... aren't they? Rule bending and rule breaking in the British Army', *Ethnography*, 11(3): 359–380.

Kivett, D. D. and Warren, C. A. B. (2002) 'Social control in a group home for delinquent boys', *Journal of Contemporary Ethnography*, 31(1): 3–32.

Klerks, P. (2001) 'The network paradigm applied to criminal organisations', *Connections*, 24(3): 53–65.

Klockars, C. (1980) 'The Dirty Harry problem', *Annals of the American Association of Political and Social Science*, 452(1): 33–47.

Knapp, N. (2007) *A Los Angeles Bouncer's Guide to Practical Fighting: Learn No-Nonsense Fighting Tactics from a Professional Bouncer*. London: Turtle Press.

Knightley, P. (1987) *The Second Oldest Profession: Spies and Spying in the Twentieth Century*. London: W. W. Norton & Co.

Kovacs, P. (1998) 'Hospice research: challenges, opportunities and rewards', *American Journal of Hospice and Palliative Medicine*, 15(5): 295–300.

Kozinets, R. V. (2010) *Netnography: Doing Ethnographic Research Online.* Thousand Oaks, CA: Sage.

Kramer, A., Guillory, J. and Hancock, J. (2014) 'Experimental evidence of massive-scale emotional contagion through social networks', *Proceedings of the National Academy of Sciences*, 111(24): 8788–8790.

Krebs, V. (2001) 'Mapping networks of terrorist cells', *Connections*, 24(3): 43–52.

Krim, R. (1988) 'Managing to learn: action inquiry in City Hall', in P. Reason (ed.), *Human Inquiry in Action*. London: Sage. pp. 144–162.

Kroger, B. (1996) 'Nellie Bly: she did it all', *Quarterly of the National Archives*, 28(1): 715.

Kruisbergen, E. W., De Jong, D. and Kleemans, E. R. (2011) 'Undercover policing: assumptions and empirical evidence', *British Journal of Criminology*, 51(2): 394–412.

Kulik, C. T., Pepper, M. B., Shapiro, D. L. and Cregan, C. (2012) 'The electronic water cooler: insiders and outsiders talk about organizational justice on the internet', *Communication Research*, 39(5): 565–591.

Kunda, G. (1992) *Engineering Culture: Control and Commitment in a Hi-Tech Corporation.* Philadelphia, PA: Temple University Press.

Kunter, B., Wilkins, C. and Yarrow, P. (1952) 'Verbal attitudes and overt behaviour involving racial prejudice', *The Journal of Abnormal and Social Psychology*, 47(3): 649–652.

Kwortnik, R. J. and Thompson, G. M. (2009) 'Unifying service marketing and operations with service experience management', *Journal of Service Research*, 11 (4): 389–406.

Langer, R. and Beckman, S. C. (2005) 'Sensitive research topics: netnography revisted', *Qualitative Market Research*, 8(2): 189–203.

LaPiere, R. T. (1934) 'Attitudes vs. Actions', *Social Forces*, 13(2): 230–237.

Latané, B. and Darley, J. M. (1969) 'Bystander "Apathy"', *American Scientist*, 57(2): 244–268.

Lawton, J. (2001) 'Gaining and maintaining consent: ethical concerns raised in a study of dying patients', *Qualitative Health Research*, 11(5): 693–705.

Lee, D. (2013) *101 Tips on How to be a Bouncer: Techniques to Handle Situations without Violence.* Amazon Digital Services LCC.

Lee, J. and Ingold, T. (2006) 'Fieldwork on foot: perceiving, routing and socializing', in S. M. Coleman and P. Collins (eds), *Locating the Field: Space, Place and Context in Anthropology*. Oxford: Berg. pp. 67–86.

Lee, Raymond M. (1995) *Dangerous Fieldwork.* London: Sage.

Lee, Raymond M. (2000) *Unobtrusive Methods in Social Research.* Buckingham: Open University Press.

Lee, S. T. (2004) 'Lying to tell the truth: journalists and the social context of deception', *Mass Communication & Society*, 7(1): 97–120.

Leo, R. A. (1995) 'Trial and tribulations: courts, ethnography, and the need for an evidentiary privilege for academic researchers', *The American Sociologist*, 26(1): 113–134.

Leveson, B. (2012) *An Inquiry into the Culture, Practices and Ethics of the Press*, Volumes 1–4. London: The Stationery Office.

Levine, R. V., Norenzayan, A. and Philbrick, K. (2001) 'Cross-cultural differences in helping strangers', *Journal of Cross-Cultural Psychology*, 32(5): 543–560.

Levine, T. R. (2014) *Encyclopedia of Deception.* London: Sage.

Lewis, M. and Saarni, C. (eds) (1993) *Lying and Deception in Everyday Life.* New York: Guilford Press.

Li, J. (2008) 'Ethical challenges in participant observation: a reflection on ethnographic fieldwork', *The Qualitative Report*, 13(1): 100–115.

Librett, M. and Perrone, D. (2010) 'Apples and oranges: ethnography and the IRB', *Qualitative Research*, 10(6): 729–747.

Lindgren, S. and Lundström, R. (2011) 'Pirate culture and hacktivist mobilization: the cultural and social protocols of #WikiLeaks on Twitter', *New Media and Society*, 13(6): 999–1018.

Linstead, S., Marechal, G. and Griffin, R.W. (2014) 'Theorizing and researching the dark side of organization', *Organization Studies*, 35(2): 165–188.

Lister, S. (2002) 'Violence as a commercial resource: situating bouncers and the use of force in context', *Journal of Forensic Psychiatry*, 12(2): 245–249.

Lister, S., Hadfield, P., Hobbs, D. and Winlow, S. (2001a) 'Accounting for bouncers: occupational licensing as a mechanism for regulation', *Criminology and Criminal Justice*, 1(4): 363–384.

Lister, S., Hadfield, P., Hobbs, D. and Winlow, S. (2001b) 'Be nice: the training of bouncers', *Criminal Justice Matters*, 45(Autumn): 20–21.

Lister, S., Hobbs, D., Hall, S. and Winlow, S. (2000) 'Violence in the night-time economy. Bouncers: the reporting, recording and prosecution of assault', *Policing and Society*, 10(4): 383–402.

Lister, S., Hobbs, D. and Winlow, S. (2001) 'The "24-hour city": condition critical?', *Town and Country Planning*, 70(11): 300–302.

Littlewood, R. (1993) 'Ideology, camouflage or contingency? Racism in British psychiatry', *Transcultural Psychiatry*, 30(3): 243–290.

Locke, J. L. (2010) *Eavesdropping: An Intimate History*. Oxford: Oxford University Press.

Lofland, J. R. and Lejeune, R. A. (1960) 'Initial interaction of newcomers in Alcoholics Anonymous: a field experiment in class symbols and socialization', *Social Problems*, 8(2): 102–111.

Loftus, B. and Goold, B. (2012) 'Covert surveillance and the invisibilities of policing', *Criminology & Criminal Justice*, 12(3): 275–288.

Lovatt, A. (1996) 'The Ecstasy of urban regeneration: regulation of the night-time economy in the transition to a post-Fordist city', in J. O'Connor and D. Wynne (eds), *From the Margins to the Centre: Cultural Production and Consumption in the Post Industrial City*. Aldershot: Arena. pp. 141–168.

Low, S. and Lawrence-Zuniga, D. (eds) (2003) *The Anthropology of Space and Place: Locating Culture*. Oxford: Blackwell.

Lubet, S. (2015) 'Ethics on the run', *The New Rambler Review*, 26 May, Northwestern Public Law Research Paper.

Lugosi, P. (2006) 'Between overt and covert research: concealment and disclosure in an ethnographic study of commercial hospitality', *Qualitative Inquiry*, 12(3): 541–561.

Lugosi, P. and Bray, J. (2008) 'Tour guiding, organisational culture and learning: lessons from an entrepreneurial company', *International Journal of Tourism Research*, 10(5): 467–479.

Lumsden, K. (2009) 'Don't ask a woman to do another woman's job': gendered interactions and the emotional ethnographer', *Sociology*, 43(3): 497–513.

Lury, C. and Wakeford, N. (eds) (2012) *Inventive Methods: The Happening of the Social.* London and New York: Routledge.

Lynch, M. (1993) *Scientific Practice and Ordinary Action: Ethnomethodology and Social Studies of Science.* Cambridge: Cambridge University Press.

Lyng, S. (1990) 'Edgework: a social psychological analysis of voluntary risk-taking', *American Journal of Sociology*, 95(4): 851–856.

Lyng, S. (ed.) (2005) *Edgework: The Sociology of Risk Taking.* Thousand Oak, CA: Sage.

Maas, P. (1973) *Serpico, The Cop Who Defied the System.* New York: Viking Press.

Mac Giollabhui, S., Goold, B. and Loftus, B. (2016) 'Watching the watchers: conducting ethnographic research on covert police investigations in the United Kingdom', *Qualitative Research*, 16(6): 630–645.

Macionis, J. and Plummer, K. (2005) *Sociology: A Global Introduction.* (3rd edn). Harlow: Pearson Education (1st edn, 2002).

MacIntyre, D. (1999) *MacIntyre.* London: BBC Books.

Mackellar, J. (2009) 'Dabblers, fans and fanatics: Exploring behavioural segmentation at a special-interest event', *Journal of Vacation Marketing*, 15(1): 5–24.

Maclaughlin, D. with Hall, W. (2002) *The Filth: The Explosive Inside Story of Scotland Yard's Top Undercover Cop.* Edinburgh: Mainstream Publishing.

MacSuibhre, S. (2011) 'Erving Goffman's *Asylums* 50 years on', *The British Journal of Psychiatry*, 198(1): 1–2.

Macyoung, M. (1996) *A Professional's Guide to Ending Violence Quickly: How Bouncers, Bodyguards and Other Security Professionals Handle Ugly Situations.* London: Paladin Press.

Madden, J. M., Quick, J. D., Ross-Degnan, D. and Kafle, K. K. (1997) 'Undercover careseekers: simulated clients in the study of health provider behaviour in developing countries', *Social Science and Medicine*, 45(10): 1465–1482.

Madge, C. (2007) 'Developing a geographer's agenda for online research ethics', *Progress in Human Geography*, 31(5): 654–674.

Madge, C. and Harrisson, T. (1938) *Britain by Mass-Observation.* London: Penguin.

Madison, D. S. (2006) 'The dialogic performative in critical ethnography', *Text and Performance Quarterly*, 26(4): 320–324.

Mahmood, M. (2008) *Confessions of a Fake Sheik: 'The King of the Sting' Reveals All.* London: Harper Collins.

Maines, D. (1993) 'Narrative's moment and sociology's phenomena: toward narrative sociology', *Sociological Quarterly*, 34(1): 17–38.

Malbon, B. (1999) *Clubbing: Dancing, Ecstasy and Vitality.* Routledge: London.

Manning, P. K. (1974) 'Police Lying', *Journal of Contemporary Ethnography*, 3(3): 283–306

Manning, P. K. (2008) 'Goffman on organisations', *Organization Studies*, 29(5): 677–699.

Manning, P. K. (2009) 'Three models of ethnographic research: Wacquant as risk-taker', *Theory & Psychology*, 19(6): 756–777.

Marlow, T. (2011) *The Bouncer: Working Stiffs*. London: Brazen Snake Books.

Mars, G. (1982) *Cheats at Work: An Anthropology of Workplace Crime*. London: Allen and Unwin.

Mars, G. (2013) *Locating Deviance: Crime, Change, and Organizations*. Farnham: Ashgate.

Marsh, P., Rosser, E. and Harré, R. (1978) *The Rules of Disorder*. London: Routledge and Kegan Paul.

Martin, C. (ed.) (2009) *The Philosophy of Deception*. Oxford: Oxford University Press.

Martin, L. J. (2010) 'Anticipating infertility: egg freezing, genetic preservation, and risks', *Gender and Society*, 24(4): 526–545.

Martellozzo, E. (2012) *Online Child Sexual Abuse: Grooming, Policing and Child Protection in a Multi-Media World*. London: Routledge.

Marzano, M. (2007) 'Informed consent, deception, and research freedom in qualitative research: a cross-cultural comparison', *Qualitative Inquiry*, 13(3): 417–436.

Marx, G. T. (1980) 'The new police undercover work', *Journal of Contemporary Ethnography*, 8(4): 399–446.

Marx, G. T. (1982) 'Who really gets stung? Some issues raised by the new police under-cover work', *Crime & Delinquency*, 28(2): 165–193.

Marx, G. T. (1988) *Undercover: Police Surveillance in America*. Berkeley, CA: University of California Press.

Mattley, C. (1998) '(Dis)courtesy stigma: fieldwork among phone fantasy workers', in J. Ferrell and M. S. Hamm (eds), *Ethnography at the Edge: Crime, Deviance and Field Research*. Boston, MA: Northeastern University Press. pp. 146–159.

Mawby, R. C. (2014) 'The presentation of police in everyday life: police–press relations, impression management and the Leveson inquiry', *Crime, Media, Culture*, 10(3): 239–257.

May, T. (2000) 'From banana time to just-in-time: power and resistance at work', *Sociology*, 33(4): 767–783.

Mayo, E. (1933) *The Human Problems of an Industrial Civilization*. New York: Macmillan.

Mazure, R. (2009) *The Infiltrator: Undercover in the World of Drug Barons and Dirty Banks Behind Pablo Escobar's Medellin Cartel*. London: Hachette Books.

McAra, L. (2008) 'Crime, criminology and criminal justice in Scotland', *European Journal of Criminology*, 5(4): 481–504.

McCleary, R. and Tewksbury, R. (2010) 'Female patrons of porn', *Deviant Behavior*, 31(2): 208–223.

McKay, S. (2015) *Covert Policing: Law and Practice* (2nd edn). Oxford: Oxford University Press (1st edn, 2010).

McKinney, J. C. (1966) *Constructive Typology and Social Theory*. New York: Appleton Century Crofts.

Mears, A. (2008) 'Discipline of the catwalk: gender, power and uncertainty in fashion modelling', *Ethnography*, 9(4): 429–456.

Measham, F. and Brain, K. (2005) 'Binge drinking, British alcohol policy and the new culture of intoxication', *Crime, Media, Culture*, 1(3): 262–283.

Measham, F. and Moore, K. (2006) 'Reluctant reflexivity, implicit insider knowledge and the development of Club Studies', in B. Sanders (ed.), *Drugs, Clubs and Young People: Sociological and Public Health Perspectives*. Aldershot: Ashgate. pp. 13–25.

Mechanic, D. (1989) 'Medical sociology: some tensions among theory, method and substance', *Journal of Health and Social Behaviour*, 30(2): 147–160.

Medford, K. (2006) 'Caught with a fake ID', *Qualitative Inquiry*, 12(5): 853–864.

Mellor, R. (1989) 'Urban sociology: a trend report', *Sociology*, 23(2): 241–260.

Melton, J. G. (1985) 'Spiritualization and reaffirmation: what really happens when prophecy fails', *American Studies*, 26(2): 82.

Menih, H. (2013) 'Applying ethical principles in researching a vulnerable population: homeless women in Brisbane', *Current Issues in Criminal Justice*, 25(1): 527–39.

Merritt, C. B. and Fowler, R. G. (1948) 'The pecuniary honesty of the public at large', *Journal of Abnormal and Social Psychology*, 43(1): 90–93.

Miethe, T. D. (1999) *Whistleblowing at Work: Tough Choices in Exposing Fraud, Waste, and Abuse on the Job*. Boulder, CO: Westview Press.

Miles, S. (2006) 'The cultural capital of consumption: understanding "postmodern" identities in a cultural context', *Culture and Psychology*, 2(2): 139–158.

Milgram, S. (1974) *Obedience to Authority: An Experimental View*. London: Tavistock Publications.

Milgram, S. (1977) 'Subject reaction: the neglected factor in the ethics of experimentation', *The Hastings Center Report*, 7(5): 19–23.

Milgram, S. (1992) *The Individual in a Social World: Essays and Experiments* (2nd edn). New York: McGraw-Hill (1st edn, 1977).

Miller, A. G. (1986) *The Obedience Experiments: A Case Study of Controversy in Social Science*. New York: Praeger.

Miller, F. G., Wendler, D. and Swartzman, L. C. (2005) 'Deception in Research on the Placebo Effect', *PLoS Medicine*, 2(9): e262.

Miller, M. (1995) 'Participant observation: reconsidering the least used method', *Journal of Contemporary Criminal Justice*, 11(2): 97–105.

Miller, R. (1998) 'Undercover shoppers', *Marketing*, 28 May: 1–4.

Millon, T. (1975) 'Reflections on Rosenhan's "On being sane in insane places"', *Journal of Abnormal Psychology*, 84(5): 456–461.

Millward, P. (2009) 'Glasgow Rangers supporters in the city of Manchester: the degeneration of a "fan party" into a "hooligan riot"', *International Review for the Sociology of Sport*, 44(4): 381–398.

Mitchell, R. G. Jr. (1993) *Secrecy and Fieldwork*. London: Sage.

Mitchell, R. G. Jr. and Charmaz, K. (1996) 'Telling tales, writing stories: postmodernist visions and realist images in ethnographic writing', *Journal of Contemporary Ethnography*, 25(1): 144–166.

Mixon, D. (1972) 'Instead of deception', *Journal for the Theory of Social Behaviour*, 2(2): 145–177.

Moberg, D. J. and Seabright, M. A. (2000) 'The development of moral imagination', *Business Ethics Quarterly*, 10(4): 845–884.

Mock, K. (2000) 'Hate on the internet', in S. Hicks, E. F. Halpin and E. Hoskins (eds), *Human Rights and the Internet*. New York: Palgrave Macmillan. pp. 141–152.

Monaghan, L. (2002a) 'Embodying gender, work and organization: solidarity, cool loyalties and contested hierarchy in a masculinist occupation', *Gender, Work and Organization*, 9(5): 504–536.

Monaghan, L. (2002b) 'Regulating "unruly" bodies: work tasks, conflict and violence in Britain's night-time economy', *The British Journal of Sociology*, 53(3): 403–429.

Monaghan, L. (2002c) 'Hard men, shop boys and others: embodying competence in an masculinist occupation', *The Sociological Review*, 50(3): 334–355.

Monaghan, L. (2002d) 'Opportunity, pleasure, and risk: an ethnography of urban male heterosexuality', *Journal of Contemporary Ethnography*, 3(4): 440–477.

Monaghan, L. (2003) 'Danger on the doors: bodily risk in a demonised occupation', *Health, Risk and Society*, 5(1): 11–31.

Monaghan, L. (2004) 'Doorwork and legal risk: observations from an embodied ethnography', *Social & Legal Studies*, 13(4): 453–480.

Monaghan, L. (2006) 'Fieldwork and the body: reflections on an embodied ethnography', in D. Hobbs and R. Wright (eds.), *The Sage Handbook of Fieldwork*. London: Sage. pp. 225–241.

Monaghan, L. F. and Atkinson, M. (2014) *Challenging Myths of Masculinity: Understanding Physical Cultures*. London: Routledge.

Morrall, K. (1994) 'Mystery shopping tests service and compliance', *Bank Marketing*, 26(2): 13–23.

Mowlabocus, S. (2008) 'Revisiting old haunts through new technologies: public (homo) sexual cultures in cyberspace', *International Journal of Cultural Studies*, 11(4): 419–439.

Mumford, E. (1959) 'Social behaviour in small work groups', *Sociological Review*, 7(2): 137–157.

Murphy, E. and Dingwall, R. (2001) 'The ethics of ethnography', in P. Atkinson, A. Coffey, S. Delamont, J. Lofland and L. Lofland (eds), *Handbook of Ethnography*. London: Sage, pp. 339–351.

Murphy, E. and Dingwall, R. (2003) *Qualitative Methods and Health Policy Research*. New York: Aldine de Gruyter.

Murphy, E. and Dingwall, R. (2007) 'Informed consent, anticipatory regulation and ethnographic practice', *Social Science & Medicine*, 65(11): 2223–2234.

Murray, T. H. (1980) 'Learning to deceive', *Hastings Center Report*, 10(2): 11–14.

Murthy, D. (2008) 'Digital ethnography: an examination of the use of new technologies for social research', *Sociology*, 42(5): 837–855.

Nathan, R. (2005) *My Freshman Year: What a Professor Learned by Becoming a Student*. Ithaca, NY: Cornell University Press.

National Union of Journalists (NUJ) (2013) *Code of Conduct* (https://www.nuj.org.uk/about/nuj-code/).

Near, J. P. (1995) 'Effective whistle-blowing', *Academy of Management Review*, 20(3): 679–708.

Near, J. P. and Miceli, M. P. (1996) 'Whistle-blowing: myth and reality', *Journal of Management*, 22(3): 507–526.

Nelson, N. (1888) 'City slave girls', 23 part series, *Chicago Daily Times*, 30 July to 27 August.

Newbold, G., Ross, J. I., Jones, R. S., Richards, S. C. and Lenza, M. (2014) 'Prison research from the inside: the role of convict autoethnography', *Qualitative Inquiry*, 20(4): 439–448.

Nicholson, I. (2011) 'Torture at Yale: experimental subjects, laboratory torment and the rehabilitation of Milgram's obedience to authority', *Theory & Psychology*, 21(6): 737–761.

Nugent, P. D. and Abolafia, M. Y. (2007) 'Imagining the "iron cage": the rhetoric of hidden emotions in critical ethnography', *Ethnography*, 8(2): 205–226.

O'Brien, K. (2009) 'Inside door work: gendering the security gaze', in R. Ryan-Flood and R. Gill (eds), *Silence and Secrecy in the Research Process: Feminist Reflections.* London: Routledge. pp. 117–132.

O'Brien, K., Hobbs, D. and Westmarland, L. (2008) 'Negotiating violence and gender: security and the night-time economy in the UK', in S. Gendrot and P. Spierenburg (eds), *Collection on Historical and Contemporary Violence in Europe.* New York: Springer. pp. 161–173.

O'Connor, D. (2010) 'Apomediation and ancillary care: researchers' responsibilities in health-related online communities', *International Journal of Internet Research Ethics*, 3(1): 87–103.

O'Connor, J. and Wynne, D. (eds) (1996) *From the Margins to the Centre: Cultural Production and Consumption in the Post-Industrial City.* Aldershot: Arena.

O'Keefe, J. (1997) *Old School-New School: Guide to Bouncers, Security and Registered Door Supervisors.* London: New Breed Publishing.

Oldman, D. (1974) 'Chance and skill: a study of roulette', *Sociology*, 8(1): 407–426.

Oldman, D. (1978) 'Compulsive gamblers', *The Sociological Review*, 26(2): 349–371.

Ortner, S. B. (2010) 'Access: reflections on studying up in Hollywood', *Ethnography*, 11(2): 211–233.

Page, R. (1973) *Down among the Dossers.* London: Harper Collins.

Palmer, C. (2010) 'Everyday risks and professional dilemmas: fieldwork with alcohol-based (sporting) subcultures', *Qualitative Research*, 10(4): 421–440.

Panzarella, R. and Funk, J. (1987) 'Police deception tactics and public consent in the United States and Great Britain', *Criminal Justice Policy Review*, 2(2): 133–149.

Park, R. E. (1925) *The City.* Chicago, IL: University of Chicago Press.

Park, R. E. and Burgess, E. W. (1921) *Introduction to the Science of Sociology.* Chicago, IL: University of Chicago Press.

Parker, H. (1974) *View from the Boys: A Sociology of Down-Town Adolescents.* Newton Abbot: David & Charles Holdings Limited.

Parker, J. and Crabtree, S. A. (2014) 'Covert research and adult protection and safeguarding: an ethical dilemma?', *The Journal of Adult Protection*, 16(1): 29–40.

Parr, H. (2000) 'Interpreting the hidden social geographies' of mental health: ethnographies of inclusion and exclusion in semi-institutional places', *Health & Place*, 6(3): 225–237.

Paterniti, D. A. (2000) 'The micro politics of identity in adverse circumstance: a study of identity making in a total institution', *Journal of Contemporary Ethnography*, 29(1): 93–119.

Patrick, J. (1973) *A Glasgow Gang Observed*. London: Eyre Methuen.

Pattison, E. M. (1974) 'Social criticism and scientific responsibility: a commentary on being sane in insane places', *Journal of the American Scientific Affiliation*, 26(September): 110–114.

Patton, M. Q. (2002) *Qualitative Research & Evaluation Methods* (3rd edn). London: Sage (1st edn, 1980).

Pauwels, L. (2010) 'Visual sociology reframed: an analytical synthesis and discussion of visual methods in social and cultural research', *Sociological Methods & Research*, 39(4): 545–581.

Pearson, G. (2009) 'The researcher as hooligan: where "participant" observation means breaking the law', *International Journal of Social Research Methodology*, 12(3): 243–255.

Pearson, G. (2011) 'A commentary on "Little Hooliganz: the inside story of glamorous lads, football hooligans and post-subculturalism"', *Entertainment and Sports Law Journal*, 9(1): 1–14.

Perez-y-Perez, M. and Stanley, T. (2011) 'Ethnographic intimacy: thinking through the ethics of social research in sex worlds', *Sociological Research Online*, 16(2).

Perry, G. (2013) *Behind the Shock Machine: The Untold Story of the Notorious Milgram Psychology Experiments*. New York: The New Press.

Perry, N. (1998) 'Indecent exposures: theorizing whistleblowing', *Organization Studies*, 19(2): 235–257.

Peshkin, A. (1985) 'Virtuous subjectivity: in the participant observer's I's', in D. N. Berg and K. K. Smith (eds), *Exploring Clinical Methods for Social Research*. Beverly Hills, CA: Sage. pp. 267–281.

Petkovic, G., Charlesworth, J., Kelley, J., Miller, F., Roberts, N. and Howick, J. (2015) 'Effects of placebos without deception compared with no treatment: protocol for a systematic review and meta-analysis', *BMJ Open*, 5(11): e009428.

Petticrew, M., Semple, S., Hilton, S., Creely, C. S., Eadie, D., Ritchie, D., Ferrell, C., Christopher, Y. and Hurley, F. (2007) 'Covert observation in practice: lessons from the evaluation of the prohibition of smoking in public places in Scotland', *BMC Public Health*, 7: 204–211.

Pettinger, L. (2005) 'Representing shop work: a dual ethnography', *Qualitative Research*, 5(3): 347–364.

Pierce, J. L. (1995) *Gender Trials: Emotional Lives in Contemporary Law Firms*. Berkeley, CA: University of California Press.

Piliavin, I. M., Rodin, J. A. and Piliavin, J. (1969) 'Good Samaritanism: an underground phenomenon?', *Journal of Personality and Social Psychology*, 13(4): 289–299.

Pimple, K. D. (ed.) (2008) *Research Ethics*. Aldershot: Ashgate.

Pine, J. (2008) 'Icons and iconoclasm: Roberto Saviano's *Gomorrah* and La Denuncia', *Journal of Modern Italian Studies*, 13(3): 431–436.

Pink, S. (2006) *The Future of Visual Anthropology: Engaging the Senses*. London: Routledge.

Pink, S. (2007a) *Doing Visual Ethnography*. London: Sage.

Pink, S. (2007b) 'Walking with video', *Visual Studies*, 22(3): 240–242.

Pink, S. (2008a) 'An urban tour', *Ethnography*, 9(2): 175–196.

Pink, S (2008b) 'Mobilising visual ethnography: making routes, making place and making images', *Forum: Qualitative Social Research*, 9(3), Article 38.

Pink, S. (2010) 'The future of sensory anthropology/the anthropology of the senses', *Social Anthropology*, 18(3): 331–340.

Pink, S. (2015) *Doing Sensory Ethnography* (2nd edn). London: Sage (1st edn, 2009).

Pistone, J. D. with Woodley, R. (1988) *Donnie Brasco: My Undercover Life in the Mafia*. New York: Hodder and Stoughton.

Platt, J. (1994) 'The Chicago school and first hand data', *History of the Human Sciences*, 7(1): 57–80.

Pleasants, N. (1998) 'Experimentation in the social sciences: cultural dope or reflexive agent? A reflexive critique of ethnomethodology', *Ethnographic Studies*, 3: 17–40.

Plowman, C. (2013) *Crossing the Line: Losing Your Mind as an Undercover Cop*. London: Mainstream Publishing.

Plummer, K. (2003) 'Continuity and change in Howard S. Becker's work: an interview with Howard S. Becker', *Sociological Perspectives*, 46(1): 21–39.

Polley, N. M. and Tewksbury, R. (2010) 'Equal protection at the erotic oasis: examining selective prosecution claims in lewd conduct cases', *Criminal Justice Review*, 35(4): 453–471.

Pollner, M. (1979) 'Self-explicating settings: making and managing meaning in traffic court', in G. Psathas (ed.), *Everyday Language: Studies in Ethnomethodology*. New York: Irvington Press. pp. 227–255.

Pollner, M. (1987) *Mundane Reason: Reality in Everyday Life and Sociological Discourse*. Cambridge: Cambridge University Press.

Polsky, N. (1967) *Hustlers, Beats, and Others*. Chicago, IL: Aldine.

Ponticelli, C. M. (1996) 'The spiritual warfare of exodus: A postpositivist research adventure', *Qualitative Inquiry*, 2(2): 198–219.

Presser, L. (2009) 'The narratives of offenders', *Theoretical Criminology*, 13(2): 177–200.

Prosser, J. (ed.) (1998) *Image-Based Research: A Sourcebook for Qualitative Researchers*. London: Falmer Press.

Prosser, J., Clark, A. and Wiles, R. (2008) 'Visual research ethics at the crossroads', Working Paper 10, *Realities*. ESRC National Centre for Research Methods, University of Manchester.

Pryce, K. (1979) *Endless Pressure: A Study of West Indian Life-styles in Bristol*. Harmondsworth: Penguin.

213

Pryce, K. (1986) *Endless Pressure: A Study of West Indian Life-styles in Bristol* (2nd edn). London: Bristol Classical Press (1st edn, 1979).

Punch, M. (1986) *The Politics and Ethics of Fieldwork*. London: Sage.

Punch, M. (1994) 'Politics and ethics in qualitative research', in N. K. Denzin and Y. S. Lincoln (eds), *Handbook of Qualitative Research*. Thousand Oaks, CA: Sage. pp. 83–97.

Purdam, K. (2014) 'Citizen social science and citizen data? Methodological and ethical challenges for social research', *Current Sociology*, 62(3): 374–392.

Queen, W. (2005) *Under and Alone: The True Story of the Undercover Agent Who Infiltrated America's Most Violent Outlaw Motorcycle Gang*. New York: Random House.

Quinn, P. (1990) *A Bouncer's Guide to Barroom Brawling: Dealing with the Sucker Puncher, Street fighter and Ambusher*. London: Paladin Press.

Raab, J. and Milward, H. (2003) 'Dark networks as problems', *Journal of Public Administration Research and Theory*, 13(4): 413–439.

Rambo, C. (2005) 'Impressions of grandmother: an autoethnographic portrait', *Journal of Contemporary Ethnography*, 34(5): 560–585.

Rank, S. G. and Jacobson, C. K. (1977) 'Hospital nurses' compliance with medication overdose orders: a failure to replicate', *Journal of Health and Social Behavior*, 18(2): 188–193.

Redhead, S. (1990) *The End of the Century Party: Youth and Pop Towards 2000*. Manchester: Manchester University Press.

Redhead, S. (ed.) (1993) *Rave Off: Politics and Deviance in Contemporary Youth Culture*. Aldershot: Avebury.

Redhead, S. (ed.) (1997) *Subculture to Club Cultures*. Oxford: Oxford University Press.

Redhead, S. (2009) 'Hooligan Writing and the Study of Football Fan Culture: Problems and Possibilities', *Nebula*, 6(3): 16–41.

Redhead, S. (2010a) 'Little Hooliganz: the inside story of glamorous lads, football hooligans and post-subculturalism', *Entertainment and Sports Law Journal Online*, 8(2).

Redhead, S. (2010b) 'Lock, stock and two smoking hooligans: low sport journalism and hooligan memoirs', *Soccer and Society*, 11(2): 627–642.

Redhead, S., O'Connor, J. and Wynne, D. (eds) (1998) *The Club Cultures Reader: Readings in Popular Cultural Studies*. Oxford: Blackwell.

Reed, K. (2007) 'Bureaucracy and beyond: the impact of ethics and governance procedures on health research in the social sciences', *Sociological Research Online*, 12(5).

Reed-Danahay, D. E. (ed.) (1997) *Auto/Ethnography: Rewriting the Self and the Social*. Oxford: Berg.

Reed-Danahay, D. (2001) 'Autobiography, intimacy and ethnography', in P. Atkinson, A. Coffey, S. Delamont, J. Lofland and L. Lofland (eds), *The Handbook of Ethnography*. London: Sage. pp. 407–425.

Reiss, I. L. (1971) 'Book review: *Tearoom Trade*', *American Sociological Review*, 36(3): 581–583.

Renninger, B. J. (2015) 'Where I can be myself … where I can speak my mind: networked counterpublics in a polymedia environment', *New Media & Society*, 17(9): 1513–1529.

Renold, E., Holland, S., Ross, N. J. and Hillman, A. (2008) 'Becoming participant: problematizing "informed consent" in participatory research with young people in care', *Qualitative Social Work*, 7(4): 427–447.

Reverby, S. M. (ed.) (2000) *Tuskegee's Truth: Rethinking the Tuskegee Syphilis Study*. Chapel Hill, NC: University of North Carolina Press.

Reynolds, P. D. (1982) 'Moral judgements: strategies for analysis with application to covert participant', in M. Bulmer (ed.), *Social Research Ethics: An Examination of the Merits of Covert Participant Observation*. London: Macmillan. pp. 185–216.

Reynolds, R. and de Zwart, M. (2010) 'The duty to "play": ethics, EULA's and MMO's', *International Journal of Internet Research Ethics*, 3(1): 48–68.

Richards, J. and Marks, A. (2007) 'Biting the hand that feeds: social identity and resistance in restaurant teams', *International Journal of Business Science and Applied Management*, 2(2): 42–57.

Richardson, S. and McMullan, M. (2007) 'Research ethics in the UK: what can sociology learn from health', *Sociology*, 41(6): 1115–1132.

Riemer, J. W. (1977) 'Varieties of opportunistic research', *Urban Life*, 5(4): 467–477.

Rigakos, G. S. (2002) *The New Parapolice: Risk Markets and Commodified Social Control*. Buffalo, Canada: University of Toronto Press.

Rigakos, G. S. (2008) *Nightclub: Bouncers, Risk and the Spectacle of Consumption*. Montreal, Canada: McGill-Queen's University Press.

Roberts, B. (2002) *Biographical Research*. Buckingham: Open University Press.

Roberts, B. (2008) 'Performative social science: a consideration of skills, purpose and context', *Forum: Qualitative Social Research [Online]*, 9(2), Article 58.

Robinson, L. (2007) 'The cyberself: the self-ing project goes online, symbolic interaction in the digital age', *New Media & Society*, 9(1): 93–110.

Roebuck, J. B. and Frese, W. (1976) 'The after-hours club: an illegal social organization and its client system', *Journal of Contemporary Ethnography*, 5(2): 131–164.

Rollins, J. (1985) *Between Women: Domestics and their Employers*. Philadelphia, PA: Temple University Press.

Ronai, C. R. (1995) 'Multiple reflections of childhood sex abuse: an argument for a layered account', *Journal of Contemporary Ethnography*, 23(4): 395–426.

Ronai, C. R. (1997) 'On loving and hating my mentally retarded mother', *Mental Retardation*, 35(6): 417–432.

Ronai, C. R. (1998) 'Sketching with Derrida: an ethnography of a researcher/erotic dancer', *Qualitative Inquiry*, 4(3): 405–420.

Ronai, C. R. and Ellis, C. (1989) 'Turn-ons for money: interactional strategies of the table dancer', *Journal of Contemporary Ethnography*, 18(3): 271–298.

Rose, G. (2001) *Visual Methodologies: An Introduction to the Interpretation of Visual Methods*. London: Sage.

Rosen, L. (1972) 'Book review: *Tearoom Trade*', *Journal of Marriage and the Family*, 34(2): 382–384.

Rosenberg, A. (2010) 'Virtual world research ethics and the private/public distinction', *International Journal of Internet Research Ethics*, 3(1): 6–22.

Rosenhan, D. L. (1973) 'On being sane in insane places', *Science*, 179(4070), 19 January: 250–258.

Rosenhan, D. L. (1975) 'The contextual nature of psycho-diagnosis', *Journal of Abnormal Psychology*, 84(5): 462–474.

Rosenhan, D. L. (1981) 'The joys of helping: focus of attention mediates the impact of positive affect on altruism', *Journal of Personality and Social Psychology*, 40(5): 899–905.

Roth, J. A. (1962) 'Comments on secret observations', *Social Problems*, 9(3): 283–284.

Roth, J. A. (1963) *Timetables: Structuring the Passage of Time in Hospital Treatment and other Careers.* Indianapolis, IN: Bobbs-Merrill.

Roth, J. A. (1974) 'Turning adversity to account', *Urban Life and Culture*, 3(3): 347–359.

Roth, J. A. (1975) 'Book review of *City Police*', *Sociology of Work and Occupations*, 2(3): 288–290.

Rothschild, J. and Miethe, T. D. (1994) 'Whistleblowing as resistance in modern work organizations: the politics of revealing organizational deception and abuse', in J. Jermier, D. Knights and W. Nord (eds), *Resistance and Power in Organizations.* London: Routledge. pp. 252–273.

Roy, D. F. (1952) 'Quota restriction and goldbricking in a machine shop', *American Journal of Sociology*, 57(5): 427–442.

Roy, D. F. (1959) 'Banana time: job satisfaction and informal interaction', *Human Organization*, 18(4): 158–168.

Rubinstein, J. (1973) *City Police.* New York: Farrar, Strauss and Giroux.

Ruby, J. (2000) *Picturing Culture: Explorations of Film and Anthropology.* Chicago, IL: University of Chicago Press.

Russell, N. and Gregory, R. (2005) 'Making the undoable doable: Milgram, the Holocaust and modern government', *The American Review of Public Administration*, 35(4): 327–349.

Russell, R. and Tyler, M. (2002) 'Thank heaven for little girls: "Girl Heaven" and the commercial context of feminine childhood', *Sociology*, 36(3): 619–637.

Ryan, J. with Thomas, F. (1987) *The Politics of Mental Handicap.* London: Free Association Books.

Sagarin, E. and MacNamara, D. (1970) 'The problem of entrapment', *Crime & Delinquency*, 16(4): 363–378.

Sageman, M. (2004) *Understanding Terror Networks.* Philadelphia, PA: University of Pennsylvania Press.

Salerno, Roger. A (2007) *Sociology Noir: Studies at the University of Chicago in Loneliness, Marginality and Deviance, 1915–1935.* London: McFarland and Company.

Sallaz, J. J. (2002) 'The house rules: autonomy and interests among service workers in the contemporary casino industry', *Work and Occupations*, 29(4): 394–427.

Sanders, B. (2005) 'In the club: ecstasy use and supply in a London nightclub', *Sociology*, 39(2): 241–258.

Sanders, T. (2005) *Sex Work: A Risky Business.* Cullompton, Devon: Willan Publishing.

Sanders, T. (2006) 'Sexing up the subject: methodological nuances in researching the female sex industry', *Sexualities*, 9(4): 449–468.

Sargent, C. (2009) 'Playing, shopping, and working as rock musicians: masculinities in "de-skilled" and "re-skilled" organizations', *Gender and Society*, 23(5): 665–687.

Sauter, T. (2014) '"What's on your mind": writing on Facebook as a tool for self-formation', *New Media & Society*, 16(5): 823–839.

Saviano, R. (2007) *Gomorrah: Italy's Other Mafia*. London: Macmillan.

Saviano, R. (2014) 'I'm a Monster', An Interview with Rudiger Sturm, *The Red Bulletin* (UK edition), pp 28–33.

Scarce, R. (2005) *Contempt of Court: A Scholar's Battle for Free Speech from Behind Bars*. Walnut Creek, CA: AltaMira Press.

Schacht, S. P. (1997) 'Feminist fieldwork in the misogynist setting of the rugby pitch: temporarily becoming a sylph to survive and personally grow', *Journal of Contemporary Ethnography*, 26(3): 338–363.

Schacht, S. P. (2004) 'Moving beyond the controversy: remembering the many contributions of Laud Humphreys to sociology and the study of sexuality', *International Journal of Sociology and Social Policy*, 24(3): 3–11.

Schein, E. H. (1989) 'A social psychologist discovers Chicago Sociology', *The Academy of Management Review*, 14(1): 103–104.

Scheper-Hughes, N. (1990) 'Theft of life', *Society*, 27(6): 57–62.

Scheper-Hughes, N. (2004) 'Parts unknown: undercover ethnography of the organs-trafficking underworld', *Ethnography*, 5(1): 29–73.

Scheper-Hughes, N. (2011) 'Mr Tati's Holiday and Joao's Safari: seeing the world through transplant tourism', *Body & Society*, 17(2&3): 55–92.

Schneider, Sara K. (2008) *Art of Darkness: Ingenious Performances of Undercover Operators. Con Men and Others*. Chicago, IL: Cuneform Books.

Schrag, Z. (2010) *Ethical Imperialism: Institutional Review Boards and the Social Sciences, 1965–2009*. Baltimore, MD and London: The Johns Hopkins University Press.

Schreer, G. E., Smith, S. and Thomas, K. (2009) 'Shopping while black: examining racial discrimination in a retail setting', *Journal of Applied Social Psychology*, 39(6): 1432–1444.

Schroeder, R. (2014) 'Big Data and the brave new world of social media research', *Big Data & Society*, July–December, 1–11.

Schutz, A. (1973) *The Structure of the Life-World*. Evanston, IL: Northwestern University Press.

Schwartz, M. S. and Schwartz, C. G. (1955) 'Problems in participant observation', *American Journal of Sociology*, 60(4): 343–354.

Scott, G. G. (1983) *Magicians: A Study of the Use of Power in a Black Magic Group*. New York: Irvington.

Scott, J. (2000) *Social Network Analysis: A Handbook* (2nd edn). London: Sage (1st edn, 1991).

Scott, J. (ed.) (2002) *Social Networks: Critical Concepts in Sociology*. London: Routledge.

Seale, C. and Kelly, M. (1997) 'A comparison of hospice and hospital care for the spouses of people who die', *Palliative Medicine*, 11(2): 101–106.

Seaton, A. V. (1997) 'Unobtrusive observational measures as a qualitative extension of visitor surveys at festivals and events: Mass Observation revisited', *Journal of Travel Research*, 35(4): 25–30.

Seaton, A. V. (2002) 'Observing conducted tours: the ethnographic context in tourist research', *Journal of Vacation Marketing*, 8(4): 309–319.

Sedgwick, P. (1974) 'Goffman's Anti-Psychiatry', *Salmagundi*, 26 (Spring): 26–51

Shachaf, P. and Hara, N. (2010) 'Beyond vandalism: Wikipedia trolls', *Journal of Information Science*, 36(3): 357–370.

Shaffir, W. B. (1985) 'Some reflections on approaches to fieldwork in Hassidic communities', *Jewish Journal of Sociology*, 27(2): 115–134.

Sharp, K. and Earle, S. (2003) 'Cyberpunters and cyberwhores: prostitution on the internet', in Y. Jewkes (ed.), *Dot.cons: Crime, Deviance and Identity on the Internet*. Cullompton, Devon: Willan Publishing. pp. 36–52.

Sheridan, D. (1993) 'Writing to the archive: Mass-Observation as autobiography', *Sociology*, 27(1): 27–40.

Sheridan, D., Street, B. V. and Bloome, D. (2000) *Writing Ourselves: Mass-Observation and Literacy Practices*. Cresskill, NJ: Hampton Press.

Shilling, C. and Mellor, P. A. (2015) 'For a sociology of deceit: doubled identities, interested actions and situational logics of opportunity', *Sociology*, 49(4): 607–623.

Shils, E. (1959, reprinted in 1982) 'Social inquiry and the autonomy of the individual', in M. Bulmer (ed.), *Social Research Ethics: An Examination of the Merits of Covert Participant Observation*. London: Macmillan. pp. 125–141.

Sikes, P. (2013) *Autoethnography*, Thousand Oaks, CA: Sage.

Silverman, D. (2001) *Interpreting Qualitative Data: Methods for Analyzing Talk, Text and Interaction* (2nd edn). Thousand Oaks, CA: Sage (1st edn, 1993).

Silverstone, D. (2006) 'Pub space, rave space, urban space: three different night-time economies', in B. Sanders (ed.), *Drugs, Clubs and Young People*. Aldershot: Ashgate. pp. 141–153.

Simmel, G. (1906) 'The sociology of secrecy and secret societies', *American Journal of Sociology*, 11(4): 441–498.

Simmel, G. (1950) 'The metropolis and the mental life', in K. Wolff (ed.), *The Sociology of George Simmel*. New York: Free Press. pp. 409–427.

Simpson, B. (2005) 'Identity manipulation in cyberspace as a leisure option: play and the exploration of self', *Information & Communications Technology Law*, 14(2): 115–131.

Simpson, B. (2006) 'From family first to the FBI: children, ideology and cyberspace', *Information & Communications Technology Law*, 15(3): 239–257.

Sin, C. H. (2005) 'Seeking informed consent: reflections on research practice', *Sociology*, 39(2): 277–294.

Sinclair, U. (1906) *The Jungle*. New York: Doubleday.

Skeggs, B. (2004) *Class, Self, Culture*. London: Routledge.

Slater, D. (1999) 'Trading sex pics on IRC: embodiment and authenticity on the internet', *Body and Society*, 4(4): 91–117.

Slater, L. (2001) *Lying: A Metaphorical Memoir*. London: Routledge.

Slater, M., Antley, A., Davison, A., Swapp, D. and Guger, C. (2006) 'A virtual reprise of the Stanley Milgram Obedience Experiments', *PLoS ONE [Online]*, 1(1).

Slavin, S. (2004) 'Drugs, space, and sociality in a gay nightclub in Sydney', *Journal of Contemporary Ethnography*, 33(3): 265–295.

Sluka, J. A. (1990) 'Participant observation in violent social contexts', *Human Organization*, 49(20): 114–126.

Smart, C. (2010) 'Disciplined writing: on the problem of writing sociologically', Working Paper 13, *Realities*. ESRC National Centre for Research Methods, Morgan Centre, University of Manchester.

Smith, A. (2007) 'Unlocking the geographies of the Mind Gym', *Ethnography*, 8(4): 425–444.

Smith, A. C. T. and Stewart, B. (2012) 'Body perceptions and health behaviours in an online bodybuilding community', *Qualitative Health Research*, 22(7): 971–985.

Smith, G. (2006) *Erving Goffman*. London: Routledge.

Smithers, J. A. (1977) 'Institutional dimensions of senility', *Urban Life*, 6(3): 251–276.

Snow, D. A., Robinson, C. and McCall, P. L. (1991) 'Cooling out men in singles bars and nightclubs: observations on the interpersonal survival strategies of women in public places', *Journal of Contemporary Ethnography*, 19(4): 423–449.

Social Policy Association (2009) *Social Policy Association Guidelines on Research Ethics*. www.social-policy.org.uk.

Social Research Association (2003) *Ethical Guidelines*. www.the-sra.org.uk.

Sosteric, M. (1996) 'Subjectivity and the labour process: a case study in the restaurant industry', *Work, Employment & Society*, 10(2): 297–318.

Sparkes, A. C. (2002) 'Autoethnography: self-indulgence or something more?', in A. P. Bocher and C. Ellis (eds), *Ethnographically Speaking: Autoethnography, Literature and Aesthetic*. Walnut Creek, CA: AltaMira Press. pp. 209–232.

Spicker, P. (2011) 'Ethical covert research', *Sociology*, 45(1): 118–133.

Spitzer, R. L. (1975) 'On pseudoscience in science, logic in remission, and psychiatric diagnosis: a critique of Rosenhan's "On being sane in insane places"', *Journal of Abnormal Psychology*, 84(5): 442–452.

Spradley, J. P. (1980) *Participant Observation*. New York: Holt, Rinehart and Winston.

Stanley, L. (2008) 'It has always known and we have always been "other" – knowing capitalism and the "coming crisis" of sociology confront the concentration system and Mass-Observation', *Sociological Review*, 56(4): 535–551.

Stanley, L. and Wise, S. (2010) 'The ESRC's Framework for Research Ethics: fit for research purpose?', *Sociological Research Online*,15(4).

Stark, L. (2012) *Behind Closed Doors: IRBs and the Making of Ethical Research*. Chicago, IL: University of Chicago Press.

Stevenson, R. and Crossley, N. (2014) 'Covert social movement networks in context: exploring change in the inner circle of the Provisional Irish Republican Army', *Social Movement Studies*, 13(1): 70–91.

Stohl, C. and Stohl, M. (2011) 'Secret agencies: the communicative constitution of a clandestine organization', *Organization Studies*, 32(9): 1197–1215.

Storm, M. (2014) *Agent Storm: My Life Inside al-Qaeda.* London: Viking Press.

Strauss, A., Schatzman, L., Ehrlich, D., Bucher, R. and Sabshin, M. (1963) 'The hospital and it's negotiated order', in E. Freidson (ed.), *The Hospital in Modern Society.* New York: Free Press. pp. 147–169.

Sturm, R. (2014) 'I'm a monster', special interview feature on Roberto Saviano, *The Red Bulletin* (UK Edition). November: 28–33.

Styles, J. (1979) 'Outsider/insider: researching gay baths', *Journal of Contemporary Ethnography*, 8(2): 135–152.

Stylianou, S. (2012) *On the Doors: Working as Britain's Hardest Bouncer, I Was Hit, Stabbed and Faced Guns – But I've Never Been Beaten.* London: John Blake Publishing.

Sugden, J. (2002) *Scum Airways: Inside Football's Underground Economy.* London: Mainstream Publishing.

Sugden, J. (2004) 'Is investigative sociology just investigative journalism?', in M. McNamee (ed.), *Philosophy and the Sciences of Health, Exercise and Sport: Critical Perspectives on Research Methodology.* London: Routledge. pp. 203–218.

Sugden, J. (2007) 'Inside the grafters' game: an ethnographic examination of football's underground economy', *Journal of Sport and Social Issues*, 31(3): 242–258.

Sullivan, M. A., Queen, S. A. and Patrick, R. C. (1958) 'Participant observation as employed in the study of a military training programme', *American Sociological Review*, 23(6): 660–667.

Summerfield, P. (1985) 'Mass Observation: social research or social movement?', *Journal of Contemporary History*, 20(3): 439–452.

Sundholm, C. A. (1973) 'The pornographic arcade: ethnographic notes on moral men in immoral places', *Urban Life and Culture*, 2(1): 85–104.

Sutcliffe, K. (2008) 'Not guilty – but who's to know?', *British Journalism Review*, 19(1): 48–56.

Suter, W. Newton, Lindgren, Henry C. and Hiebert, Sarah J. (1989) *Experimentation in Social Psychology: A Guided Tour.* Boston, MA: Allyn and Bacon.

Swanton, O. (1997) 'Gangchester: bright lights, big trouble', *Manchester Evening News*, 15 December.

Swanton, O. (1998) 'Gang law', *Mixmag*, February (Issue 81): 68–76.

Swinden, E. (2000) 'Bouncers in world of guns and drugs', *Manchester Evening News*, 6 December.

Swinden, E. (2000a) 'The danger on the doors', *Manchester Metro News*, 8 December.

Swinden, E. (2000b) 'Bouncer revelation man leaves the country', *Manchester Evening News*, 10 December.

Taber, N. (2010) 'Institutional ethnography, autoethnography, and narrative: an argument for incorporating multiple methodologies', *Qualitative Research*, 10(1): 5–25.

Taylor, J. (2011) 'The intimate insider: negotiating the ethics of friendship when doing insider research', *Qualitative Research*, 11(1): 3–22.

Taylor, S. J. (1987) 'Observing abuse: professional ethics and personal morality in field research', *Qualitative Sociology*, 10(3): 288–302.

Tedlock, B. (1991) 'From participant observation to the observation of participation: the emergence of narrative ethnography', *Journal of Anthropological Research*, 47(1): 69–94.

Tetzlaff-Bemiller, M. J. (2011) 'Undercover online: an extension of traditional policing in the United States', *International Journal of Cyber Criminology*, 5(2): 813–824.

Tewksbury, R. (1995) 'Adventures in the erotic oasis: sex and danger in men's same-sex, public, sexual encounters', *Journal of Men's Studies*, 4(1): 9–24.

Tewksbury, R. (1996) 'Cruising for sex in public places: the structure and language of men's hidden, erotic worlds', *Deviant Behavior*, 17(1): 1–19.

Tewksbury, R. (2002) 'Bathhouse intercourse: structural and behavioral aspects of an erotic oasis', *Deviant Behavior*, 23(1): 75–112.

Tewksbury, R. (2004) 'The intellectual legacy of Laud Humphreys: his impact on research and thinking about men's public sexual encounters', *The International Journal of Sociology and Social Policy*, 24(3/4/5): 32–57.

Tewksbury, R. (2008) 'Finding erotic oases: locating the sites of men's same-sex anonymous sexual encounters', *Journal of Homosexuality*, 55(1): 1–19.

Tewksbury, R. (2010) 'Men and erotic oases', *Sociology Compass*, 4(12): 1011–1019.

Thomas, D. (2012) *Narcissism: Behind the Mask*. Brighton: Book Guild Publishing.

Thompson, Geoff. (1994) *Bouncer.* Chichester: Summersdale.

Thompson, Geoff. (1999) *On the Door.* Chichester: Summersdale.

Thompson, Geoff (2001/2009) *Watch My Back: A Bouncer's Story.* Chichester: Summersdale.

Thornton, Sarah. (1995) *Club Cultures: Music, Media and Subcultural Capital.* Cambridge: Polity Press.

Thurman, N. (2008) 'Forums for citizen journalism? Adoption of user generated content initiatives by online news media', *New Media & Society,* 10(1): 139–157.

Thurnell-Read, T. (2011) 'Off the leash and out of control: masculinities and embodiment in Eastern European stag tourism', *Sociology*, 45(6): 977–991.

Tillman-Healy, L. M. (2001) *Between Gay and Straight: Understanding Friendship across Sexual Orientation*. Walnut Creek, CA: AltaMira Press.

Tillman-Healy, L. M. (2003) 'Friendship as method', *Qualitative Inquiry*, 9(5): 729–749.

Tober, D. M. (2007)' Kidneys and controversies in the Islamic Republic of Iran: the case of organ sale', *Body & Society*, 13(3): 151–170.

Toch, H. (1993) 'Good violence and bad violence: self-presentations of aggressors through accounts and war stories', in R. B. Felson and J. T. Tedeschi (eds), *Aggression and Violence: Social Interactionist Perspectives*. Washington, DC: American Psychological Association. pp. 193–206.

Tolich, M. (2010) 'A critique of current practice: ten foundational guidelines for autoethnogaphers', *Qualitative Health Research*, 20(12): 1599–1610.

Tomlinson, A. and Yorganci, I. (1997) 'Male coach/female athlete relations: gender and power relations in competitive sport', *Journal of Sport and Social Issues*, 21(2): 134–155.

Toynbee, P. (1971) *A Working Life*. London: Hodder & Stoughton Ltd.

Toynbee, P. (2003) *Hard Work: Life in Low-pay Britain*. London: Bloomsbury.

Trautner, M. N. (2005*)* 'Doing gender, doing class: the performance of sexuality in exotic dance clubs', *Gender and Society*, 19(6): 771–788.

Treadwell, J. and Garland, J. (2011) 'Masculinity, marginalization and violence: a case study of the English Defence League', *British Journal of Criminology*, 51(4): 621–634.

Trifari, R. (2008) *My Life as a Bouncer: 50 True Stories*. Bloomington, IN: iUniverse

Tuda, P. N. and Pathak, P. (2014) 'Growing corruption: is whistle blowing the answer', *Management and Labour Studies*, 39(2): 208–218.

Tumminia, D. (1998) 'How prophecy never fails: interpretive reason in a flying-saucer group', *Sociology of Religion*, 59(2): 157–170.

Tunnell, K. D. (1998) 'Honesty, secrecy, and deception in the sociology of crime: confessions and reflections from the backstage', in J. Ferrell and M. S. Hamm (eds), *Ethnography at the Edge: Crime, Deviance and Field Research*. Boston, MA: Northeastern University Press. pp. 206–220.

Turbide, O., Vincent, D. and Laforest, M. (2010) 'The circulation of discourse: the case of deprecating remarks on trash radio', *Discourse Studies*, 12(6): 785–801.

Turkle, S. (1984) *The Second Self: Computers and the Human Spirit*. New York: Simon & Schuster.

Turkle, S. (1995) *Life on the Screen: Identity in the Age of the Internet*. New York: Simon & Schuster.

Turkle, S. (1999) 'Cyberspace and identity', *Contemporary Sociology*, 28(6): 643–648.

Tuskegee Study of Untreated Syphilis in the Negro Male (1972) Tuskegee, AL: Tuskegee Institute.

Twemlow, C. (1980) *Tuxedo Warrior: The Tales of a Mancunion Bouncer*. Chichester: Summersdale.

Underwood, M. K. (2005) 'Observing anger and aggression among preadolescent girls and boys: ethical dilemmas and practical solutions', *Ethics & Behaviour*, 15(3): 235–245.

Urbas, G. (2010) 'Protecting children from online predators: the use of covert investigation techniques by law enforcement', *Journal of Contemporary Criminal Justice*, 26(4): 410–425.

Van Den Hoonaard, W. C. (2011) *The Seduction of Ethics: Transforming the Social Sciences*. Toronto: University of Toronto Press.

Van der Geest, S. and Sarkodie, S. (1998) 'The fake patient: a research experiment in a Ghanian hospital', *Social Science & Medicine*, 47(9): 1373–1381.

Van Dongen, E. and Fainzang, S. (1998) 'Medical anthropology at home: creating distance', *Anthropology & Medicine*, 5(3): 245–250.

Van Hoof, J. J., Moll, M. and Constantinescu, M. (2009) 'Selling alcohol to underage adolescents in Romania: compliance with age restrictions in Pitesti', *Revista de Cercetare si Interventie Sociala (Review of Research and Social Intervention)*, 27: 82–91.

Van Maanen, J. (1979) 'The fact of fiction in organisational ethnography', *Administrative Science Quarterly*, 24(4): 539–550.

Van Maanen, J. (1988) *Tales of the Field*. Chicago. IL: University of Chicago Press.

Van Maanen, J. (1991) 'The Smile Factory: work at Disneyland', in P. J. Frost, L. F. Moore, M. Reis Louis, C. C. Lundberg and J. Martin (eds), *Reframing Organisational Culture*. London: Sage. pp. 58–76.

Van Maanen, J. (2010) 'A song for my supper: more tales of the field', *Organizational Research Methods*, 13(2): 240–255.

Van Vorst, M. and Van Vorst, B. (1902/1903) 'The Woman that toils', *Everybody's Magazine*, September 1902 to January 1903.

Varni, C. A. (1972) 'An exploratory study of spouse-swapping', *The Pacific Sociological Review*, 15(4): 507–522.

Varon, J. (2004) *Bringing the War Home: The Weather Underground, the Red Army, and Revolutionary Violence in the Sixties and Seventies*. Berkeley, CA: University of Berkeley Press.

Vincent, N. (2006) *Self-Made Man: My Year Disguised as a Man*. New York: Atlantic Books.

Vincent, N. (2010) *Voluntary Madness: My Year Lost and Found in the Loony Bin*. New York: Vintage Books.

Von Hoffman, N. (1970) 'Sociological snoopers', *The Washington Post*, 30 January.

Vrooman, S. S. (2002) 'The art of invective: performing identity in cyberspace', *New Media & Society*, 4(1): 51–70.

Wacquant, L. (1992) 'The social logic of boxing in black Chicago: toward a sociology of pugilism', *Sociology of Sport Journal*, 9(3): 221–254.

Wacquant, L. (1995) 'Pugs at work: Bodily capital and bodily labour among professional boxers', *Body & Society*, 1(1): 65–93.

Wacquant, L. (2000) *Body and Soul: Notebooks of an Apprentice Boxer*. New York: Oxford University Press.

Wacquant, L. (2005) 'Carnal connections on embodiment, apprenticeship, and membership', *Qualitative Sociology*, 28(4): 441–471.

Wainwright, P. (2009) 'Undercover nurse struck off the professional register for misconduct', *Nursing Ethics*, 16(1): 659–661.

Walden, T., Singer, G. and Thomet, W. (1974) 'Students as clients: the other side of the desk', *Clinical Social Work Journal*, 2(4): 279–290.

Walker, C. R. (1922) *Steel: The Diary of a Furnace Worker*. Cambridge, MA: Atlantic Monthly Press.

Walker, D. (2011) *God in a Brothel: An Undercover Journey into Sex Trafficking and Rescue*. New York: InterVarsity Press.

Wallis, R. (1977) *The Road to Total Freedom: A Sociological Analysis of Scientology*. New York: Columbia University Press.

Wallraff, G. (1969) *13 Undesired Reports (13 Unerwunschte Reportagen)*. Cologne, Germany: Rowohlt Taschenbuch.

Wallraff, G. (1977) *Lead Story*. Cologne, Germany: Kiepenheuer & Witsch.

Wallraff, G. (1985) *Lowest of the Low (Ganz Unten)*. Cologne, Germany: Kiepenheuer & Witsch.

Wallraff, G. (2009) *Reports from the Brave New World*. Cologne, Germany: Kiepenheuer & Witsch.

Walsh, P. (2005) *Gang War: The Inside Story of the Manchester Gangs*. London: Milo Books.

Ward, D. (2000) 'I don't want to get no bullet over no bullshit', *The Guardian*, Education section, 6 December.

Ward, J. (2008) 'Researching drug seller: an "experiential" account from "the field"', *Sociological Research Online*, 13(1).

Ward, J. (2010) *Flashback: Drugs and Dealing in the Golden Age of the London Rave Scene*. London: Routledge.

Warwick, D. P. (1982) 'Tearoom Trade: means and ends in social research', in M. Bulmer (ed.), *Social Research Ethics: An Examination of the Merits of Covert Participant Observation*. London: Macmillan. pp. 38–58.

Watson, R. (2009) 'Constitutive practices and Garfinkel's notion of trust: revisted', *Journal of Classical Sociology*, 9(4): 475–499.

Watt, S. and Scott Jones, J. (2010) 'Let's look inside: doing participant observation', in J. Scott Jones and S. Watt (eds), *Ethnography in Social Science Practice*. London: Routledge. pp. 107–125.

Watts, G. (2005) *I'm Asking You Nicely*. London: Highland Books.

Wax, M. (1977) 'On fieldworkers and those exposed to fieldwork: federal regulations and moral issues', *Human Organization*, 36(3): 321–328.

Weatherford, J. (1986) *Porn Row*. New York: Arbor House.

Webb, B. (1898) 'The diary of an investigator', in B. Webb and S. Webb, *Problems of Modern Industry*. London: Longmans, Green & Co. pp. 1–19.

Webb, E. J. (1981) *Nonreactive Measures in the Social Sciences*. Dallas, TX: Houghton Mifflin.

Webb, E. J., Campbell, D. T., Schwartz, R. D. and Sechrest, L. (1966) *Unobtrusive Measures: Nonreactive Research in the Social Sciences*. Chicago, IL: Rand-McNally.

Weinberger, A. (1981) 'Responses to old people who ask for help: field experiments', *Research on Aging*, 3(3): 345–368.

Weiner, B. (1975) 'On being sane in insane places: a process (attributional) analysis and critique', *Journal of Abnormal Psychology*, 84(5): 433–441.

Welch, G. (2010) *In the Land of Believers: An Outsider's Extraordinary Journey into the Heart of the Evangelical Church*. New York: Metropolitan Books.

Westmarland, L. (2001) 'Blowing the whistle on police violence: gender, ethnography and ethics', *British Journal of Criminology*, 41(3): 523–535.

Wheaton, B. and Tomlinson, A. (1998) 'The changing gender order in sport: the case of windsurfing subcultures', *Journal of Sport and Social Issues*, 22(3): 252–274.

Whine, M. (1999) 'Cyberspace: a new medium for communication, command and control by extremists', *Studies in Conflict and Terrorism*, 22(3): 231–245.

Whitaker, E. (2005) 'Adjudicating entitlements: the emerging discourses of research ethics boards', *Health*, 9(4): 513–535.

Whiteman, N. (2010) 'Control and contingency: maintaining ethical stances in research', *International Journal of Internet Research Ethics*, 3(1): 6–22.

Whitinui, P. (2014) 'Indigenous autoethnography: exploring, engaging, experiencing "self" as a native method of inquiry', *Journal of Contemporary Ethnography,* 43(4): 456–487.

Wieder, D. L. (1974) *Language and Social Reality: The Case of Telling the Convict Code.* The Hague: Mouton.

Wiens, A. N. (1971) 'Book review: *Tearoom Trade*', *Contemporary Psychology,* 16(7): 430–432.

Wiles, R., Grow, G., Charles, V. and Heath, S. (2007) 'Informed consent and the research process: following rules or striking balances', *Sociological Research Online,* 12 (2).

Williams, W. (1920) *What's On The Worker's Mind By One Who Put On Overalls To Find Out.* New York: Charles Scriber & Sons.

Willis, P. (1977) *Learning to Labour: How Working Class Kids Get Working Class Jobs.* London: Saxon House.

Wilson, A. H. (2002) *24-Hour Party People: What the Sleeve Notes Never Tell You.* London: Channel 4 Books.

Wilson, A. M. (1998) 'The use of mystery shopping in the measurement of service delivery', *The Service Industries Journal,* 18(3): 148–163.

Wilson, R. E., Gosling, S. D. and Graham, L. T. (2012) 'A review of Facebook research in the social sciences', *Perspectives on Psychological Sciences,* 7(3): 203–220.

Wilson, V. P. (2007) *Fair Game: My Life as a Spy, My Betrayal by the White House.* New York: Simon & Schuster.

Winlow, S. (2001) *Badfellas: Crime, Tradition and New Masculinities.* Oxford: Berg.

Winlow, S. and Hall, S. (2009) 'Living for the weekend: youth identities in northeast England', *Ethnography,* 10(1): 91–113.

Winlow, S., Hobbs, D., Lister, S. and Hadfield, P. (2001) 'Get ready to duck: bouncers and the realities of ethnographic research on violent groups', *British Journal of Criminology,* 41(3): 536–548.

Wirth, L. (1928) *The Ghetto.* Chicago, IL: University of Chicago.

Wirth, L. (1938) 'Urbanism as a way of life', *American Journal of Sociology,* 44(1): 1–24.

Wolf, D. (1991) 'High risk methodology: reflections on leaving an outlaw society', in W. Shaffir and R. Stebbins (eds), *Experiencing Fieldwork: An Inside View of Qualitative Research.* London: Sage. pp. 211–223.

Wolff, H. K. (1964) 'Surrender and community study: the study of Loma', in A. J. Vidich, J. Bensman and M. R. Stein (eds), *Reflections on Community Studies.* New York: Wiley. pp. 233–263.

Wolff, M. (1973) 'Notes on the behaviour of pedestrians', in A. Birenbaum and E. Sagarin (eds), *People in Places: The Sociology of the Familiar.* New York: Praeger. pp. 35–48.

Woodward, K. (2008) 'Hanging out and hanging about: insider/outsider research in the sport of boxing', *Ethnography,* 9(4): 536–561.

Woodward, R. and Jenkings, K. N. (2011) 'Military identities in the situated accounts of British military personnel', *Sociology,* 45(2): 252–268.

Wortnik, Jr. R. J. and Thompson, G. M. (2009) 'Unifying service marketing and operations with service experience management', *Journal of Service Research,* 11(4): 389–406.

Wynhausen, E. (2005) *Dirt Cheap: Life at the Wrong End of the Job Market*. Sydney: Pan Macmillan.

Yancey, W. W. and Rainwater, L. (1970) 'Problems in the ethnography of the urban underclass', in R. W. Habenstein (ed.), *Pathways to Data*. Chicago, IL: Aldine. pp. 78–97.

Yea, S. (2010) 'Trafficking in part(s): the commercial kidney market in a Manila slum, Philippines', *Global Social Policy*, 10(3): 358–376.

Yee, N., Bailenson, J. N. and Ducheneaut, N. (2009) 'The Proteus Effect: implications of transformed digital self-representation on online and offline behaviour', *Communication Research*, 36(2): 285–312.

Young, M. (1991) *An Inside Job: Policing and Police Culture in Britain*. Oxford: Clarendon Press.

Zaman, S. (2008) 'Native among the natives: physician anthropologist doing ethnography at home', *Journal of Contemporary Ethnography*, 37(2): 135–154.

Zickmund, S. (1997) 'Approaching the radical other: the discursive culture of cyber-hate', in S. G. Jones (ed.), *Virtual Culture: Identity and Communication in Cyberspace*. Thousand Oaks, CA: Sage. pp. 185–205.

Zimbardo, P. (1973) 'On the ethics of intervention in human psychological research: with special reference to the Stanford prison experiment', *Cognition*, 2(2): 243–256.

Zimmerman, D. H. (1969) 'Task and troubles: the practical bases of work activities in a public assistance organization', in D. A. Hansen (ed.), *Explorations in Sociology and Counselling*. Boston, MA: Houghton Mifflin, pp. 264–284.

INDEX